HR Strategy

HR Strategy

(2nd Edition)

Creating Business Strategy with Human Capital

Paul Kearns

AMSTERDAM • BOSTON • HEIDELBERG • LONDON • NEW YORK • OXFORD
PARIS • SAN DIEGO • SAN FRANCISCO • SINGAPORE • SYDNEY • TOKYO

Butterworth-Heinemann is an imprint of Elsevier

Butterworth-Heinemann is an imprint of Elsevier
The Boulevard, Langford Lane, Kidlington, Oxford, OX5 1GB
30 Corporate Drive, Suite 400, Burlington, MA 01803, USA

Second Edition 2010
Reprinted 2010

British Library Cataloguing in Publication Data
A catalogue record for this book is available from the British Library

Library of Congress Cataloging-in-Publication Data
A catalog record for this book is available from the Library of Congress

ISBN: 978-1-85617-815-0

For information on all Butterworth-Heinemann
publications visit our website at www.elsevierdirect.com

Printed and bound in China
10 11 12 13 14   8 7 6 5 4 3 2

Working together to grow
libraries in developing countries

www.elsevier.com | www.bookaid.org | www.sabre.org

ELSEVIER   BOOK AID
International   Sabre Foundation

Contents

4. So What is the Best Theory on Managing People?

5. Are you Mature Enough for HR-Business Strategy?

6. Who Will Develop the HR-Business Strategy?

7. Strategic Value Measures and Management Tools

8. What Factors have the Biggest Influence on the Value of an HR-Business Strategy?

9. Due Diligence and Reporting on Human Capital

About the Author

Paul Kearns has worked in the HR field since 1978 and established his strategic HR consultancy, PWL, in1991. He has been teaching HR-business strategy at MBA level for over 10 years.
His other books include:
The Value Motive (Wiley, 2007)
Evaluating the ROI from Learning (CIPD, 2005)

Paul can be contacted at:

Personnel Works Limited
PO Box 109
Bristol
BS9 4DH
UK
Phone +44 (0) 117 914 6984
Web www.paulkearns.co.uk
Email info@paulkearns.co.uk

Preface to the 2nd Edition

Having worked in the field of human resource management (HRM) for over 30 years all I have ever hoped to do is offer what I believe to be the best advice available. I encourage you to enter this book with a healthily, sceptical attitude though. Nothing can be taken for granted or at face value in HRM, there are no guarantees and no Magic Pills that actually work. So the first, golden rules of HR Strategy are work it out for yourself, use your common sense, make sure it fits your own particular set of circumstances and don't expect an easy ride.

I wrote the 1st Edition of 'HR Strategy: Business Focused, Individually Centred' back in 2002 (published in 2003) and took a very critical look at what was going on in HR departments; particularly in the US and the UK. I asked whether organizations had anything that could be accurately referred to as an 'HR strategy' and concluded they were all wide of the mark. I still hold to that worldview today but I think events in the intervening years have clearly demonstrated that organizations get the HR functions they deserve. The typical HR department is increasingly bogged down in transactional work and a legalistic bureaucracy that leaves little time for anything else other than reacting to immediate, day-to-day issues. Yet many of these issues would never arise if employee expectations, the demands placed on them, their development and the complete psychological contract were managed more strategically. The advent of 'e-HR' has done nothing to change the foundations on which HR operates and the savings claimed from the use of greater technology in personnel administration have yet to be substantiated.

One particular development that has made me think long and hard of course is that I am now writing in the middle (or even still the beginning?) of what will probably turn out to be the biggest global depression since the 1930s. So do events on this scale make me want to alter the thesis at all? The simple answer is no, even though I never expected to see so many companies imposing pay freezes and even my premier exemplar, Toyota, laying workers off, working short time and reducing salaries accordingly. These developments may well shake an organization to its roots but they do nothing to undermine the key principles that will always underpin HR strategy – it has to be dynamic enough to move with the business strategy and yet be anchored in some solid, unchanging principles that will stand the test of time. That is why I did not feel the need to change one word of the 'CEO's welcome letter' suggested in the 1st Edition (see again here in Chapter 4). It was designed to have perpetual relevance simply because no one can ever guarantee a job for life: it always anticipated that the worst could actually happen. Now it has.

Meanwhile, the most noticeable development in HR since the 1st Edition has been the increasing amount of rhetoric around the term 'human capital management' (HCM), but without any clarity of thought as to whether it marks a genuine departure from conventional HRM or not. I have tried my best here to provide such clarity but while sterile, academic debates will probably continue about the role of HRM and HCM, ad nauseam, they have been overtaken by the seismic, real world events we are now witnessing with quantitative easing and the re-capitalisation of the banks at huge long-term cost to economies and their future taxpayers. This has led to some forecasters predicting the death of capitalism as we know it but I think such reports are much exaggerated. Moreover, any strategist should beware of letting their fundamentals be swayed in the face of such upheaval; recessions come and go, but the one thing that does not seem to change over time is human nature and that is what HR-business strategy is aiming to harness, the best value from each of us for the greatest good of all concerned.

One big and embarrassing lesson that HR professionals have to learn from failed banks, and their CEO's who employed 'people' directors, heads of learning, leadership development, compensation and benefits, organisational development and diversity is that their methods obviously did not work. They are guilty as charged on two strategic, counts – failure to maximise value and failure to minimise risk. This is not just a banking phenomenon though and HR strategy failure can become a matter of life or death.

The National Audit Office (NAO) in the UK reported that more than 2000 people died as a result of NHS hospital errors or accidents in 2004–2005 (*The Times*, 3 November 2005). In 2007 another NAO study (2005 figures reported in *The Times* on 19 December 2007) revealed that premature babies in some areas were more than twice as likely to die as in others. Obviously many factors would contribute to these terrible statistics but the NAO criticized a failure 'to share lessons across the NHS', something an HR-business strategy would be designed to address. It would also ensure that processes and communications were working effectively that might have prevented another type of error (reported in *The Times* on 8 November 2007) identified by a Coroner, at an inquest into the death of a 19-year-old soldier in a roadside explosion in Iraq in 2004, who said the British Army's supply chain 'appeared chaotic and lacking in clarity' and the soldier would have survived if the bomb-jamming equipment, which had been in stock for two weeks, had been fitted. These are stories about dysfunctional organizations. No individual is to blame because the whole system is failing.

The picture is no rosier in manufacturing with the US automotive giants, Ford and General Motors, negotiating Government bailouts to make up for their management failings. We must also take note that two of these companies defined modern American management methods in the twentieth Century and employed many senior managers with MBAs from the most prestigious business schools, who are themselves having to take a long hard look at what they have been taught. Fortunately the 'creative destruction' built into capitalism means we will continue to learn from these failures and eventually a much stronger version of the model will surface. So there can be no better time to reconsider what the word 'management' should mean in the twenty-first Century. My own answer to that question is business strategy has to have a fully integrated HR strategy built into it – hence my new use this time around of the compound term **HR-business strategy**, a much better descriptor of the indivisible and inseparable nature of what is required.

Other developments that have been increasingly conflated with HR strategy are corporate social responsibility (CSR), business ethics, environmentalism and diversity. Whatever the laudable aims of such endeavours they have served to cloud the waters of organizational strategy and make the role of a CEO much more problematic because many more stakeholders now have to be considered. These issues have a natural appeal to the psyche of many HR practitioners, who have a preoccupation with fairness and societal concerns in their DNA. Some will promote these as part of what they see as the campaigning role of HR but rarely do they develop a coherent way of reconciling these valid societal issues with the harsh world of a globalized economy. I tried to offer some answers to this conundrum in the 1st Edition and I have re-doubled my efforts here (and in 2007 in 'The Value Motive'). No longer can any CEO just offer profit, or any purely financial ratios, as testament to their effectiveness or organizational success. If these societal issues are to play any strategic part at all they will have to be properly factored into the total equation.

In the 1st Edition I made the point that the ultimate owner of the HR strategy has to be the CEO; only they can make HR-business strategy work so why not put them centre stage? I am even more convinced now that this is the only way forward and so have borrowed Machiavelli's device (in *The Prince*) of writing the 2nd Edition from the standpoint of an adviser to the CEO. It is unlikely that many CEOs will purchase this book themselves, however, so I am hoping the primary audience of HR professionals and those who want to be HR strategists will hand it to them after digesting the lessons herein. Even though the book 'talks to' the CEO it is designed as an HR director's practical guide, an *aide memoire* or even a script for them to open up a more meaningful and focused dialogue with the board and the rest of the executive about what an HR-business strategy really means and, more importantly, what it could be worth in hard currency.

One trend that has not abated since the 1st Edition is the plethora of new management gimmicks, fads and supposed breakthroughs that continues to plague those who seek to become professional managers. An appetite for newness, as opposed to genuine innovation, is not only symptomatic of an unscrupulous consultancy market but also organizational 'leaders' who have actually run out of ideas themselves. I persevere with my long-running campaign against such Magic Pills in the hope that professional, evidence-based management will eventually become the predominant methodology. Interest in evidence-based management has grown significantly since 2002 and the American Academy of Management is now taking the subject seriously enough for it to counter such faddism (see Denise Rousseau's comment in Chapter 6). I hope that this book will further the cause of evidence-based, general management and be a sharp spur to evidence-based, strategic HR management.

As far as any additional content in this edition is concerned there are new sections on human systems (only covered very briefly in the earlier edition) and more on where and how human capital management fits into a holistic HR-business strategy. I have also added a section on learning strategy, for two reasons. One, organizational learning is probably the most fertile area for creating huge value from people and therefore demands much more attention at board and executive level than it currently attracts. Two, learning strategy has to be a subset of HR-business strategy; a viewpoint that is still not fully accepted by many who call themselves learning or organizational development specialists.

Finally, it is worth emphasizing that while the 1st Edition attempted to lay down a very solid, theoretical platform this edition provides much more practical, step-by-step guidance: or at least as much as any 'practical' guide to strategy can. In that sense the two editions could be more accurately described as Parts 1 and 2. I hope readers of both will see them as complementary even though there are significant areas of overlap. The 1st Edition led directly to me teaching a regular, elective, MBA programme on HR strategy for mature students (mainly non-HR). A significant number of them have since become convinced that the disciplines I teach, under the HR-business strategy banner, should be a mandatory part of the core MBA programme. I couldn't agree more and will now be teaching it as a core management programme from 2010 onwards.

I hope you enjoy this 2nd Edition, if 'enjoy' is the right word. Whether it makes you a more enlightened manager or not, it has been written in the hope that it should help you to create more value for yourself, your organization, your people and, most important of all, for your fellow human beings.

Paul Kearns
31 March 2009

Executive Introduction and Overview

WHICH DOOR DO YOU WANT TO OPEN?

The easiest way to get an instantaneous impression of what this book is all about is to imagine you turn up at your organization next Monday and you find there are now two entrance doors – one marked 'Your company – minus HR-business strategy' and the other 'Your company – plus HR-business strategy'. Read the scenarios of what you might encounter as you enter in Table A and then decide which you might prefer.

FIGURE A Which door do you want to use?

Door 1. Minus HR-Business Strategy	Door 2. Plus HR-Business Strategy
You come across someone you take to be a junior manager who is very polite but looks rather anxious. He says 'Good morning Mr. (insert your surname) – have you got a minute please?'	You come across someone you take to be a junior manager who is very polite and says 'Good morning (insert your preferred name) – have you got a minute please?'
You are not sure what to make of this, especially first thing on a Monday morning - it is unusual that a junior manager would come to you direct.	You see nothing unusual in this. You have always made time to get out and meet people, talking openly to them and listening.
You try to be as approachable as you can but are slightly worried so you say – 'sure, come into my office'. You are also conscious this could be a complete waste of time on what is already planned to be a very busy day.	You know this person will not be wasting your time because your managers are well versed in a system that says they can raise any important issue directly with whoever they deem it most appropriate. They also work in a culture where this is encouraged as perfectly acceptable behaviour.
As you both walk towards your office your PA gives the junior manager a strange look, wondering what is going on? You ask for two coffees.	The manager says it is quite a sensitive subject but should only take about 15 minutes. So you move into your office where your PA welcomes you both with a smile and asks if you want coffees – they are well used to this sort of thing.
You sit down with the manager and try to make him feel comfortable, he tells you his name is Bill and where he works. You ask him what exactly he wants to talk about?	Phil, the manager, says that he is worried that the new delivery schedules that were introduced two weeks ago are unworkable and something needs to be done about it – immediately.
The manager says he is worried that his own boss is paying lip service to the new delivery schedules that were introduced two weeks ago. This worries you because it looks like Bill is blowing the whistle on his boss and this strikes you as disloyal. You tell Bill you will look into it. Bill leaves the office looking even more worried than when he entered.	You quickly check that Phil has already done his best to get this sorted with the relevant people but experience tells you he probably has. Usually you are only asked to get involved as a last resort. Phil says this is one of those occasions. You do not perceive any of this as disloyalty, just the normal way of working.
Bill thinks his job might be on the line.	You thank Phil for bringing it to your attention. Phil is not worried about jeopardising his position.
Your first concern is to phone Bill's head of department to find out what sort of person he is. After that your main concern is that you do not want this issue to be blown out of proportion. You tell his boss to 'sort it out'.	You know this is a big issue so you call a short meeting to resolve it straight away. No one at this meeting feels Phil has let them down in any way or undermined their authority.

THE BASIC THESIS BEHIND HR-BUSINESS STRATEGY

This is a book on how to maximize the value of your organization by maximizing the value of your people – who we might refer to as your 'human' capital. The goal is always more value. The *means* for achieving more value from people we will call HR-business strategy – the title is completely irrelevant but we have to hang the idea on something. What really matters is that you fully understand what HR-business strategy means in practice. It is probably not going to be what you think it is and it is likely to be very different to what your HR director has been telling you. It is not a written document so much as a declaration of long-term intent; a relentless journey towards making every facet of your organization work in harmony.

HR-business strategy can also be defined as a conscious and explicit way of managing your organization's human capital to gain a competitive advantage. It can be viewed as a new, generic, business strategy in its own right. However, HR issues cannot be treated as a separate exercise from the development of the business strategy. HR-business strategy makes the two inseparable and indivisible.

While the aims are simple and clear the formulation, development and implementation of HR-business strategy is a highly complex and difficult process to instigate. Over time though, with determination and leadership, everyone in the organization will begin to understand the founding principles of the strategy (e.g. only do things that are fit for purpose, only do things that will create value) and these will guide their actions and behaviour every day. You will have to manage them less. They will want to contribute more and will obtain much more satisfaction from doing so.

Most organizations that have a sizeable HR function think they already have an HR strategy and if you believe this to be the case then you can check this now by applying this quick but rigorous test.

HR-BUSINESS STRATEGY CHECKLIST – DOES YOURS PASS THE TEST?

1. Do you have a clear vision and mission that has been communicated to all employees?
2. Do you have a clear business strategy, if so what are the top three strategic objectives?
3. Do you work to clear principles that every employee will find easy to understand and simple to follow (e.g. honest feedback is crucial)?
4. When you developed your business strategy was anyone allocated, at the same time, the specific task of considering all of the strategic HR implications?
5. Does that person have a full seat on the team that produced the business strategy?

6. Could you state clearly what key HR issues stem from each of the strategic objectives? For example, if increasing market share is a key strategic objective are the people driving this objective working well as a team? Do they have all the necessary skills? Does one person own this objective and have total accountability for it? Have you communicated what will happen if the objective is not achieved?

7. Have you identified and resolved any conflicting objectives (e.g. increasing market share while cutting advertising spend?)

8. Have you specifically communicated to key people how they have to add value in order to achieve these objectives? (e.g. the marketing team have to get greater brand exposure with a much smaller budget?)

9. Have you communicated to all employees that the achievement of the existing strategic plan will move the baseline to a higher level of expectation? If so do you think they welcome this challenge?

10. Have you ensured that you will get honest enough feedback and useful information to monitor how well they are all doing?

If you do not pass this test comfortably then read on but this is how the text is structured from here.

STRUCTURE OF THE TEXT

Because of the highly complex nature of HR-business strategy the book is structured in as logical sequence as possible covering:

- The purpose of having an HR-business strategy
- It's potential value
- It's use as an additional, generic strategic option
- How it would start to work in practice as part of the strategic planning process
- The need to re-visit conventional models of people management
- Replacing management fads with organizational maturity
- Identifying who might help produce HR-business strategy and what skills they need
- How measures of performance will have to change
- What other indicators reveal how well the organization is doing at a very deep, sustainable level
- How to produce a human capital report
- Where HR-business strategic thinking might develop in the future

Chapter 1

What is the Purpose of HR-Business Strategy?

PREDICTING THE FUTURE FOR YOUR PEOPLE

Producing a strategy is all about predicting the future or, more accurately, winning the argument about what the future might hold. Yet life is so complex that boards of directors can prove to be just as fallible in this endeavour as any other, mere mortals. The boardroom is not somewhere to expect absolute truths, only best guesses. The most we can hope for is that these guesses are based on the best evidence available. Furthermore, CEO's have to convince their peers they have a strategy for creating the greatest possible value from all of the capital at their disposal and that has to include achieving the greatest returns from their 'human' capital as well.

Whatever strategy you dream up though it will have to be competitive. We should not have to remind ourselves of this fact, but Kenichi Ohmae made it so plain in his classic book *The Mind of the Strategist* (McGraw-Hill 1982) and hinted at the need for a really effective people strategy when he said

> *What business strategy is all about – what distinguishes it from all other kinds of business planning – is, in a word, competitive advantage. Without competitors there would be no need for a strategy ….. Corporate strategy thus implies an attempt to alter a company's strength relative to that of its competitors in the most efficient way.*

What better way is there to '*alter (your) company's strength relative to that of (your) competitors*' than to ensure you manage your people better than they manage theirs? We will eventually push this case even further in suggesting that any business strategy that does not explicitly and consciously integrate with an HR strategy will no longer qualify as the best strategic option. Stakeholders will not be getting the value they should expect if you fail with your people.

As with all 'simple' advice though let us not be fooled into thinking this will be easy. Really serious issues quickly mount up as soon as you try to put a strategy for people management into practice. Consider, for example, what difficulties you would face in telling all your employees that you now expect as much value as possible from everyone, and your chagrin at realising you have not already done so! Never mind, we will come back to that later. For now the first step, or should we say hurdle, is how will you predict what the future holds for your employees whilst also ensuring they might want to take this journey with you?

How good are you already at making predictions about your business, its markets and customers? However impressive your track record might be there are no guarantees your next prediction will be well founded. Stakeholders should expect that your strategic predictions are at least based on the best information available and have been subjected to the most rigorous analysis. Only then can your strategy provide a robust springboard for action. It is self-evident and inevitable that organizations with the most accurate predictions will enjoy the highest rates of success.

Yet history has a habit of reminding us that we get predictions horribly wrong. One only has to look at the global credit crunch of 2008–2009 to realize that even the experts – economics professors, investment analysts and financial regulators are all fallible human beings. Spot-on prophecies are sometimes uttered, but because the news is not what the crowd wants to hear, they are drowned out. Peter Schiff, President of Euro-Pacific Capital, famously predicted in a television debate on America's CNBC in August 2006 http://www.youtube.com/watch?v=LfascZSTU4o that the USA was heading for a debt crisis. His co-debater, a previous adviser to the Reagan government, took precisely the opposite view declaring that the US economy was in great shape. They could not both be right, of course, and history duly declared Schiff the winner, but only when it was too late to prevent the disaster.

It is because life is precarious that we crave some semblance of certainty and direction from our leaders. One prediction we can make, with absolute certainty, is that having the wrong strategy will always lead to disaster. The only matters left open to debate are how long it takes before catastrophe strikes and how much longer before we acknowledge our mistakes and learn some painful lessons. In times of societal upheaval and change we can be talking very lengthy timescales indeed before we realise some of society's worst mistakes: take political strategies of socialism versus capitalism, or how to tackle global warming.

The determined leader will never dodge or shy away from the sheer size of the challenge though. Trying to avoid making predictions is not an option because you stop being a leader and become a victim of circumstance. So any prediction is better than none and to choose the best option you need to be a prescient predictor of human behaviour over substantial periods of time. Fortunately, this is not half as difficult as it sounds. Human nature is highly predictable, particularly the combined behaviour of large numbers of people, in fact worryingly so.

Psychologists Solomon Asch and Stanley Milgram, in the 1950s and 1960s, performed some of the most infamous experiments on human behaviour. Asch just confirmed much of what we already knew that social pressures on individuals to conform can result in them consciously providing incorrect information. The guinea pigs in his groups were the only persons who were not aware of the experiment and so conformed against their own common sense and better judgement. Milgram's experiments in obedience found that, in a controlled experiment, participants would obey instructions to administer electric shocks to people they had never met, simply for failing in a laboratory test. These findings are still controversial today, but we need to be alert to the possibility that organizational culture can be such that bizarre and dangerous behaviour can be exhibited by employees in the work environment, who would not behave in such a manner in their own home or when left to their own devices.

However we behave, it took many thousands of years for us to evolve into what we are today and this is not likely to be undone or undergo any radical change within one or two generations. It might seem distasteful to have to remind ourselves of what human beings are capable of but we can predict with a high degree of confidence, based on historical evidence, that we will still be witnessing wars, famines, genocides and totalitarian regimes in the future simply because we have not found a way to eliminate them yet.

We are also likely to have more asset bubbles and financial crashes if we do not do something to prevent them, but what can we do ? The same, primal, human urges that caused the Dutch tulip mania of 1637, the South Sea Bubble of 1720 and the Wall Street 'crash' of 1929 are the very same as the human behaviours that led to the asset bubble and the credit crunch of 2007. Nothing much changes when we are talking about man's most basic instincts and there will always be those, in the absence of any external constraint, who will allow their desires to rule their lives without considering the consequences of obesity, indebtedness or infidelity. This is not intended to infer any moral or value judgement on such individuals, simply to accept that these 'weaknesses' pose serious challenges, if not threats, to the way we all live.

They require complex, strategic solutions and, like love, the course of true strategy is unlikely to run smooth. If it were easy everyone would be doing it, but then it would offer no competitive advantage. It is precisely because strategy is so difficult that it offers such great opportunities. Its value lies in its complexity and the inability of the majority of CEOs to master it. Any CEO can produce an operating plan, but that is a very distant cousin to strategy and from a much lower order. Moreover, how many CEOs can develop a sustainable business strategy when the average tenure of a FTSE 100 CEO is less than 5 years? Fewer still could produce an HR-business strategy.

Large supermarket chains such as WalMart or Tesco can make an educated guess as to what their customers will buy every week. Most of their shelves would be stacked according to historical experience and their logistics would operate likewise. Business and operating plans work reasonably well when customer behaviour does not change too much in the short term. Plans can be cruelly exposed though when the world around them starts to change. Tastes can change, as with organic foods or when customers prefer ethical or Fairtrade products. Such developments force changes that demand a well-conceived, coherent HR-business strategy.

Supermarket policies on the quality, standard and shape of vegetables they think customers want will change when prices rise steeply: knobbly carrots and oddly shaped bananas suddenly become acceptable. Bureaucrats and legislators in the EU also changed their regulations to allow these, previously prohibited, misshapen produce onto the shelves but neither the supermarket managers nor the Brussels bureaucrats could be said to be acting strategically: a strategist would have stuck to some solid principles. Not so the EU, the arguments that justified laws outlawing the ugly and defenceless vegetables of yesteryear were suddenly unceremoniously jettisoned in the face of economic reality. No wonder the EU does not command the respect of all its citizens, when they act in such a fickle and decidedly un-strategic way.

A strategic change in the way supermarkets operate would acknowledge that a change in vegetable policy affects many aspects of the business, not just the shelf stacker. The procurement teams would not just buy different quality produce they would develop a different contract and relationship with their suppliers. This would require them to move away from their previous, rigidly enforced, standards and towards adopting an alternative negotiating stance. If they just ditched their high quality farmers for lower quality producers what would happen when low prices and higher incomes returned? New strategies always involve fresh thinking and different behaviours.

New strategies invariably mean moving into uncharted waters and this comes with risk, management paradoxes and apparent contradictions – neatly summed up in the oft-quoted phrase – 'the biggest risk of all is to take no risk'. Any CEO could be forgiven for wanting as much of a steady state income stream as possible, especially as they realise that change is likely to lead to disruption and cost. So strategy is as much about managing these risks as it is about opening up new opportunities. Trying to avoid risk stifles innovation. This is the very same dilemma that faces banking regulators, who have to weigh the cold hand of regulation against the wealth-generating advantages of unfettered entrepreneurialism. HR-business strategy should be viewed in precisely these same terms, needing to control employees whilst simultaneously wanting to allow them full rein to realize their greatest potential.

This will always be a complex balancing act because there is no such thing as a perfect strategy and all strategies, by virtue of the dynamic environment in which they exist, have to be dynamic. Conventional, textbook, economic theory produces a construct of perfect competition where customers have perfect knowledge of products and prices and can express their buying decisions through the existence of perfect markets bringing purchasers and suppliers together, in perfect equilibrium. Yet, in reality, we all know how imperfect markets are and many organizations make good profits from those imperfections. The Internet has certainly provided much better market and price information for purchasers, but the range of features and options on many products and services are just too complex for ready comparisons to be made, whether they are insurance policies or digital cameras. Some companies could even be accused of having a deliberate policy of confusing customers so that they cannot always find the lowest price comparisons so easily. This criticism could justifiably be laid at the door of most mobile/cell phone companies' tariffs.

Not all CEOs will see life as a series of bear traps though. They will relish the buzz that comes from taking risks, while their more conservative executives take a step back. Shareholders' expectations might impose pressures on a CEO to exploit all market opportunities, but even they know that there is a thin dividing line between acceptable risk taking and outright gambling. CEOs should never be tempted to gamble though, especially if they are tempted by big bonuses that pay out if they win but incur no consequence if they lose. Gamblers never make effective managers, even if their gambles sometimes pay off. They might talk about their successful 'strategies' and dedicated gamblers will try and convince you they have 'foolproof' systems but when the coin is tossed or the roulette wheel spun they can do absolutely nothing to influence the outcome; they are as much the victims of luck as anyone else.

Dedicated strategists are still subject to the same laws of probability but will consciously manage probability to increase their likelihood of winning, including contingencies to ensure they make more winning calls than duds: such as intelligent hedging on foreign exchange transactions and commodities. Hedge fund managers take manipulating probability to the extreme, with highly mathematised risk models but they can also get it wrong and anyone who eschews any sort of formula would be rightly regarded as a mere punter. No CEO would see that as a compliment.

We should not move on, however, without acknowledging that there are other serious schools of thought that suggest strategizing itself is a pointless exercise. Proponents of chaos theory intimate that strategists can never hope to control all of the external variables (e.g. competitors, innovations, environmental issues, natural disasters) and are therefore doomed to suffer the vagaries of the famous 'butterfly effect'; where the smallest and innocuous occurrence a long way away can throw all their calculations out. Chaos theory is correct in reminding us that we live in a chaotic world but chaos, by definition, cannot be managed. We can only react to it, as with a tsunami, and even if we accurately predict it we do not have the technology to prevent it.

So when it comes to getting the best out of people, this is the starting point for our journey along the road towards HR-business strategy. People cannot give of their best in a chaotic organization; it has to be a conscious effort. It might prove to be a Herculean effort, but it should be worth it as long as we ensure we are as well prepared for the battle as possible. What better place to learn some important lessons then than from some of the best strategic thinkers that ever existed, those engaged in the art of war? Let us also stress the word 'art' here because however scientific we try to make the subject of strategic people management, it is always likely to be as much art as science.

HR-BUSINESS STRATEGY AND THE ART OF WAR

The Concise Oxford Dictionary is very clear what strategy is:
strategy n.

1. *The art of war*

2a. *the management of an army in a campaign*

2b. *moving troops into favourable positions*

This definition is entirely concerned with military matters and yet we can easily read straight across to the notion that we should regard our employees as our 'troops' in a 'war' or campaign against competitors or potential opponents, some of whom we do not even know exist yet. So our aim should be to move them into a position where they can perform at their best. Managers have a great deal to learn from military strategists and probably the most important lesson is that *the ultimate effectiveness of any individual 'soldier' is determined, primarily, by the strategy they are working to rather than their own capabilities*. The wrong strategy renders everyone ineffective and risks lives. The American 'shock and awe' tactics used at the start of the Iraq war in 2003 was part of a strategy guaranteed to result in a significant number of casualties, on both sides. The British troops' tactics in Basra were part of a different type of strategy. General Petraeus is now widely regarded as having completely rewritten military strategy in the way he mounted a 'surge' to deal with embedded insurgents. These represent three different strategies with different probabilities of survival, irrespective of the inherent capabilities of the soldiers concerned. This is a very serious matter – all strategies are essentially 'people' strategies and always have serious consequences for peoples' lives and livelihoods.

All organizations work in the same way. Many good workers end up redundant because their CEO gets the business strategy wrong. Retailer Woolworths, in the UK, shut down in 2009, after 99 years in business, with the loss of thousands of jobs after the failure of a series of CEOs to produce a successful strategy. It might be instructive therefore to try and imagine just what it might feel like for you to be a military leader in a war zone, not as an academic exercise, but to encourage you to think long and hard about the burden of responsibility that making 'people' decisions should impose on a CEO.

So imagine that you are an army general and have just been dropped into a war zone with a thousand troops at your disposal. All you can see in front of you is a ridge about half a mile ahead and you have been told that on the other side of this ridge is the enemy. You do not know what they look like. You have no idea how many there are. You have no intelligence about their arms, equipment, positions, their battle readiness or the state of their supply lines. One thing you know for certain though is that they are aware of you and if you do not defeat them first they will be doing their utmost to defeat you. Is this any different to any commercial 'war zone' with many unknowns? So what do you do?

When this scenario was put to a group of HR directors on a strategy workshop some years ago the first reply given was 'I'd retreat'. This might tell us something about the courage, character and determination of the average HR director, but she was told that retreating was not an option because not only would the enemy be in hot pursuit they would also have the psychological 'upper hand'. Sitting there and doing nothing was not allowed as an option for the same reason; they might attack at any minute and catch you unawares and unprepared (a bit like Google et al. creeping up on Microsoft). No, the only answer to getting you safely and successfully out of this situation is to devise a better strategy than your enemy, to be at least one step ahead. Strategists take the initiative.

No one ever knows how many strategic options are available, but one thing is for certain: if a computer model presented you with all of the possible permutations then one of them would have to be the first choice because it would be *relatively* better than all the others. Of course, no one is ever going to present you with such a clear-cut answer on a plate. In the world of financial derivatives the scientific, computer-generated, mathematical models used for trading proved to be just as fallible as the people who programmed them. Computer geeks who want to get their revenge on their colleagues often take great delight in telling them that one day computers will be more intelligent than we are. If that is so, it might be a good idea to teach them how to plug themselves in first. In the meantime, there is no higher authority or absolute arbiter available to tell you whether you have chosen the 'right' or 'wrong' strategy.

Asking a CEO whether they have the right strategy is the wrong question. No one will be able to answer it without the benefit of 20:20 hindsight. Was 3G a successful strategy for most mobile telecommunications companies that paid billions for the licences? They failed to generate as much revenue as anticipated. So while we can never judge the success of a strategy until after the event (ex post), the impartial observer (and shareholder) can still legitimately ask in advance (ex ante) whether the strategy chosen was deemed to be the best of all the available options at the time. Strategy is a very unforgiving subject. It demands that we think extremely carefully and apply as much foresight and wisdom as we can muster.

Returning to the war zone scenario, other workshop participants, when put under pressure to respond, feel inclined to say that it is just not realistic. Generals and their troops do not just get dropped into war zones without military intelligence and, even if they did, they would only be able to act 'tactically' rather than strategically. You might have some sympathy with those who try to wriggle out of difficult situations in this way; it is only to be expected from most human beings who do not like to make difficult decisions. 'Military intelligence' is often referred to as a perfect oxymoron and history books are replete with military blunders that arose out of poor intelligence. The Charge of the Light Brigade was a classic example, but Vietnam was hardly a great success and the then Defence Secretary Robert McNamara later admitted (in the documentary 'The Fog of War', 2003 – absolutely required viewing for all

HR-business strategists, on how not to do it) that one of the great 'lessons' learnt, after the event, was "know your enemy' – doh!'

There are two crucial points that these HR directors had not acknowledged. First, many companies face 'unfair' questions and find themselves in situations that are not of their own making, but they cannot just walk away. Think of food producers who suddenly find a crank has laced one of their products on the supermarket shelves with poison. Second, whilst there will always be a need for short-term tactics, the whole point of studying strategy is to minimize the occasions when the organization is likely to leave itself open to such risks (i.e. the food producer has a tamper-proof packaging policy, tightens up security procedures, ensures every part of the supply chain process is watertight etc.). So no one is allowed to duck these issues.

The ones who still do not want to play this game sometimes adopt a 'gung-ho strategy' (an oxymoron if ever there was one) where they give the order to fix bayonets and mount a full-scale attack by charging over the ridge. As with any gamble, this sometimes pays off, but the laws of probability are not on their side. Moreover, what sort of esprit de corps is generated by a general who always has this as their preferred modus operandi? So perhaps we do not need to spend too long discussing the strategic merits of gung-ho HR strategies either. One workshop participant, with a more intelligent and reflective approach, suggested they would immediately send out a small reconnaissance party to see if they could see what was going on over the ridge, which sounds eminently sensible. In fact, you do not really need to have any military experience to at least consider this common sense option. Strategy without intelligence will always be a rather hit-and-miss affair.

One type of very relevant intelligence, for the general who knows that looking after their troops is the best way to fight the enemy, is their readiness and preparedness for action. For example, how about their existing field positions? Are they all in one tight group or are they spread out over the surrounding area? A tight formation makes you susceptible to heavy casualties from an unseen mortar attack. Are there any natural defences or cover at your disposal, such as rocks, ditches or trees? If you do have to retreat where will you retreat to? Have you got any idea in which direction you would need to head and what obstacles or terrain you might face? What about communications with your own troops? What is their present frame of mind? Are they hungry and tired? Are they well aware of the threats that face them and psychologically prepared? Also, are you a general that already inspires confidence due to a successful track record in military campaigns behind you?

Another dimension we have not covered yet is the context in which you have to operate. If this scenario were set in the early nineteenth century the expectations of the troops would be very different from those in World War II and different again from troops sent into conflicts in the present day. Modern armies may well have the world's media watching their every move and this would influence their behaviour and actions, as was only too apparent in the Iraq war of 2003 and the treatment of prisoners at Abu Ghraib. A true strategist should never underestimate the importance of context, particularly cultural context.

HR-BUSINESS STRATEGY IS INHERENTLY COMPLEX

This simple scenario is intended to offer a very small insight into the complexities of strategic thinking with an emphasis on the people dimension. Anyone of reasonable intelligence can understand all of the *tactical* considerations that were highlighted in this example. The complexity comes from having to understand the interrelationship between all of the various variables; the separate elements that have to work together to make up a complete strategy. It is a rare combination of science and art, of joining all the separate elements into one coherent whole that is the real, intellectual challenge. It is a challenge that sorts the mere managers from the leaders. HR-business strategy, as with any type of strategy, is not about the individual 'battles' but the waging of a complete war against the competition. It is the common thread that ties each individual's actions into a common cause. Effective strategies should, by definition, produce effective MOs (modus operandi). The ethos, principles, values and objectives of the organization should all be encapsulated within an HR-business strategy.

War can be a very dirty business though and discussing morality might seem irrelevant when someone is in a situation of kill or be killed. Machiavelli, infamous for espousing a philosophy of the ends justifying the means, appeared to be devoid of any morality when advising his masters on just such matters. In 'The Prince' http://www.constitution.org/mac/prince12.htm he raises the question of how a prince should hope to be regarded by the populace in a newly won territory:

> ... whether it is better to be loved than feared or feared than loved?

and responds to his own question by saying

> ... one should wish to be both, but, because it is difficult to unite them in one person, it is much safer to be feared than loved, when, of the two, either must be dispensed with.

When reading such apparently cold and cruel sentiments the student of HR-business strategy could be forgiven for thinking Machiavelli has little to teach us about getting the best out of people, but this would probably be a misinterpretation of Machiavelli's genius. For example, he refers to the relative merits, or otherwise, of using mercenary troops when conducting a campaign:

> Mercenaries and auxiliaries are useless and dangerous; and if one holds his state based on these arms, he will stand neither firm nor safe; for they are disunited, ambitious and without discipline, unfaithful, valiant before friends, cowardly before enemies...they have no other attraction or reason for keeping the field than a trifle of stipend, which is not sufficient to make them willing to die for you.
>
> The Prince, 12

He adds that he '*should have little need to labour this point*' probably because it is so obvious that any 'employer' who hires mercenaries is never likely to get the best out of such people compared to regular, loyal, committed workers. A lesson that was obviously not learnt by the subprime mortgage and banking industry when it employed mercenary, mortgage salespeople and derivatives traders.

Machiavelli is as relevant today as he ever was because he had that rare quality of teaching us some fundamental, universal truths, but many still find his bleak picture of human nature unpalatable. Anyone holding to a more rose-tinted view is unlikely to address the most serious human issues though. HR-business strategy is not about being nice to people, it is about turning man's most basic, selfish and often belligerent instincts to the good of mankind. It is about encouraging people to use their most admirable qualities and values to create as much value for society as possible, whilst subduing their worst, natural inclinations. This presents HR-business strategy in its true light, as part of a grand, master plan for society; a point that will become more obvious as we progress through each chapter. However, for now, we need to keep our feet firmly on the ground at an individual organization level. You, as a CEO, have an organization to run today, so what might a working definition of HR-business strategy be? What will lend it immediate relevance and import?

An HR-business strategy is a conscious and explicit attempt to maximize organizational value by gaining a sustainable competitive advantage from human capital.

This is a definition that should serve you well for the foreseeable future assuming you want your organization to have as high a value as possible.

SO WHAT IS A HIGH-VALUE ORGANIZATION?

If you asked a market analyst to produce a list of high-value organizations they would probably use market capitalization (share price × number of shares) as their measure. This is a very conventional approach, but it is a very narrow view of what constitutes value and is susceptible to market fluctuations and can be influenced by questionable 'buy' and 'sell' notices from investment analysts. You might not be able to control many of these external factors, but you can have a significant effect on the human capital at your disposal.

'Making good profits' does not qualify you for the high-value league table. Take the reinsurance industry based in the city of London as an example. Until about 10 years ago, traditional reinsurance companies in the city were run along very similar lines to each other and then a very unusual CEO called Matthew Harding came along who took over Benfield Reinsurance and started to rewrite the reinsurance business rulebook. He started by making some very simple, but fundamental, changes to the way he did business: like listening to what customers really wanted and ensuring claims were settled promptly. He attracted a great deal of profitable business in the process. At one stage Benfield employed only 65 people and yet made a profit of £30,000,000; a profit per head of £461,000. One of their erstwhile nearest rivals employed 120 people and made approximately £1,000,000 profit (only £8,333 profit per employee) in the same year. Both companies worked in exactly the same market and both generated profits but the value comparison is stark and compelling.

Part of the 'secret' to Harding's success was sweeping away old-fashioned, inefficient and ineffective processes, thereby enabling a significantly higher amount of value to be created by each employee. There was nothing intrinsically different in the people he employed; they were not imported from another planet. They may have had to adapt to new ways of working, but basically they were the same people who could only have generated £8,333 profit if they worked for a competitor. The value of troops is always dictated by strategy.

Despite such startling results though, Benfield might still not join the premier league. A high-value organization *maximizes* its potential value. Getting the competitive business strategy right, and the right people, made an incredible difference but there was no HR-business strategy at work here. An HR-business strategy at Benfield would have produced even more value. Who would be looking for an HR-business strategy though, when the business is already doing so well? Only those who are never satisfied will want both; '*the world belongs to the discontented*' (Robert Woodruff former Chairman, Coca Cola).

Only CEOs who have infinite ambitions will want to avail themselves of what HR-business strategy really has to offer and predicting how much value it could add should quickly check whether it is worth it. Those who talked about people being an asset never managed to put a value on it. So why not try to calculate what this 'asset' might actually be worth? It is a tough question, and one that most HR directors would duck, but it has to be addressed if we expect HR-business strategy to be taken as seriously as it needs to be.

Imagine that your company does not have an HR-business strategy. Now quickly calculate what a 1% increase in revenue or profit would be worth in £'s? Alternatively, what would a 1% reduction in your cost base be worth? If you work in a not-for-profit sector, such as health care or higher education, imagine what a 1% increase in patients treated or students educated would look like in terms of funding? These could be very sizeable figures, depending on the sort of business you are in, but they might still not be exciting enough. So we need to extrapolate these figures.

In Fig. 1.1 the value proposition of HR-business strategy is represented in terms of company performance on the *Y*-axis and a 10-year timescale on the *X*-axis. Graph 1 predicts how your company will perform over 10 years without an HR-business strategy. Graph 2 shows what might happen with a strategy. What it also highlights is the time lag involved. If you formulate an HR-business strategy today (year 0) the full effects will not really start to kick in for about 3 years. This makes sense when you think about it. If Continental Airlines wants to copy Southwest Airlines the pilots and staff who were used to one way of working would take some time to change.

This is not intended to be just another hypothetical, what if, exercise. This is a simple, and very practical, management tool. Its purpose is to find out where

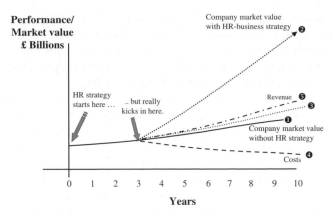

FIGURE 1.1   HR-business strategy is only interested in looking for maximum potential.

an HR-business strategy could have the biggest impact. It flushes out any assumptions and helps a CEO to articulate not only what might happen in the future but also what people practices might be required. In a European beverage company (soft and alcoholic drinks) this template was put in front of the new CEO who had, until recently, been the company's finance director. The sequence of questions shown below is a brief summary of a real dialogue that was held with him (in 2005) and how he responded on this particular occasion. It is worth remarking that the graphs drawn at the time were no more than a rough outline on a notepad – no technology, fancy graphics or 3-hour PowerPoint presentation required. HR-strategists just do it.

HR strategist to CEO: 'Draw a line (like 1) on this chart for how you hope the business will grow over the next 10 years'.

CEO: (draws a slightly steeper line – 5) 'I think we will do slightly better than that'.

HRS: 'I think we could do a great deal better if we had an HR-business strategy – so I would draw this line (2)'.

CEO: 'To get that increase in business would require a significant increase in CAPEX and I don't want to go down that road yet'.

HRS: 'OK, but can we look specifically at what you want to achieve on revenue then?' (draws line 3)

CEO: 'I'm happy with how sales and revenue are doing for the time being'.

HRS: 'OK, so what about reducing your cost base?' (draws line 4)

CEO: 'I think we are pretty cost conscious, don't forget I used to be the FD (laughs) and we constantly review costs'.

HRS: 'If you are happy with sales revenue and cost then I have only one more question – what sort of graph would you draw for how you want customer satisfaction to improve?'

CEO: 'Now that's the only issue that worries me at the moment – and what worries me even more is that we don't have any data to produce such a graph for what our customers think of us'.

HRS: 'Well regardless of the lack of data, why not try drawing a graph anyway and give your best guess as to the room for improvement?'

CEO: 'I don't need a graph, I think the opportunity is huge. One of our main customers has just informed me, personally, that we have serious problems with our relationship because a delivery was left *outside* his premises last week!'

That is all this tool is used for – a simple way of working through the broad options available for significantly improving the business. So in that sense it is a prioritizing tool. The rest of this dialogue then drilled down into all of the possible issues with improving customer service. At every step though, the mantra was – which of these will provide the most value in the long term?

But why does it have to be a 10-year view? Well, partly because training and developing people takes time, cultures do not change overnight; structures and processes all take time before the benefits really start to accrue. In this particular case one suggestion for the CEO was simply to go onto the shop floor and get some immediate feedback from staff about whether they knew how unhappy the customers were? If this were a huge supermarket chain and the question was asked 'how much more value could we get from every checkout operator?' a 1% improvement this year (e.g. a 1% take up in store cards following personal recommendations by the checkout operator?) might be achievable. As it really starts to take hold though, think what 1% more value would look like from mobilizing many thousands of employees? This is not just about saving money though. The saving could fund an all-out price war against slower moving competitors.

One of the key reasons Toyota has managed to move so far ahead of its rivals is that it has been getting more value out of every single employee, every day, for over 50 years. This is why Ford and GM have done their best to copy what Toyota has been doing. Ford themselves must have thought so at some stage because they have tried to do virtually everything Toyota does. They have tried to introduce total quality management, a philosophy of kaizen (continuous improvement) and if you visited a Ford or GM factory today you will find just-in-time deliveries, problem-solving techniques (Six Sigma anyone?) quality circles and many other techniques used so effectively by Toyota. Yet, despite all of their efforts, they have failed in their 'replication strategy'. Why? Well if they had listened to strategy guru Michael Porter many years ago they would have realized that

Sustainable advantage comes from <u>systems</u> (our emphasis) of activities that are complementary. Companies with sustainable competitive advantage integrate lots of activities within the business: their marketing, service, designs, and customer support. All those things are consistent, interconnected and mutually reinforcing. As a result, competitors don't have to match just one thing; they have to match the whole system. And until rivals achieve the whole system, they don't get very many of the benefits.

Maybe this is something all of the other car companies still have to learn (although Honda seems to have got the message): the whole system has to work as one if you are to have any chance of achieving Toyota's levels of efficiency and effectiveness. A business strategy that does not incorporate an integrated HR strategy is never going to achieve a completely '*consistent, interconnected and mutually reinforcing*' system.

THE TOYOTA WAY

Toyota is an extremely rare example of just such a business. It is a complete system in every sense. This is why, if we are to use it as an exemplar case study, it should carry a WARNING: THIS CASE STUDY IS THE EXCEPTION! It is a perfect example of an integrated HR-business strategy, although this is a term that would not come from the lips of Eiji Toyoda, a member of the family that founded the company in 1937. Yet, he could not possibly have hoped to achieve the same success without having a workforce that was working for the company every step of the way. A workforce that valued secure employment; who could see their best mutual interests would be served by not having a confrontational industrial relations environment; who were willing to come to work always thinking of ways to work better and being prepared to learn various tools and techniques to constantly reduce costs. Sure, the same workforce wants a reasonable level of pay, terms and conditions, but is willing to ensure that its target number of cars is produced at the end of each and every shift, come what may.

The Toyota strategy is a complete and holistic strategy. The system is indivisible and cannot be deconstructed or copied piecemeal. When other manufacturing companies, not just automotive, try to copy the Toyota Production System (TPS), (such as Honeywell who, as late as 2005, called their version the Honeywell Operating System or HOS) they do not achieve anything like the same benefits because they have only a poor and pale imitation of TPS. The most glaring omission is usually an absence of people strategy and a culture created specifically to drive the TPS.

A management development specialist at a workshop in 1999, who was very proud to be working for BMW, made no attempt to hide his scepticism about the virtues of Toyota as an employer. He took great delight in pointing out that he, personally, knew several people who worked for Toyota who did not regard them as anything other than a hard-nosed, obsessive business that did not particularly look after their employees well and were planning to leave the company. Whether this anecdotal evidence has any veracity or not, the fact remains that Toyota continues to employ over 200,000 people (even after the recent cuts), mainly loyal employees, from whom it manages to create huge value when compared to its nearest, particularly American, rivals. BMW's success is built on totally different foundations.

There is no idealism at play here. No organization is likely to achieve a 100% employee satisfaction rating and working for Toyota might not suit a great many people, but then that is not the point. Toyota will themselves openly admit that it is not the sort of place that everyone wants to work. This is perfectly in keeping with an HR-business strategy that aims to attract and retain people who are most suited to the organization's objectives. HR-business strategies work better, more often, with more employees than poor or non-existent strategies. If the BMW manager had criticized Toyota in terms of its performance, relative to BMW, and suggested that BMW achieved more value from its staff he would have a much stronger and more convincing argument. It is unlikely he would have found any evidence to do so.

Anyone who works for Toyota, as a supplier, will soon realize that one of its key strengths is the clear set of simple principles that everyone in the business understands and follows: principles such as 'fit for purpose', which have been enshrined in Toyota's ways of working since the beginning. They have stood the test of time and still continue to guide their actions and their decisions every day. It is solid principles that form the strongest foundations.

In 2009, as with every other major automotive manufacturer, Toyota is facing probably the toughest market conditions for many years. It is no more immune to the downturn than any other company but, paradoxically, this is where its long-term strategy will reap even greater rewards. It had already been building up a significant proportion of its workforce from subcontracted agency staff in order to allow it flexibility as times changed. So it is now able to slim down with less pain than the severe redundancies inflicted on Ford and GM. More importantly, as the worldwide automotive industry adapts to a rapidly shrinking market, those companies that survive intact will 'steal' future business from the companies that disappear because their short-term plans could not cope.

Lessons in HR-business strategy from Toyota

There are several key lessons here for anyone wanting to develop an HR-business strategy:

- the business strategy and the HR strategy are one and the same
- the greatest benefits come from the holistic application of sound principles over many years
- the highest levels of management must not only understand the holistic, systemic, nature of the strategy but give their complete commitment to it
- the principles must be durable even in the face of the most difficult and unforeseeable circumstances
- simple principles can be explained to any level of employee and once they follow them their daily actions can be regarded as directly contributing to business strategy
- in this way a grand strategy also becomes a strategy for individuals in the organization

There is much more to be learnt from the Toyota way and many organizations are beginning to wake up to this, but none of them will be able to emulate Toyota unless they understand the HR strategy aspects of their business strategy.

It is a pity that more good examples are so hard to come by and that the intervening years since the first edition of this book have not unearthed many more success stories. This is certainly not because organizations do not try. The main reason is that organizations are bedazzled by initiatives rather than more contemplative strategies. The worst are proprietary and generic 'solutions' (try reading *Fish! A Remarkable Way to Boost Morale and Improve Results*, Hyperion, 2000) developed by someone else *outside* your organization. They usually follow a well-worn, tried-and-tested cycle of failure. They start with hype, followed by a big-bang launch and end in disillusionment and recrimination. Such initiatives never gain the requisite commitment and ownership from the people who have to make them work. A greater problem is that the use of outside consultants tends to make the whole process a detached and abstracted exercise. This flies in the face of the fundamental principles of holistic, systemic thinking. This might sound pretty sophisticated, but at least Toyota gives us plenty of confidence to try harder.

Chapter 2

HR-Business Strategy is a New, Generic Option

A 'NEW', GENERIC, STRATEGY

Strategy is a future-looking process, while its impact can only be assessed with the benefit of hindsight. You only know you reached a 'tipping point' after it tipped and you only realize where the peak of the Sigmoid Curve was when you are sliding down the other side of it. Neither of these concepts is of much practical use to the strategist. Sony's original Walkman may have changed the face of mobile entertainment, but its minidisk technology inaccurately predicted what future customers wanted.

Ever since Michael Porter wrote his seminal work *Competitive Strategy. Techniques for Analysing Industries and Competitors* (Free Press, 1980), it has been generally accepted that there are only a finite number of generic strategies. Porter originally referred to cost leadership and product, or value, differentiation as the two main, generic strategies with a third being a focused (or niche) strategy. Other writers, such as Hamel and Prahalad, have told us of a core competence strategy – concentrate on what you are good at – (in *Competing for the Future*, Harvard Business School Press, 1994) and more recently Renée Mauborg and W. Kim Chan would have us believe that you can create clear water between you and your shark-like competitors with a *Blue Ocean Strategy* (Harvard Business School Press, 2005) – a concept already known to most of us as a USP (unique selling proposition). World-weary executives, who have heard it all before, might just regard all of these as statements of the blindingly obvious dressed up in the latest design of Emperor's new clothes.

Formulating a strategy is one thing though, implementing it successfully is another. If you are happy enough with your present strategy you could pick up another book by Kaplan and Norton (*The Balanced Scorecard – Translating Strategy into Action*, Harvard Business School Press, 1996) to make sure implementation follows four generic perspectives (financial, customer, efficiency and innovation). Does any CEO really need all of this advice though? Strategic thinking is as old as civilization and has been practised in military, political and business contexts for many, many years. So is it likely that anyone has come up with any genuinely innovative strategies that have not been considered before?

Several decades of exponential growth in MBA programmes have plagued CEOs with 'new' fads and fashions and the vast array of management books available only serves to confuse anyone seeking a clear way forward. This is the classic paradox of choice; too much apparent choice creating uncertainty and prevarication. Perhaps this book could be seen as just another fad if it were not for the fact that we want to revisit some very old ideas, such as 'look after your people well and they will look after the business'. We will not be following any lessons for military leaders in Sun Tzu's 'The Art of War' though, because military leaders did not have to *ask* their troops to go into battle, they ordered them. Neither will we be looking to the 'dark satanic mill' owners of the industrial revolution for advice as their employees also had little choice in the matter. The only 'employment' legislation of the time was the Master and Servant Act, which tells us all we need to know.

Some employers still take the view though, that employees should be grateful they have a job and recessions only serve to reinforce this attitude, but treating people as expendable commodities is unlikely to provide a high value, sustainable strategy. High values and enlightened attitudes are never mutually exclusive, quite the opposite, they are perfectly complementary. So no CEO should think they are being asked to choose between a business strategy and an HR strategy; both are mutually inclusive.

Even when times were hard in the nineteenth century, enlightened leaders like Robert Owen in New Lanark in Scotland (see www.robert-owen.com) realized that a caring attitude to employees could make good business sense as well as creating a better type of society in which to live. If you have never heard of Robert Owen though, or of any of the other famous business philanthropists (Rowntree, Hershey, Cadbury – business philanthropists were often Quakers and seemed to like their chocolate), it is probably because their management methods did not become mainstream. Perhaps they were not entirely able to square the circle of hard-nosed capitalism with individual and societal benefit? Perhaps they were naïve or maybe just ahead of their time? Strategy involves such lengthy timescales it is often difficult to know the difference but there must be something in this idea of getting the best out of people by looking after them. It is just common sense.

In much of the recent academic literature on HR strategy and in HR circles generally, there has been great play made of the concepts of employee engagement and talent management. The simple notion that *how you manage your people* will influence your business performance is generally well accepted. However, like most blindingly obvious ideas, it is much easier to say than to do because it involves reconciling potentially conflicting forces. For example, hospital patients want to get well; nurses want to give excellent care; a ward manager wants to keep costs down; taxpayers want low taxes (until they become patients themselves) and governments just want the figures to look good. That is why a strategy is required in the first place; it is the only way to plot a course through a range of diverse perspectives. Then there is the issue of whether your people can deliver the strategy. Can that be taken for granted? Probably not, otherwise why did academics like Kaplan and Norton come to the conclusion that an *implementation* scorecard was necessary?

Even if you get this far, the toughest judges will be asking whether your strategy is the best option among all those available. We might guess that most 'successful' CEOs (in conventional terms) would just reply to this question by saying 'look at my results'. The only problem with that simplistic response is what results should we look at? Existing profits? The current cost base? Market share? Customer satisfaction? Or are there better indicators that offer deeper insights into longer-term, underlying strengths and weaknesses? For example, how innovative are you and what is your average product development cycle time? This could be a particularly telling point in industries like pharmaceuticals where any delay can cost billions in cash flow. Similarly, when Ford and General Motors used to make a profit, were their senior executives aware of the deep-seated malaise that had infected their business: a disease that eventually led to their junk bond, credit rating from Standard & Poor's?

REPORTING ON STRATEGY

The banking crisis of 2008–2009, the collapse of Lehman brothers, the Madoff Securities Ponzi scandal and many other recent events have only served to reinforce mounting concerns with the way we audit, analyse, manage and report on organizational performance. So we have to start reporting on organisations holistically, in much greater depth and, most important of all with a new perspective on the way human capital is managed. This approach will have to incorporate a full, rigorous and robust analysis and an assessment of what returns the organization is managing to accumulate. In doing so, we should be able to discern those organizations that are managing to achieve competitive advantage and high value *from their people* and those who still regard 'human resource management' as at best a tedious, administrative chore and at worst an annoying, operational irritant that gets in the way of running the business.

We are raising serious issues of corporate governance here that were already being discussed some years before the credit crunch of 2007 started. In the UK the government's Department for Trade and Industry did more than most to try and produce a workable framework for assessing the value of human capital. It created a special Accounting for People Taskforce to pull together current thinking on the subject with a view to making recommendations for a new, annual, Operating and Financial Review (OFR) to be completed by the top FTSE companies.

The first hurdle it had to overcome was to establish a clear definition of 'human capital management' (HCM). While the term had gained currency since Gary Becker's work in the 1960s (see *Human Capital: A Theoretical and Empirical Analysis*, with Special Reference to Education University of Chicago, 1994) there was still no common definition or proprietary model for

HCM and there has been no clear delineation between 'human capital management' and 'human resource management'. So, for now, we will use the terms 'HCM' and 'HR-business strategy' interchangeably, but we will adopt the definition of HCM offered by the Taskforce in its report published in October 2003 because this captures the very essence of both: (http://www.berr. gov.uk/files/file38839.pdf)

Human capital management is an approach to people management that treats it as a high level, strategic issue and seeks systematically to analyse, measure and evaluate how people policies and practices create value.

Regardless of what else the taskforce did or did not achieve, this definition fits perfectly with the sort of HR-business strategy that we are suggesting any CEO might want to build. However, it is a definition loaded with meaning, so we need to really understand each of the key words as they set a very tough challenge:

High level – HCM is not something that can be delegated to the HR team or middle management. Its implementation demands sponsorship, ownership, commitment and involvement from the highest level possible.

Strategic – HCM is inherently strategic; it cannot be detached or bolted on, ad hoc or piecemeal.

Systematically – it has to happen systematically, which means its success will be entirely dependent on having effective HCM systems in place.

Analyse – without deep and incisive analysis the problems will be ill-defined and the solutions ineffective.

Measure – without a philosophy of accountability and management by measurement, and the selection of the right measures, HCM will be nothing more than a bureaucratic paper chase.

Evaluate – evaluation has to be a management mindset backed up by closed-loop, feedback systems and a willingness to hear not just the good news but the bad as well. The organization has to learn from its mistakes and evaluation is a crucial part of changing the culture from 'seeking-to-blame' to one of problem prevention and quality assurance.

Value – measures on their own say very little until true value has been assessed and this has to mean value with £ signs.

In the event, the government dropped the OFR reporting requirement. What really let the Taskforce down though was a complete absence of any meaningful HCM data supplied by the case study organizations in their report. All reported standard personnel data such as absence and staff turnover figures without any clear £ sign benefits attributed to HCM. The hype surrounding HCM had completely overtaken reality of HR practices on the ground; a very common problem.

A real HR-business strategist would never be taken in by such rhetoric as he or she would seek direct and causal connections to be made between a continuous trend in organizational improvement and human capital practices. If we look at the Royal Bank of Scotland as an example, this had been a darling of the stock market for its audacious takeover of Natwest bank and for taking a huge share in Bank of China in 2006. It is not surprising, therefore, that its Chief Executive, Fred Goodwin, was asked to join the Taskforce and add his endorsement:

> *Accounting for People helps provide organisations with the framework to demonstrate the effectiveness of their people strategies and their impact on business performance.*

This is the same Fred Goodwin who was known in the City as 'Fred the Shred' for making profits by brutally cutting costs and who reluctantly resigned in October 2008 after the UK government had, in effect, nationalized the bank to save it from collapse.

You do not have to be the shrewdest analyst to cut through this PR gloss, but to really get under the skin of an organization, to see how its heart is beating, how its major organs are functioning and whether it is in good general shape is a highly skilled job; the organizational equivalent of a neurosurgeon. Such analysts will not jump to the conclusion that the companies with the 'best' financial results must be the best managers of human capital and will not be taken in by spurious statistics. Their analysis will be evidence-based and the evidence they seek will have to be very convincing.

WHY MOST EXISTING HR 'STRATEGIES' ARE NOT WORTHY OF THAT NAME

There is still a widely held misconception that HR strategy is something that can be produced in isolation from the business strategy; with a life of its own. This type of thinking is best exemplified in this statement from a former VP of HR from US telecom company Verizon:

> *I worked with the business presidents and general managers running the lines of business. I said, "Here's the HR strategy now let's brainstorm what questions you need answered from a human capital perspective. What are the questions that are keeping you up at night?"*

(from www.HR.com, 18 June 2001)

Any CEO worth their salt should immediately be able to spot the 'deliberate mistake' here (have you?). This VP's mental framework is completely upside down and the wrong way around. Shouldn't the issues that are 'keeping you awake at night' have been the first questions the VP of HR should have asked, not the last? They should have been the very issues on which to focus the HR-business strategy, not something bolted on as an afterthought. This also begs the very obvious question – on what basis did the VP of HR originally formulate his own HR 'strategy'?

One can only assume that he must have had some sort of HR strategy template to work to, regardless of the business strategy at Verizon: a generic template that could be applied regardless of context. Perhaps this tells us something about the mindset of such senior HR professionals – they believe in something generically known as 'best-practice' HR. If that is the case then this would represent the very antithesis of HR-business strategy: copying practices when the sole purpose of strategy is to do exactly the opposite – differentiation.

Copying a competitor's strategy might seem like a survival strategy but it is not. Even business school case studies encourage copying – 'do what Jack Welch did at GE or Lou Gerstener did at IBM'. Why? If another strategist has already done it they have already creamed off all the competitive advantage from being first mover. Even if you managed to copy everything they did (the whole system as Porter would say) you would never catch up with them, only follow in their wake. It is for this reason that strategic case studies are a particularly inappropriate way to teach HR-business strategy. Finding out how World War 1 was won did not help much with World War 2 and the 'war on terrorism' is a very different type of 'World War' again.

The US automotive manufacturers have been copying Japanese manufacturers for years, or at least thought they were. They should have been much bolder but bold strategic moves mean taking risks that your faint-hearted competitors choose not to. As a CEO you should be expecting your HR director to produce an HR-business strategy that does things your competitors have never even dreamed of.

Instead, your HR director is probably just trying to support your business plan. This is wrong, both conceptually and in practice, and leads to a series of policies that add no value in their own right (e.g. let's do talent management – yes but doesn't everybody do that?). It also relegates HR thinking to a purely reactive, operational matter. Imagine asking the sales and marketing director to develop a sales and marketing strategy *after* the finance director, R&D director and operations directors have all put together the business strategy. When we hear HR directors talking about making sure their HR 'strategy' is 'aligned' with the business strategy it is an admission that they have already missed the boat.

Even suggesting the HR and business strategies are linked and integrated has missed the point; they have to be conceived as one, simultaneously. In other words, if you have a business strategy that does not incorporate HR strategy then you are already guilty of having produced a suboptimal strategy. You will not have factored into the strategic equation the possibility of achieving the most value from your people. It is HR-business strategy's extra, highly fertile, human ingredient that rivals will find so very difficult to replicate; more difficult than any other type of generic strategy (e.g. technology led, cost leadership, market domination). You only reap these benefits though, if it is built into your vision and you have the leadership ability and strength of character to make it happen.

DEVELOPING YOUR OWN HR-BUSINESS STRATEGY

So on what basis do you start to formulate your strategy? Well you do not have to use a different strategic planning framework, only an adaptation of a classical model. The strategic planning framework or hierarchy, shown in Fig. 2.1, is a classic textbook approach and probably very close to what you already use. It could also be described as common sense as it is likely that any intelligent CEO, without any formal training in strategy, would come up with a similar sequence of decision-making steps. It is applied in most types of organization, including commercial, public sector, not-for-profit, third sector and social enterprises. There is a strong likelihood though, if you are a freethinking CEO, that you already possess a healthily sceptical attitude to any 'textbook' approach. You will have learnt, from your own experience, that it is much easier to describe such models on paper than to make them work in the real world. Do not think for one moment though that HR-business strategy is some ivory tower, academic exercise. Very soon, you will feel how real it is for you and your organization. So let us revisit this textbook model and translate it into a very practical, modus operandi.

We will look at each individual aspect of this complete framework throughout the rest of the book, but first it must be stressed that this is not meant to be a mechanistic, tick box, process. It is intended to represent a holistic, social, paradigm. A paradigm is like a religion; it is infused with a deep-seated philosophy about why we are here on this earth. It works best when it provides meaning and purpose to peoples' lives and should not be treated as a simplistic, sequential set of steps devoid of human consideration. The two-dimensional representation in Fig. 2.1 does not do justice to the concept as it cannot capture the multidimensional structure of the paradigm, its intrinsic fluidity or dynamism. As we explore each facet we will try to illustrate just how organic this paradigm needs to be if it is to grow to have a life and momentum of its own.

FIGURE 2.1   The total framework for HR-business strategy is centred around value and human values.

Vision

What this model actually says is that for strategy to work well you, at the top of the organization, have to hold a clear vision of what the future holds so that you can set a course or direction. So have you already decided on your own predictions about the future? Even if you feel you have a crystal clear vision, the next question is how much do you want to share it with your Chairman or your executive colleagues? Once you nail your colours to a particular mast you have to defend them so it is only to be expected that you might not want to commit yourself to such a clear-cut course of action. These are the human nature aspects that dry academic texts rarely bring to the fore and yet it is in acknowledging and addressing such human frailties that the true strength of HR-business strategy lies.

Let us take the banking sector as an example. We now realize that many top bankers did not predict the future at all well, although we should not jump to the conclusion that all banking leaders are the same. Wells Fargo bank wisely resisted the temptation (and the pressure of their shareholders) to get involved in sub-prime mortgage derivatives and is likely to benefit greatly from the weakness of their former competitors. So those who have a vision, and stick to their principles (a sacrosanct banking principle used to be 'never borrow short to lend long'), are more likely to thrive in the long term whereas those who provided no clear strategic direction or merely reacted to short-term pressures have reaped their just deserts.

Assuming that you have a clear vision, and are planning to share it with your closest colleagues, how do you put it into words and what should be included? This short list should help.

- How is the world likely to look in the future and what are the implications for your organization?
- How ambitious do you want the organization to be?
- What sort of markets do you want to be in?
- What types of products and services do you want to provide?
- What type of organization do you need to be – both in reality and as perceived by others – in terms of its values, principles and stability?
- Do you have a view on the implications of changing technology?
- What sort of employer do you want the organization to be, how would you like it to be perceived and what do you expect from employees?

Vision only sets a general course and does not attempt to delve into specifics. It will not have any numbers attached to it or specific timescales. This is probably why you might be tempted to move swiftly onto the mission statement, which at least sets out clear strategic goals, but this would be a mistake. Vision means a great deal to your employees, at every level. What do you stand for as CEO? Are you a man or woman of principle and integrity? Why would anyone want to follow you, never mind give their all for your 'cause'? The Oxford dictionary definition of a 'principle' is a 'fundamental truth or law, a personal code of conduct'. Another way of looking at this is the principles that people adhere to influence their behaviour. If we get the right principles, it follows that we get the sort of behaviour we need. HR-business strategists understand the power of principles.

Admittedly, principles are difficult to stick to and no one sticks to their own principles 100% of the time, which is why we admire and respect those people who do: they have raised their game above that of the ordinary man. The majority of us try to stick to the principle of honesty, but every one of us has told a lie at some time; white or otherwise. This does not necessarily mean that we are totally dishonest or lesser mortals. Our normal behaviour will gravitate towards expecting and giving truthful answers but we will let our standards slip on occasions, especially when put under abnormal pressure (e.g. our boss has just asked why we did not hit our target). Having principles that mean something, and continually trying to work more closely to them, provides a very solid foundation on which to develop excellence and they should not change much, if at all, over time.

If vision is this important then failing to articulate a vision is a gross omission. Employees like strong leadership and are much more likely to engage wholeheartedly with an organization when it matches their own values and aspirations. They will also trust an employer who tells them exactly in which direction they are heading. When Richard Branson says Virgin will put tourists into space he has a good track record of making things happen and attracting people who want to join him on his exciting journeys, both literally and metaphorically. Other CEOs take what they believe to be the easy way out: why would they commit themselves to a vision that they might not be able to deliver? This is the Vision Paradox: failing to declare a vision might seem like a safe bet but it is exactly the opposite. CEOs that do not have a vision, or are not prepared to commit themselves, cannot expect commitment from their employees. It is a recipe for long-term decline and failure. Civil service organizations, in particular, in the UK, the EU and the UN are all failing because of a lack of vision.

So start now by writing down, as succinctly as you can, what your vision is. Now pass it to a trusted colleague and ask them 'what does this mean for you personally? Whichever way you communicate your vision though, everyone who reads it will view it from a very personal perspective. We are all intrinsically egocentric, the centre of our own universe and will naturally ask ourselves what are the implications for me? What about my career aspirations, security of employment, rewards, effort, job satisfaction and what sacrifices might I be expected to make in my family and personal life? When they have a clear vision to consider they might come to the conclusion that they do not want to stay (especially if an ambitious CEO is likely to expect ambitious and hard-working staff). Fortunately, this is the first part of a natural, self-selection process that will build a stronger bond with those who relish this challenge and simultaneously, and equally importantly, send a very strong signal to the disengaged that maybe their futures lie elsewhere. Clear vision is the cornerstone of a win–win strategy but it also marks the first step towards your mission.

Mission (or Value Statement)

Robert Townsend used to run car hire firm Avis Rent-a-car and said it took him 6 months to produce Avis's succinct mission statement to 'become the number one in *driverless*, hire vehicles'. This meant that managers employed in the *chauffeur-driven* division would not have a future with the new Avis. Canon famously stated they just wanted to 'beat Xerox', which sent a very clear message. These are classic mission statements – concise and yet profound.

Townsend was also well known for his best selling 1970 book *Up the Organisation: How Groups of People Ought to Conduct Themselves for Fun and Profit* (a later edition had the particularly relevant subtitle – 'How to Stop the Corporation from Stifling People and Strangling Profits') in which he advised that the 'personnel' function should be no more than a one-person department. If we visit Avis Europe's website today http://www.avis-europe.com/content-310 we see that its European HQ in the UK has an HR team that is probably much more than one person based on the information they provide:

Human Resources

The HR team works as business partners to managers to enable them to deliver their objectives. They have specialist expertise in recruitment, employee relations, performance management and salaries and benefits. The learning and development team supports the business by identifying talent and developing employees to their full potential.

We will consider how well such HR functions are doing in Chapter 5, but in the meantime one wonders what Robert Townsend (who died in 1998) would have made of this? Would he ask where did it all go wrong or was this just another case of an inaccurate prediction by a CEO of the future of organisational management? If he actually had a one-person, personnel department in the 1960s (he was head of Avis from 1962 to 1965) they would have helped him get rid of the people in the chauffeur-driven division. Presumably the present European CEO thinks there is a need for a larger HR team today. What you need to consider is can you deliver your mission without some expertise on HR-business strategy?

While you ponder that one, it is worth alerting you to the possibility that your mission statement could be perceived as meaningless, anodyne and perfunctory unless you put a great deal of thought into it. In fact you should really be thinking in terms of a 'value' statement. What Robert Townsend should have added to his mission for Avis were the words '... and make a profit'. If he were the CEO of a non-profit organization he might have said '... and provide the best we can at the lowest cost'.

Whatever your current mission statement says here are some simple tests to ensure it provides a basis for developing a meaningful HR-business strategy.

THREE MISSION STATEMENT TESTS

1. Does your mission statement clearly declare what success looks like?
2. Does it include both value (hard £ value) and values (what we believe is important)?
3. Would it guide an employee's behaviour consistently?

Here are a few examples to try out these tests, all taken off the Web on 9 January 2009:

The BBC's Mission

> *To enrich people's lives with programmes and services that inform, educate and entertain.*

This fails the first test. How many peoples' lives does the BBC have to enrich and how much enrichment/informing/educating/entertaining is required? What share of the total audience does it have to win? If you were a TV producer for the BBC what does 'enhancing lives' mean for you? Does it mean top quality Shakespearean drama or does it mean the Gerry Springer show? Who is the arbiter and what criteria would be followed?

It fails the second test because it does not factor in costs to indicate hard value. The BBC had an income of £5 billion in 2008 of which £3.5 billion came from licence payers and government grants. So how much of this money actually ended up 'enhancing lives'? If a new TV programme did not attract many viewers does that still count as 'value'?

It also fails the third test of what does it mean for an individual employee because it is so nebulous and vague. Organizations in the creative and media sectors find it particularly difficult to articulate what their goals are but that is even more reason, not less, to provide a clear steer for everyone, employees and customers alike.

Google's Mission

> *Google's mission is to organise the world's information and make it universally accessible and useful.*

First test – who says it is useful?

Second test – if this is Google's mission in 2009 then it seems to run counter to the self-censorship with which they placated the Chinese authorities back in 2006. Mission statements that appear to be hypocritical or where espoused values run counter to practices send very conflicting signals to employees and fail the third test. This is a perennial problem with drafting mission statements (and probably why Townsend took 6 months on Avis's); we want to galvanize everyone behind a common purpose, but it is difficult to do that in one short statement.

Third test – what does 'useful' mean to you?

Virgin Atlantic's Mission

1. To grow a profitable airline
2. Where people love to fly
3. And where people love to work

This is not only a very simple mission statement it is also very clever. It actually gives the impression that these are the *three priorities, in a particular order,* and profitability comes first; everything else is secondary. The message is clear and powerful, if the airline isn't profitable it will cease to exist. Second, it puts the customer's needs ahead of the employees (just) because that's why and how the company exists. Yet it includes in number 3 wanting to make the company a great place to work, presumably because Richard Branson and the CEO believe that 1 and 2 will not be achieved without 3.

This passes all three tests, success is measurable, the customer is valued (not treated as a captive audience) and although it wants its employees to enjoy their work the *purpose* of their work is not engagement but the number 1 priority of profitability. Clarity of purpose is highly motivational.

As with vision, some CEO's think that a mission statement is just another mechanical step: something to put on the notice board, but not necessarily to be lived and breathed by them or their executives. They think that the most important step is the next one, strategy, and that they can start their planning process off at this stage. This type of CEO prefers action to contemplation but we shall soon see why contemplation is crucial for a sustainable model of organizational success.

STRATEGY

If you do not include a mention of your employees needs in your mission statement you have already sent a very negative signal that they are not part of the big picture; their interests are not as important as stakeholders. More importantly, as you move into strategizing mode, they won't feature uppermost in your mind. They will just have to do whatever your strategy demands: another subliminal, negative signal.

Take Microsoft's business strategy, which has always been painfully obvious to its competitors – maintain a monopoly at all costs and kill off any competition wherever possible, by whatever means. This has been a very successful strategy in the past, because it was conceived at the dawn of a brand new industry that lent itself to a natural monopoly (a common, universal, computer operating system and business software platform). Several successful lawsuits later, including the EU fine for Microsoft's attempt to restrict competition in the media software market and a more recent one in February 2008 of $1.3 billion, should have told Microsoft loudly and clearly what society thinks about its strategy. Yet Microsoft's mission and values are still apparently

To help people and businesses throughout the world realise their full potential

Whether this is totally hypocritical or not should not be our main concern here, although how many of Microsoft's employees really engage with such underlying values? Our task here is to produce a guide for CEO's to create value through their people so we need to judge the way companies like Microsoft and Google perform, not by a simplistic look at profits, or by any public declaration of their espoused values, but by a shrewd analysis of whether they are getting their people to realize their full value. This will not be answered by asking employees whether they enjoy working there, or even if they are really engaged or committed to the 'cause'. No, it will only come from an in-depth appraisal of the long-term, sustainable, hard value of the business. So let us start to do this by looking at a selection of some well-known, global businesses (most of which were reviewed in the first edition) to see how they have fared when judged against this type of analysis?

Table 2.1 contains two types of data (latest figures collected in February 2009) on the companies listed; their market capitalization and position in the

TABLE 2.1 What Does Market Capitalization Tell Us about HR-Business Strategies?

Company	Market capitalization 2002	Market capitalization 2009	Global 500 ranking 2009 (2002)
Toyota	106.36	107	22 (28)
Daimler (Chrysler)	46.02	35.8	73 (81)
Honda	41.40	84.4	147 (97)
General Motors	33.87	2.4	Not in FT500 (126)
Nissan	33.01	Part of Renault	227 (131)
Ford	28.63	6.4	Not in FT500 (156)
GE	372.08	160.6	3 (1)
Microsoft	326.63	178.9	7 (2)
IBM	179.21	117.1	27 (12)
Verizon	125.26	14.8	55 (19)
Google	N/A	102	56 (N/A)

FT Global 500 rankings. We should, therefore, be very wary of reaching any firm conclusions based on such limited data. It is also worth noting that market capitalization (shares × share price) is a very volatile measure, particularly at a time when share prices around the world have collapsed in the wake of the credit crunch and recession. So what questions are prompted by this data and what other data would we need to obtain better insights into how well these companies are performing?

If we first look at the automotive group at the top of the table, one of the most obvious points to note is the collapse in value of Ford and General Motors and the corresponding resilience of Toyota; especially when we realize that these three companies are all similarly sized in numbers of vehicles produced. So how can Toyota create so much more value from their operations? Also, what is it that Honda (a much smaller producer) is doing so well that they have managed to make significant strides forward (a doubling in market value) over the same period, in a very mature market that has overcapacity?

If we lined up experts in sales and marketing, customer service, finance, automotive production, technology and R&D to help us with this analysis they would all have a view on why the figures are the way they are. One suggestion for Ford and GM's demise is their concentration on producing gas-guzzling SUVs that are no longer in demand in the North American market. Other analysts point to GM's high pension and health costs for employees (and ex-employees) adding too much to the cost of each vehicle produced, making them uncompetitive.

Let us accept these two observations at face value for now. If you were Ford or GM's CEO what would you do about putting these problems right? Presumably, you would change the range of vehicles you produced and try to negotiate different rewards and benefits with the unions. Neither of these problems have quick-fix solutions though. They are both symptoms of the deep-seated malaise that has existed at these two companies for many years (certainly since the first edition in 2003) and the steady decline in market value has consistently reflected this.

When GM approached the US Congress for a bailout at the end of 2008, their unions were not prepared to take a pay cut, partly because they didn't see their members as being responsible for the decline of the company, even though they had negotiated their very costly benefits for their members. Union negotiators are very good at wanting an equal share of rewards without an equal sense of responsibility for the company's ability to pay. Even the most obvious decision to change the vehicle mix is going to have to address the problem of changing the behaviour of those executives who had happily been producing SUVs thinking the market was always going to be profitable. These executives are going to have to get out of their comfort zone and start earning their salaries again. Addressing attitude change is always high on the list of what is required when trying to change strategies and an HR-business strategy needs to ensure that attitudes for the future do not remain entrenched in any particular business model.

The market values of the next four companies on the list (GE, Microsoft, IBM, Verizon) are obviously all showing significant drops due to market turmoil so we cannot read too much into that. However, their relative positions in the FT500 are also slipping (Ford and GM have disappeared from these rankings) and Microsoft, particularly, should be concerned about where Google might be in a few years time. So again, if you were the CEO of any of these businesses what strategy would you employ to change their fortunes? Market capitalization analysis might not provide you with many answers so what other indicators might be useful in helping you decide what changes to make?

The answers lie in exploring each and every one of the integrated elements shown in the framework in Fig. 2.1 and looking for opportunities to create some more value. However, you need to be very careful that while we look at them in the right order and attach the right priority to each we should keep reminding ourselves that this is not just a framework, it is a holistic and dynamic system, and systems theory tells us that if you change any part of the system you have changed the whole system. Just like the human body, if your diet is wrong or you don't get enough exercise your whole system will start to suffer. So perhaps we should have a look at how other companies have tried to get this right?

THE 'BEST' BUSINESSES DO NOT NECESSARILY HAVE THE BEST HR STRATEGIES

In the Personnel Today Awards of November 2006 the award for the 'Best HR strategy in line with business' went to the AA (no not that one – the UK's Automobile Association), a vehicle breakdown and recovery company with a long history. Recently though, it had been bought by private equity partners who had put their 'man', Tim Parker, in as CEO to achieve better returns. Also, in the same journal in November 2006, there was an article about the AA entitled 'AA denies ban on taking time off over winter' reporting that it had 'struggled to cope last summer' (the busy period) and now the union was waging a campaign against the company because it had made 'too many redundancies' (patrols had been reduced from 3500 to 2087) in order to reduce costs. The union threatened it would have 'employment tribunals coming out of its ears'. If this is what the *winner* of the 'Best HR strategy' award was doing one can only wonder what havoc the runners-up in this competition must have been wreaking.

Any CEO with intelligence should be able to do a better job than this, surely? Unless, of course, your aim is to make a fast buck and an even swifter exit. It is natural for organizations to tend towards complacency unless they are shaken up and the AA had plenty of fat for Tim Parker to trim and render down into a fortune for himself and his private equity partners. http://www.telegraph.co.uk/finance/migrationtemp/2805935/Business-profile-Prince-of-Darkness-to-the-rescue.html. There is nothing wrong in making an inefficient organization more efficient and you don't need to consider people at all if your single goal is short-term financial gain. What governments and citizens should be asking though is why do organizations let themselves become the targets of private equity. If the AA was already getting the best value from its people, with an HR-business strategy, there would have been no fat to trim. Private equity does not represent a new or higher value management model. It is not rocket science and requires little or no understanding of organizational DNA. An HR-business strategy would aim to achieve even better, longer-term, financial returns by managing the patrols better and without leaving paying customers stranded by the side of the road during the summer. HR-business strategy has to be a win–win for all concerned.

Regardless of the aims of any strategy the actions and behaviours of the people in the business will be dictated by the business and operating plans; this is where the strategy becomes real. If McDonalds decides that it wants to sell products other than just burgers and fries then the people who work in McDonalds have to learn how to make and serve pizzas or tortillas. The strategic decisions of today inevitably become the most basic operational tasks of tomorrow.

Let us not kid ourselves. There are many businesses around the world today, without any formal HR-business strategies, which are hugely successful for all sorts of reasons. They don't have to gain a competitive advantage from managing their people if their competitors do not have a clue what an HR-business strategy looks like. The source of their success could therefore simply lay in them having a unique business model or product (Google?), first-mover advantage (Nintendo Wii?) or simply providing the right product at just at the right time (steel companies finally making money from China and India's exponential growth). Luck can play a large part in a company's success in the short term but luck, on its own, will not provide long-term, sustainable success.

The key issue here is that investors and key stakeholders (taxpayers in the case of public sector bodies) need to know which factors are having a significant influence on an organization's fortunes and performance and whether they are likely to last. A speculator will aim to make money on short-term movements in share price, regardless of the underlying strength of the business. We might witness less undesirable speculation if we could all spot when a business is well run. This is why *human capital reporting* is now seen as a crucial perspective to complete the picture provided by more conventional analyses. Human capital reporting requires a new type of organizational 'detective' with a new set of skills, tools and techniques (see Chapter 9). Their job is to unearth performance and sustainability indicators that tell us the organization is not only managing its people well but also managing very predictable, strategic risks. The most obvious human risk is letting people operate outside the bounds of their competence, capability or authority. The lessons from rogue traders like Nick Leeson at Barings in 1995 have obviously not been learnt by the banking sector or Société Générale who found that they had their own rogue trader in Jerome Kerviel in 2008.

So why don't we start developing these detective skills by focusing on just one particular industry – airlines? In Table 2.2 we have a collection of typical business data for each of three key players – British Airways (BA, global, scheduled carrier), Ryanair (budget operator in Europe) and Southwest Airlines (budget operator in the USA). We will view this data, not through the eyes of a finance director or a marketing specialist, but through an HR-business strategy lens. Let us be absolutely clear though, what the objectives of this exercise are:

- We want to be able to judge which airlines are being managed the best, and that means in their totality
- We particularly want to ask questions about the relative 'people management' capabilities in each company
- We need to know which airlines are likely to be operating the most successful and sustainable business models

Now, just before you start to consider and assimilate this data, you might like to consider the sequence of thought processes and calculations that your brain automatically undertakes when presented with a spreadsheet or similar layout of business data to that shown in Table 2.1. You might ask yourself how often, if ever, your business brain is exposed to 'people data' when you use it for analysis? It is worth noting that the number of 'employees' shown here was not readily available from the financial statements used to garner this data and had to be obtained separately.

TABLE 2.2 Which Airline Gets the Best from their People?

All figures collected on 8 January 2009 and converted to $'s at £1 = $1.50	British Airways	Ryanair	Southwest
Passengers (million)	33	55	101
Employees	45,140	3,500	34,545
Planes	245	165	520
Airports served	300+	150	64
Revenue (billions)	$13.11	$3.66	$10.78
Pre-tax profits	$1.32 billion	$594 million	$2.78 billion
Operating margin	10.0%	19.79%	7.5%
Share price	$2.65	$4.31	$8.94
Market capitalization (billions)	$4.06	$6.32	$6.61
Market value per employee	$88,746	$1,805,712	$191,344

Of course, there is a great deal of data here and we cannot even vouch for its accuracy (remember Enron, WorldCom, Parmalat et al.) not only because it is gleaned from a variety of sources but also simply because auditors and accountants not only make errors but will also, intentionally, produce misleading information, 'cook the books', or want to put a gloss on potentially disappointing results.

It is also questionable whether we are ever able to compare 'like-with-like' between different companies, at different stages in their history and organizational development, in different market contexts and jurisdictions. So any analysis of such data is fraught with difficulty before we even start and there is no intention here to retread the same sort of detailed, conventional analysis that you, as a CEO, or your finance director would normally expect. Our objective is to encourage you to see performance indicators from a different angle. There are many revealing indicators that a company cannot cover up or obfuscate and top of this list is employee behaviour, because customers and even the general public will tell you how they are performing.

In BA's case there have been several serious industrial relations disputes at its main London Heathrow airport base over the last 5 years. It also had a disastrous move to its new Terminal 5, when even its own staff could not come to work because security would not let them through. Obviously, both of these factors will have reduced BA's potential profits significantly and that, in itself, is a problem for them. However, our real interest is what these indicators tell us about the culture at BA and its long-term prospects. It is not just the fact that the terminal opening was an embarrassing shambles, but that no operational manager was able to get the message across to the executive team, or the board, to delay the opening. What does this tell us about governance at BA? Moreover, how can an airline with such terrible employee relations hope to survive, long term, against competing airlines that do not have such impediments? An HR-business-investment analyst would not recommend holding a long-term position in BA shares, even if they were happy to hold on to shares themselves in the short term for speculative reasons.

Ryanair is a very different type of airline to BA, but it has ambitions and is currently attempting to buy Irish state airline Aer Lingus, which would make it much more of a direct threat to BA. So is it any better at managing its people? Apparently not, if we believe many stories posted on the web about the shabby way it treats its staff (many of whom are employed by a separate company – Crewlink). In fact its CEO, Michael O'Leary, is famous for his focused, cost-obsessive, business model and his view that if anyone wants to work with Ryanair they have to accept whatever the company deems appropriate. At the moment this business model is working very well, based on the returns Ryanair manages to produce, but how would Michael O'Leary's views have to change if Southwest Airlines set up a European operation in direct competition? Southwest Airlines is fêted for its enlightened management attitude to its employees and also for its 69th straight quarter of profit. Its business strategy and its people strategy are one and the same. It has its own mission which emphasizes this, even if it does fail the 'value' test, it would not do any of this if it could not make a profit

The Mission of Southwest Airlines

The mission of Southwest Airlines is dedication to the highest quality of Customer Service delivered with a sense of warmth, friendliness, individual pride, and Company Spirit.

To Our Employees

We are committed to provide our Employees a stable work environment with equal opportunity for learning and personal growth. Creativity and innovation are encouraged for improving the effectiveness of Southwest Airlines. Above all, Employees will be provided the same concern, respect, and caring attitude within the organization that they are expected to share externally with every Southwest Customer.

Ryanair makes its staff pay for their own uniforms and is even considering making passengers pay £1 to use the onboard toilet. European passengers will fervently hope to see the day that Southwest does compete with Ryanair.

It is worth noting that BA does not even appear to have a mission statement or declared purpose in life as several ex-customers appear to have been searching for one without success – one remarking

'I would like to know the mission statement/corporate purpose of British Airways. I have searched everywhere'.

http://www.flyertalk.com/forum/british-airways-executive-club/887213-what-mission-statement-british-airways.html

So where do we go from here? Well, imagine that you have just been made the CEO of either BA or Ryanair, and your task is to improve its long-term performance and viability, what would be your immediate priorities? A previous CEO of BA, Rod Eddington, slashed jobs so would you do the same? Could you slash jobs at Ryanair when it is already so obsessed with cost? Perhaps you need first to decide what is in the best long-term interests of the business and simultaneously start considering how you bring the employees with you on that strategic journey? You would also have to have a strategy that managed out those who did not want to take part. This is something BA has signally failed to do. Its industrial relations climate and culture today is not fit for any strategic purpose and it can only afford its poor industrial relations because it has many lucrative slots at Heathrow that keep unwanted competitors at bay and are worth millions. If BA should ever have to relinquish these slots would the business model survive?

Of course, you could decide to pay a fact-finding visit to Southwest Airlines to find out what makes them so good, but how would you turn a Ryanair into a Southwest? As we will continually reveal throughout this text, copying a competitor's HR-business strategy is probably the most difficult job a CEO can take on. Even just telling employees that you wanted to improve the company would elicit thousands of personal, selfish, reactions. So how would you communicate to every single employee to make sure they all understood the message and were committed to helping you to achieve your goals?

Perhaps the first thing to do is get it clear in everyone's head that the way you run the business and the way you manage people will have to be one and the same thing. So let us move our analysis on and ask how well other CEO's manage this, particularly difficult, balancing act?

THE HR-BUSINESS STRATEGY MATRIX

Figure 2.2 is a simple matrix that attempts to plot the relative positions of most of the companies referred to in this book in terms of how effective their business and HR strategies are. This is based on a very thorough analysis using the full range of human capital management indicators and insights spread throughout the text.

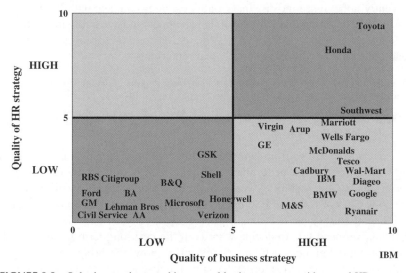

FIGURE 2.2   Only the very best combine a good business strategy with a good HR strategy.

The matrix plots the qualities of 'HR strategy' and 'business strategy' to produce a combined appraisal. Organizations that are the best at combining and integrating both appear in the top right quadrant. Companies where the business strategy is succeeding, for now, without an effective HR strategy, fall into the bottom right. Companies that have neither a good business strategy nor an HR strategy are in the bottom left. You will notice that no one is shown in the top left quadrant simply because the probability that a company can have a good HR strategy whilst its business strategy is very poor is somewhere between negligible and impossible.

Toyota, Honda and Southwest are deemed to have earned a place in the top right quadrant primarily because they have business strategies that are indivisible from their HR strategies. In each case, the way employees work and behave is integral to their offering. Even though the global recession of 2009 is putting them all under severe pressure and leading both Toyota and Honda to lay workers off, they will still be around when Ford and GM have disappeared off the map.

This matrix is intrinsically impressionistic; it is not intended to be a typical business audit. In order to produce a more detailed, strategic analysis we will have to use a whole range of tools and measures that get under the organization's skin: indicators that you can use to guide your own thinking on how well you are managing your human capital (see Chapter 9). But let us reiterate once more, this is not trying to show how HR strategy is *aligned* with business strategy, our construct is entirely different. At best, alignment produces weak versions of strategy and at worst it happens too late in the strategy formulation process. So we are now challenging the very foundation of conventional HR theory and if we want to build HR-business strategies on solid foundations we need a better theory. The first bit of theory we need to re-visit is the theory of organization design, which will incorporate structural, cultural and systemic design principles and complete our explanation of the application of the framework in Figure 2.1.

Chapter 3

What does a Strategic HR-Business Look and Feel Like?

SOME GOLDEN RULES AND PRINCIPLES OF STRUCTURAL, ORGANIZATION DESIGN

There are some simple principles, lessons and guidelines that all HR-business strategists should follow when designing an organization. Those shown below are just a distillation of many and can be regarded as the core principles, but often organizational pressures (e.g. appointment of non-executive directors, unforeseen external pressures) are hard to resist, but these best principles should not be given up lightly. Principles are the deep wells of sustainability during the longest drought.

(a) Organizations are not democracies. Some are more democratic than others but they all need leadership and therefore a hierarchy of some sort. No apologies need to be made because the only alternative to a series of reporting lines is no reporting lines at all, otherwise known as anarchy.

(b) Someone should always be ultimately accountable for whatever the organization does.

(c) The purpose of an organization is not to create jobs.

(d) Do not be seduced by terms such as the 'virtual organization'. It is a meaningless phrase. 'Virtual' organizations may refer to geographically dispersed organizations or those where electronic communication is the only link between various outposts. These factors may present some operational difficulties, but they are still real organizations in every sense of the word.

(e) An organization chart should always aim to reflect reality, even though it rarely does in practice. A title or position should never be an attempt to give credibility to managers who cannot earn it for themselves. Regardless of who the organization chart says is in control, staff will generally deal with those who they regard as being in control. The de facto organization structure rules, so why not have the courage to get the chart to match it?

(f) Do not try to 'con' your employees into thinking they are more important by drawing your organizational pyramid upside down. It is about as convincing as a magician's three-card trick.

(g) Do not employ prima donnas or those too precious to accept open criticism. Premier league footballers come very expensive and do not guarantee a winning streak: a point recently amplified by the atrocious performance of many overpaid derivatives traders and senior banking executives.

(h) Never give anyone power or authority in excess of their own capability: a very obvious rule and yet one that most organizations break on a regular basis.

(i) Ambition and talent are not always equal and very rarely do the superambitious have the talent to match. Never confuse the two when succession planning.

(j) Personal effectiveness should not be construed as organizational effectiveness. You might employ a 'brilliant' product designer, but that does not mean you will achieve an acceptable profit margin on the goods they design. Brilliant engineers have often cost their organizations dearly even though their engineering excellence is unquestionable.

(k) Every time a new post is suggested, the key question is how will this role add value? If there is no clear answer you have not put enough thought into the decision. Management layers only add value if they manage a higher value performance from those who report to them.

(l) Most managers can only cope with about six to eight direct reports. Certainly never go over 10 because none of them will be managed as effectively as they could be.

(m) The number of direct reports should be even smaller when each position is highly technical. Technical staff, who understand the technology better than their boss, create a dangerous situation and a very awkward relationship.

(n) The executive team should reach agreement on which are *key* positions. They should be identified as such on an organization chart and have successors identified. The risk of losing key people should be closely and regularly monitored. You should go to the ends of the earth to keep them because they will take so much of your potential value with them (but see g above).

(o) Anyone suggesting a matrix organization had better get the culture right first. Never give anyone two bosses, no matter what the justification may be. This leads to all sorts of political games and playing the priorities of one boss off against another.

(p) Organization charts that change too often are a symptom of bad organization design. Some organizations change their structures so often that the latest chart is never up to date. Every time the organization structure changes, it automatically means everyone directly affected has a new role. No one can change their role that often, or that quickly, and still be completely effective. HR-business strategists should counsel against all changes unless they are absolutely necessary and where the ramifications are fully considered.

(q) There is no reason why the principles of empowerment or flexibility should be constrained by an organization's desire to adhere to a principle of systematic control. Even empowered employees will ultimately be accountable to someone. Empowerment is actually more to do with the system than it is culture. Anyone can have a great idea but they should not be empowered to try it out without putting it through a system to check that it works. Innovation outside the system is as likely to sap value as it is to add value.

(r) Avoid simplistic silos and 'stove pipes' of technical, production, marketing and finance. Why not put some technical people in marketing as a balance, or vice versa. Production people will have to produce what sales can sell, but only at a given cost. It is better to get this dialogue working before the final production design is agreed.

(s) Never appoint anyone in a managerial position purely on technical merit; another obvious point yet a classic managerial fault. There is a very high probability that they will not be as brilliant a manager as they are a technician and, when they realize that, they will hide their managerial inadequacies behind a screen of overelaborate, technical expertise (and make everyone else's life more difficult in the process).

(t) Never appoint someone just because they are 'the best of the bunch'. If you cannot get the right person in the right role, then maybe you need to respecify or redesign the role.

So much for structural considerations, but the structure is only one building block. Equally important are systems and both structure and system have to be designed in a way that melds the two together.

SYSTEMS

Wanting to be a high-value organization automatically means wanting to subscribe to the philosophy of never-ending, continuous improvement. This is the pursuit of perfection (or zero defects if you prefer) whilst fully acknowledging that perfection is unattainable. The journey is more important than the goal and the only way to bring everyone with you on this long and difficult journey is to develop an HR-business strategy that makes their best interests and the organization's best interests one and the same. In organizations without an effective HR-business strategy the number of people in the organization with the inclination, never mind the capability, to constantly seek more value will be strictly limited. HR-business strategy tries to enlist every employee in that search. More than that though, the HR-business strategy aims to create the system, the structure and the processes to achieve that end. So, if someone on the shop floor has a good 'added value idea' it will have every chance of being captured and realized only if there is a system designed to do exactly that. There are many reasons though, why putting such a system in place is extremely difficult.

We all frequently use the words 'system' and 'systematic' when we talk about how our organizations operate. How many of us though actually stop to consider the power of the word *system*? Do you actually know what a system is and how would you go about trying to design one? Dictionary definitions do not help much and the word itself is overused. Where is the commonality, for example, between a payment system, a computer operating system and a road system? The answer lies in the following, working definition:

An organisational system is a means for making sure that what you plan to happen actually happens.

Payment systems make sure customers pay and suppliers get paid on time. Computer operating systems make sure the computer operates. A road system makes sure you can transport goods or people from a to b. All these systems have checks built into them. Part of the payment system includes generating a reminder for late payers; a diagnostic tells you whether the software has loaded properly; a series of road signs makes sure you end up where you need to be. Organizations have to have effective systems if they are to make sure they deliver what the customer needs.

System is an especially powerful concept when allied with the main elements of HR-business strategy, but what does it look like? We can produce the paper forms that constitute the payment system, or draw a map of a road system and we could even produce the code from a computer operating system, but how do you draw a human capital system? That is exactly what Fig. 3.1. tries to do.

This is supposed to be like a subatomic particle diagram but only a selection of the 'subatomic' human capital systems are shown for illustration purposes. The complete 'atom' is the HR-business strategy and each of the 'satellites' represents a system in its own right but is interconnected with all the other systems. So what does each of the human capital satellites mean in practice?

Acquisition and development system – this system has to ensure you acquire the right knowledge, skills and talent and can develop any enhancements as necessary. This means some attempt has to be made to identify and assess appropriate skills and talents. The system should apply throughout the organization from the highest to the lowest levels. There are plenty of tools and instruments available on the market for the process but the *system* should aim to remove anyone from a position where they do not possess the necessary skills/talent/knowledge. That is why it is directly linked to the 'satellite' of the performance system.

Performance system – assesses everyone's performance against agreed criteria, all of which are directly seen to be connected to the organizations

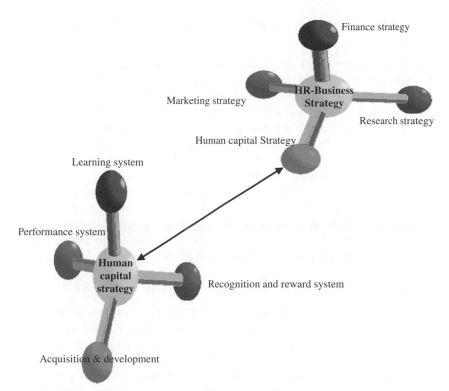

FIGURE 3.1   The complete human capital system is like many interlinked satellites.

strategic, value objectives. There will be several processes involved (appraisal, performance measurement, performance review), but the system will not tolerate underperformance for any longer than the maximum time allowed. Where individuals are trying to develop to improve their performance they will inevitably have to rely on another linked 'satellite' – the learning system.

Learning system – that sees every improvement opportunity as a learning opportunity. If a performance objective is achieved (e.g. customer complaints fall) the learning system ensures the lessons are captured (via an intranet or knowledge management database?) and disseminated to ensure everyone learns and remembers for the future. However, this satellite needs to be linked to and supported by the recognition system.

Recognition and reward system – that acknowledges which individual, team or department seems to be making the most progress. The recognition aspect can be backed up with simple awards or monetary rewards if appropriate. If the system is working well nobody should feel their contribution to improvement is unrecognized and individual managers and/or team colleagues will have a habit of acknowledging each other's contributions, even if tangible rewards do not always follow. Senior managers will regularly ask for examples of these occasions to check the system is alive and well.

The simple key to all of this is that everyone should be conscious that the systems are in place and working effectively, if not perfectly: there is no such thing as a perfect system where human beings are involved. It is the willingness to keep trying to make the system work better that is the prime motivator. Take talent management, any manager should be capable of answering the question 'where is the talent in your team?' If they are unable to answer this either there is no system in place or the system is not working properly. Equally, if employees feel that they have untapped talent or potential then they should know how to have that self-belief checked out within the system. The first question the system will ask them is how they believe their untapped talents will add value? That will always be the gateway to the whole system.

Now if you thought explaining human capital systems is difficult, wait until we look at the interplay between human systems and culture.

HUMAN SYSTEMS AND ORGANIZATIONAL CULTURE

Organizations are obviously much more complex than just a series of mechanical or administrative systems. Project management, knowledge management and budgeting are also governed by systems and are often too dependent on imperfect IT systems, which the IT specialists, in turn, blame on poor specification of requirements. However, the main limiting factor is the people who design and use them. A lack of cooperation within a project team, an unwillingness to pass on information or share knowledge and playing the budgeting system to make sure you have some funds hidden away for a rainy day are all very natural, predictable, human tendencies. Therefore organizations have to be very clever in designing systems that are inherently human yet bring out the best rather than the worst in people. Human systems designers, rather counterintuitively, should anticipate the worst aspects of human nature and then design in features to try to guarantee that such tendencies are eliminated, or at least minimized wherever possible.

Think of what a traffic light system is meant to achieve? All systems have a purpose, and in this case a dual purpose of ensuring traffic flows as smoothly and as safely as possible. The machinery of the lights themselves is only a part of the system; what make the system work are the common values of road users, drivers and pedestrians. Systems work best when they are 'human systems', that is, when everyone knows and accepts the part they have to play. There are some countries where exactly the same types of mechanical lights do not constitute a system, simply because many citizens choose to ignore them. If there is no 'policing' of the system, or no consequences for transgressors, then it will fail. Now let us apply this type of thinking to something that is so important to most large corporations – project management. So do you have a project management system and is it 'human'?

Take proprietary project management methodology Prince 2 as an example, for which there are numerous training courses available. Then consider how many projects in your experience come in on time, within budget and actually deliver what was originally required? It is particularly ironic that the roots of this methodology lay in the IT industry when one considers how many IT projects have failed over the years. Yet, you do not have to be a genius to spot why projects that have not been designed according to human system design principles go wrong including

- Unclear objectives at the outset that produce 'camel' projects designed by a committee with conflicting agendas.
- Imposed time and cost constraints that no one is prepared to challenge because of the fear culture that exists; which encourages the overbudgeting tendency to build in room for manoeuvre.
- The same culture views anyone challenging delivery dates or other critical path deadlines as being negative and career limiting.

These are just a very small sample of the most obvious cultural impediments. So if companies persist in sending everyone on a Prince 2 course the HR-business strategist should at least design in the necessary human elements that successful project management systems require. This could well include anonymity for those who want to disagree with the project objectives or constraints and allowing them to be aired fully before the project starts. Such a system would require the project leader not only to address these concerns, but also to be held accountable for any subsequent slippage.

There are plenty of large, public projects where these principles can be applied. Defence projects in particular tend to be large and very expensive. The UK Ministry of Defence (MOD) decided in 1997 to go ahead with a project to design and build a new Astute class submarine. By 2004 it was already overrunning its budget by £1 billion and 43 months late and was finally launched in June 2007. According to the Select Committee on Public Accounts – http://www.publications.parliament.uk/pa/cm200304/cmselect/cmpubacc/383/38305.htm

> The Astute submarine programme suffered from technical and project management difficulties. The Department and (contractor) BAE Systems (sic) acknowledge that they had misunderstood the risks and costs and underestimated the impact of the move of submarine design from the Department to a Prime Contractor. In particular, they underestimated the shortfall in skills and expertise in submarine design.

So here was a defence critical project that cost billions and no one had a system for ensuring that the requisite skills were available. That might have been a big mistake, but what will prevent it happening again? What has been learned and applied? Has the prevailing culture of starting projects without adequate planning changed? The evidence is plain that rushing things often causes more delays and costs but attitudes at the MOD and BAE Systems have been shaped over many years by similar project overruns that they now accept it as the norm, without question and become inured to any criticism or scrutiny.

Organizational learning is extremely difficult within such a culture and such attitudes can permeate whole sectors of industry. Take IT providers as an example. What is the prevailing attitude among IT systems salespeople? That they win the contract and then make their money out of specification and customer requirement changes? Is it in the interests of such companies to make sure they help the client get it right first time? Let us take a look at IT projects for UK government departments. A story headed 'Secret computer deals that are costing the taxpayer billions' in *The Times*, 2 February 2009 revealed that the original estimated cost of the 10 largest IT contracts in the UK public sector was £17 billion. The predicted overspend on these is £18.6 billion with a total predicted cost of IT running at £102 billion by 2013.

This is not just confined to one particular department either. Alongside the big spenders at the MOD are Revenue and Customs, the Police, NHS (original cost £2.3 billion, now £12.7 billion), Prisons and the Courts service. Hamel and Prahalad may not have come up with anything new in their 'core competence' theory but here we seem to be witnessing the completely opposite effect, a UK civil service that has a *core incompetence* in introducing IT systems. Alternatively, we could simply regard this as clear evidence that the civil service has entirely the wrong human systems in place. The HR-business strategist would immediately want to look at the competence of the government's negotiators and IT specifiers. They would also want to be able to pay whatever it takes to recruit some hard-nosed, contract negotiators from the private sector to deal with the hard-nosed, savvy, contract negotiators in the private sector. Admittedly, to do so would require one or two radical changes to civil service reward policy.

Whatever type of human systems the HR-business strategist encounters they will always have two, prime concerns:

1. **Risk management** – the need to ensure all human systems are as foolproof as possible so the organization does not endanger anyone or leave itself open to litigation (e.g. pilot licences are up to date and in order).
2. **Value maximization** – the value system is watertight, in that value does not seep out (e.g. lax cost controls, project overruns and delays) and that the human inputs into the system (e.g. skills, rewards) produce the right people producing the best value possible.

It is an organizational fact of life that the most valuable human systems are the most difficult to create. This is precisely why HR-business strategy offers an advantage that is so difficult for competitors to replicate. This is easy to understand when one thinks back to the traffic light example. There the key ingredient is trust. If you do not trust your fellow citizens to obey the red light, then there is no point the light being there because you will have to proceed with caution. You would, in effect, produce your own system that had a sole purpose of personal survival. Unfortunately though, this would not help traffic to flow and the result would be total congestion. This is just yet more evidence that 'whole systems' cannot be constructed from individual departments, teams or people doing their own 'thing'.

Now let us move up another gear to consider what human system would be required to ensure all of your people will willingly share their knowledge and expertise with each other: bearing in mind that everyone knows knowledge is power? Also, how do you design a learning system to ensure the organization always learns from its mistakes? These human systems will be worth their weight in gold.

If you quickly want to check what an absence of a learning system looks like just ask yourself what happened the last time a serious mistake was uncovered in your company? Was there a search for the 'culprits' and a desire to punish – this is what happens in a seeking-to-blame culture that you might have helped to create. Or was it just swept under the carpet; maybe you did not even hear about the last big mistake because of the fear culture you have created? Would there have been a well-understood, systematic sharing of the lessons learnt? Had the same mistake been made before? Honda follows a principle that everyone can make a mistake, but they should never make the same mistake twice. This strikes the right balance, very simply, between trying to run a safe and successful business whilst always having to accept a degree of human fallibility.

Assuming that you are now convinced of the need to concentrate some considerable effort on developing human systems there is a ready-made list shown in Table 3.1 that should be regarded as the absolute minimum necessary for a true HR-business strategy.

AVOIDING DEFAULT MODE

Strategy is a conscious decision to cope with whatever challenges you might face. Therefore, by publicly declaring that you have a strategy you are acknowledging your determination to do everything possible to avoid being a victim of circumstance or slipping into the default modes of complacency and inertia. So what might a default culture look like? This is highly predictable. If no one takes the lead on strategy then individual managers can quite rightly start to decide, for themselves, what they think is acceptable. Without a single, coherent, strategy there is no basis for accountability – the marketing director can chase market share and the sales director can chase sales, but the finance director will probably want profitability. Default 'strategies', a perfect oxymoron, are always a recipe for disaster and will inevitably lead to internal politics, in-fighting and everyone blaming everyone else when things inevitably go wrong. This is precisely what we are witnessing now due to the default global, financial strategy that failed to install a proper regulatory system. So default culture is really bad news and any attempt at a conscious strategy has to be the preferred option.

TABLE 3.1 HR-Business Strategy Human Systems

System	Purpose – to ensure …	Sample indicator
Communication system	Employees have understood instructions and objectives	Install a simple system that requires feedback, from a random sample of recipients of any communication, to check understanding
Employee development system	Employees develop their value potential	All employees should be able to articulate the value objectives of their own development
Employee engagement system	Employees are fully engaged	Engagement survey, but one that includes specific questions on connections with value
Knowledge (intellectual capital) management system	Ideas are captured and used effectively	A systematic way of collecting and assessing all ideas for value
Learning system	The individual and the organization learn what they need to know	Double-loop feedback systems are in place (see Chris Argyris)
Performance management system	All employees are performing to the best of their ability	Regular appraisal of not just individual performance but how they contribute to the value chain
Reward and recognition system	Maximum individual contribution is continuously sought and encouraged	Incidents where conscious efforts are made to acknowledge extraordinary performance
Talent identification system	All relevant talents are used effectively	Formal assessment based on building track record data

Default culture is also, inevitably, a command and control culture. If everyone is working to their own agenda, executives cannot afford for any of their own team to be supporting anyone else's. This also means executives are unable to challenge each other's agenda. This is precisely what happens in civil service departments when cabinet ministers fail to show the courage and leadership necessary to produce a coherent strategy. It is much easier for political 'leaders' (sic) to utter vague policy statements ('every child matters') then place the matter in the 'safe pair of hands' of their senior civil servants. For 'safe pair of hands' though, read 'do not embarrass your Minister'.

Illegal immigration provides a perfect example of this failing. No minister will admit publicly that illegal immigration is out of control, or even attempt to produce accurate figures as accurate figures mean greater accountability. The job of the Permanent Secretary is simply to ensure the Minister, and the Government, are *seen* to be addressing the issue. When 'maintaining an image' becomes the purpose of the 'system', though we should not be surprised if most civil servants focus on that end rather than on actually getting to grips with the problem.

This is how insidious and pernicious the absence of HR-business strategy can be. The vast majority of civil servants come to work to do a good job, not to play political games (we will substantiate this presumption with Fig. 6.1, the bell-shaped curve). However, we are programmed to survive and the majority of us know we can only survive *within* the existing culture and system; anyone who does not fit in is stigmatized as a troublemaker or has to resort to whistle blowing. Either way, innovation is stifled, if not crushed and little value is created. A more optimistic view suggests that the vast majority of human beings also evolved with a conscience and a strong sense of fairness and those who have enough talent to choose where they work, and cannot stomach such political machinations, will decide to leave. This then creates a vicious cycle of deterioration in the calibre of people in the organization. This is why the traditional, civil service, 'management' model is in a vicious downward spiral. We are all witnessing its death throes in the form of one large project failure and initiative after another.

If we needed any more evidence to back up this assertion it is provided by a story in the *Sunday Times* as recently as 22 March 2009. A 'cultural audit' report commissioned from a 'human resources consultancy' by the UK's Foreign and Commonwealth Office had to be suppressed because of its damning conclusions. These included the 'tragic' descent into mediocrity of a civil service department known for hiring the brightest Oxbridge talent. Even the brightest were reduced to 'automatons' 'submitting wholesale to the culture of committees, sub-committees, working groups and steering groups', everything other than providing a valuable service it seems. A similar report on any civil service department is likely to find traces of the same disease.

We have stumbled across another, sacrosanct, general principle that all HR-business strategists will know only too well – 'bad people drive out good'. Incompetent managers cannot cope with more talented underlings so get rid of them; bad university lecturers drop the standard of marking to keep their pass rate high, the university gets a bad reputation and loses the lecturers who want to maintain high standards. This is exactly the same principle as the economist's law that 'bad money drives out good' (originally Gresham's Law from the sixteenth century when debased currency drove people to hoard coinage with a higher metal value), which has stood the test of time so well. We can see how it applied in the securitized (sic), mortgage-backed derivatives market. Toxic debt drove out good debt and toxic dealers drove out those with integrity.

Corruption can plague all organizations, it is a very pernicious but highly predictable element that subsists very close to the surface of any populace. When peers of the realm or members of parliament are found to be corrupt the whole system appears likewise and completely undermines the legislative process and any honours bestowed. Citizens who are doing great work, often voluntarily, should be honoured and our public approbation should not be diminished by a system that is tarnished. However, when a Permanent Secretary or a business CEO receives a knighthood, and the general perception is that they have presided over failure, the credibility of every honour or award in the same scheme is devalued, not just those specific cases. The case of four UK Peers wanting fees for lobbying on behalf of clients http://www.timesonline.co.uk/tol/news/politics/article5864538.ece has tarnished the whole reputation of the House of Lords, not just those who sought the payments.

A default culture also tolerates much lower standards of competence. One Whitehall Mandarin, *Sir* John Gieve, left his post as Deputy Governor at the Bank of England in March 2009 (*Sunday Times* 1 March 2009), in the wake of the collapse of the financial and banking system, to do a '3-month spell' as a visiting fellow at Harvard. He had spent 3 years at the Bank with responsibility for financial stability and before that he had been the Permanent Secretary at the Home Office, where his department was branded 'not fit for purpose' and guilty of 'systemic failure' by his boss, the Home Secretary, John Reid. Why anyone would choose someone guilty of presiding over 'systemic failure' as guardian of the UK's financial stability is beyond the ken of anyone outside the arcane world of permanent secretaries. However, it is further evidence, if it were needed, of the failure of the selection, transfer and promotion system for senior civil servants (and Harvard professors?). No doubt students at Harvard will learn a great deal about the power of systems from Sir John.

This is not a criticism of individual civil or public servants, per se, but of those who perpetuate a system and culture that is so obviously unfit for any modern purpose and cannot possibly hope to achieve high value. This type of culture is characterized by the definition of a 'good employee' being one that keeps their mouth shut and 'bad employees' those that want to ask awkward questions. History tells us that tyrants thrive in such a culture. What is really sad though is that it does not have to be like this. There is no immutable law that says the head of a civil service department has to foster a culture of fear and reprisal for staff that step out of line, even though there is ample evidence that this is currently a common feature. Things can change, tyranny is unsustainable and so the HR-business strategist aims to change them.

However, the HR-business strategist realizes that none of these things can be tackled in isolation. The culture of the organization dictates the systems in use. Anyone who has ever tried to complain about a civil service department will know what this feels like; you are up against 'the system' but no individual civil servant accepts responsibility for the system or is prepared to be held accountable by it. The 'system' is designed to ensure that many different people, ideally in completely separate departments, handle the complainant so that no single department has any sole authority to resolve the matter. If there is a strategy at play here it is probably best described as one of attrition; wear the complainant down until they go away.

Of course, civil services are just one obvious example of the important interplay between cultures and systems and the brightest civil servants obviously know exactly what they are doing. Their defence, if they felt that they needed defending, is that everyone has to work 'the system' they are given. This is a self-perpetuating system that has no beginning and no end. No one admits to designing it this way, it just evolves like a stalactite from a relentless drip of political interference, policy changes and spin. It happened by default, by history and by human beings doing what human beings do in the absence of strategic leadership. It is a system of atrophy and that is why its removal will always be top of the HR-business strategist's to do list.

The UK Ministry of Defence (current cost approximately £35 billion) controls a combined, armed service that has earned a reputation for being one of the best in the world. One of its highest cost areas is obviously weapons procurement and in one of its own magazines (Preview, November 2005) under the heading 'Look after management and the costs will look after themselves' the Deputy CEO of Defence Procurement was well aware that its strategic objective of moving towards a 'through-life' approach to operating and maintaining equipment, such as fighter aircraft and naval vessels, demanded a similarly 'through-life' view on how it manages its people stating

> In the Civil Service, we recruit some extremely bright people... and we look after them well for the first two years or three years, then we tend to lose them.

Worse still, some of these bright people might go on to join the very contractors who contribute to the high cost of Defence Procurement and use their talents to get as much profit out of their MOD contracts (and taxpayers) as possible. The need for an HR-business strategy here is paramount and urgent. How do you keep the best people who can keep contractor costs down to a minimum whilst still providing the best equipment available?

These issues are not confined to civil service departments or any other particular sector. They are generic, organizational problems and require constant vigilance and attention to keep them at bay.

The HR-business strategist will aim to design a high-value culture and system and needs a robust framework for doing so. These two facets are represented in Fig. 2.1 by the two large, interconnecting and overlapping circles and, in reality, they are the connective tissue, the bonds that keep the organization cohesive. A CEO should consider each to be very important but if we have to recommend in which order they come then culture has to be first.

So how would you describe the culture in your own organization (bearing in mind of course that yours is just one perception among many)? Would you even know how to start to answer this question or know what factors to consider? Here is one description of what the culture is like at Microsoft, seen through the eyes of a former employee who worked as a Windows developer (quoted in the UK *Sunday Times* 18 June 2006):

> *Deep in the bowels of Windows (the business unit) there remains the whiff of a bygone culture of belittlement and aggression. Windows can be a scary place to tell the truth.*

So do you want the culture of your organization to be one where it is a 'scary place to tell the truth' and, if so, is that what you want to base your business strategy on? Probably not, but then moving to other extreme, allowing anyone to say exactly what they want to whomsoever they want, is equally scary. A Microsoft employee could tell a customer the 'truth' – that what they really need is a better product or service already offered by someone else or that if Microsoft did not have a monopoly it could drop its prices dramatically? Neither of these options sound like they are a recipe for success, do they? So what other words might we choose to describe the culture? How about asking whether your people should trust and respect each other? Do your senior managers demand respect by right and status or do they have to earn it like everyone else? Do you welcome open communication or should everything be shrouded in a veil of secrecy? Do you want managers spending hours preparing fancy presentations or would you rather they use a flipchart, as long as the information is clear?

This culture stuff is all pervasive and it is instructive to ask people in the organization, on a regular basis, to describe just how it feels to work there, even though this means you have to be prepared to hear some painful news. We all know that culture is very important and we all live in a culture, either by design or by default, but it is incredibly difficult to change or manage it. So let us move onto redesigning the system, which should be a little bit easier.

Of course system and culture are always entwined, whether you like it or not. If colleagues work in an environment of little trust they will always want to cover their backs and double-check everything. All approvals will require at least two, if not more, signatures. There is a direct, inverse relationship between trust and control: the less you trust people the more systems you have to install to control them. That is why we have parking meters because we do not trust citizens to only park for a short period before moving on to allow others to use the space. Good managers install systems that impose the minimum control necessary. Control freaks, defined by their constant feeling of insecurity, love rigid systems irrespective of value considerations.

A simple organizational example of a general principle of trust could be the payment of expenses. If you trust employees not to abuse expenses then you do not need to have copies of every single receipt (even if the tax authorities do because they have learned not to trust anybody). Also, you will not have to put price limits on what hotels they can stay in, because they will be reasonable and appropriate. They will be more inclined to be reasonable, of course, if you are always seen to be saving money whenever you can and not paying yourself bonuses without clear justification. If you are all in this together then they should feel that by saving the company money it is in their own interests of long term job security, not your pension pot. Why else do you think employees at Toyota have become so obsessed with reducing costs?

The paradox of rigid systems is that while they are installed to control people they often fail because they are not human friendly and people will work around any system they regard as too rigid. The system fails precisely because it is too rigid. Imagine installing a 'system' of automatic spikes that puncture the tyres of anyone who tries to beat the traffic lights. Even if it succeeded in stopping them it would result in total congestion as each deflated car has to be removed. Moreover it would only encourage idiots to mount the pavement to go around the lights. Interestingly though, it is not only 'idiots' who want to bypass the system. What happened to the auditing 'systems' at Enron and the documents shredded by supposedly intelligent Arthur Andersen employees? Or the financial regulators of banks who allowed some banks to completely disregard well accepted banking conventions? Whatever systems are in place, human beings are very good at subverting or bypassing them altogether. All systems are at the mercy of human fallibility and a predictable willingness to comply so we need to start replacing mechanical, bureaucratic systems with more human systems.

The other, inseparable, elements in the framework in Figure 2.1 are *process* and *roles*, which together with organization structure form a 'golden triangle', the 'reinforced steel' that provides the underlying strength of the organization.

THE GOLDEN TRIANGLE – STRUCTURE, PROCESS, ROLES

In engineering a triangular frame is one of the sturdiest forms of construction (as you will notice on any bicycle) but we have already noted that when a design is too rigid it is the architect of its own failure. In earthquake zones the most rigid structures are actually more likely to collapse than those with built-in flexibility. Some organizations feel they have more flexibility if they become matrix organizations, where reporting lines and processes tend to be relatively fluid. The aim is to combine the best elements of control, adaptability and cooperation but often they appear to be a 'matrix' on paper only. If so, they are unlikely to produce any more value than some of their more rigid, hierarchical counterparts.

The worst matrix organizations have usually missed the whole point. All organizations need some form of command and control, based on clear reporting lines; how else do you keep everyone pulling in the same direction? However, we do not have to have our behaviour dictated to us every day by where we sit on the organization chart. If Tom reports to Dick, but has to work closely with Harriet on a large project, then Tom should not feel shackled to Dick. He will want to do his best for Harriet without always having to refer back to Dick (are you still following this?). There will be occasions though when Tom needs to check back with Dick (e.g. the project is taking too much of his time and needs someone to backfill for him) but these occasions should be few and far between. Flexible, adaptable organizations like this may still look like conventional hierarchies, in organogram terms, but will be *acting* and *behaving* like cooperative communities. This is more to do with the right culture encouraging the right relationships than it is with how you draw the organization chart. However, a concentrated look at processes might help. Processes, as with structures, can be rigid or flexible but can be defined as

A series of steps that turns inputs into outputs.

A brewing process turns water, malt, hops and yeast into beer. An invoicing process turns work done into a customer remittance. A combination of surgical and nursing processes turn ill patients into healthy ones. In other words, all of the time, energy and money that go into the organizational system are converted into value by processes.

Figure 3.2 is a complete sales process (made up of three subprocesses) starting with reception taking an enquiry and ending by getting paid for delivering the goods. The different shadings indicate which departments are involved in the process. The sorts of questions we need to ask from an HR perspective are

- Is the process as efficient as it could be in terms of time and cost?
- Is the process effective at converting inputs (enquiries) into outputs (payments for goods sold)?
- Are the roles of each individual in the process well designed?
- Are the individuals as capable and fully trained to perform their role as they can be?
- Should we put some of these people in the same team?

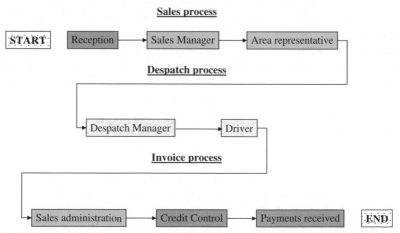

FIGURE 3.2   A complete, end-to-end, process reveals where everyone fits in the value chain.

Your value chain is a combination of all the processes you use and a break in any one of these processes (the invoice is not delivered to the right address) will reduce value. Processes are best viewed as a plumbing diagram that is potentially full of leaks. What you want is as smooth and easy a flow as possible without any leaks at all. Processes are also very measurable, and therefore very manageable, in terms of time, cost and output.

Structure and process should fit together like a hand in a glove but they rarely do. This is an area where the HR-business strategist is simultaneously presented with a huge task and a correspondingly huge opportunity. For example, the new product development process should involve everyone who has a contribution to make: someone, say, from sales, marketing, production and distribution. Yet, the way many organizations are structured immediately militates against this. Each function has its own boss and maybe none of them own, or has any direct responsibility for, the product development process in its entirety. The CEO may get very frustrated when they see in-fighting and poor cooperation but then they should acknowledge that this is a direct consequence of the way they designed the organization or allowed it to default. People tend to behave the way the design of the organization encourages them to or, worse still, forces them to.

It might be worth looking at how one company, Arup, deals with this conundrum.

Some lessons in flexible organisations from Arup

Danish engineer Ove Arup set up Arup in 1946. All new recruits read a speech he wrote. In it he says there are two ways to approach work, the 'Henry Ford' way, where work is a necessary evil and the alternative which is to make work interesting and rewarding. The company has grown by 15-20% a year for the past two decades and by 25% in the previous year. All of this was achieved without acquisition or increasing borrowing but it has a record of starting a new business every two or three years. The company is owned indirectly by its staff and is run by a trust, which has to act in the interests of the staff. It regards itself as a meritocracy rather than a democracy. The present Chairman, Terry Hill joined the company in 1976 after working alongside some Arup people. He said one of the things that attracted him was "They treated you like a human being, not just another resource." Having worked for a government department he found Arup a very loose and freethinking organisation and puts some of their success down to "a balance of freedom and accountability". When it comes to finding new recruits the company is highly unconventional. Rather than hire for specific vacancies when it finds someone really good it tends to make a space for them. Wherever it can it shares work and knowledge across its global operation and posts problems on its internal system with the aim of solving them within a day wherever possible.

Taken from an interview with Terry Hill reported in Sunday Times – Business on 20 July 2008.

Trying to draw the lessons from Arup on paper would never do them justice. Their system/culture could be best described as 'collegiate' and what pertains there today emanates directly from the company's founder. It would not suit everybody. Some engineers and architects might find this level of flexibility uncomfortable and feel more secure in a more tightly controlled environment. Arup must still have its own processes and everyone who works there must be reasonably clear about their role at any point in time. Yet, it appears that it is their common understanding of the 'loose rules' of the game that makes it work. Can you imagine trying to create this atmosphere and environment yourself in your own organization? Maybe it is particularly suited to a professional practice? It would certainly be difficult for any other consulting architectural or engineering group to copy a 'formula' that has been honed over 60 years.

Regardless of the environment created at Arup you can certainly start to look at the processes and roles in your own organization and how well they meld together with the structure. Although it should be emphasized here that we should not confuse 'job titles' with roles. Job titles, and their attendant job descriptions, can be relatively easily written down on paper (e.g. an Area Manager has to 'monitor performance of subordinates'), but roles are much more defined by shared values and relationships (the Area Manager sees their role as a trusted and respected coach to his team, to help them perform).

Changing a business strategy inevitably involves some form of restructuring and any new CEO will be tempted to make their mark, very visibly, by changing the organization chart. This is the most obvious first step for a CEO and, in order to bring it under control, you will want to make sure there are clear reporting lines, responsibilities and accountabilities and, of course, you will move your own preferred 'troops' into favourable positions. Publishing the chart is a declaration that you are in control and everyone is meant to adhere to it – in theory.

In practice, organization charts can and do change all too often and this breeds indifference. Why should someone bother to build a relationship with a new boss or colleague if experience tells him or her that the chart might change again at any time and with little notice and even less justification? Furthermore, close colleagues do not ditch each other just because the organization chart has changed. So the frequency with which organization charts change can be a very telling indicator of organization cohesion, or lack of it. In the worst cases no one bothers to update the chart because the situation is regarded as just too damn unpredictable.

One point often missed during restructuring is the extent to which the three corners of the processes/structure/roles triangle are the separate, yet interdependent, legs of a three-legged stool and should always change in synch. Take a look at Fig. 3.3 and imagine that you lose an area manager (Area 1 Manager) in the 'Existing' organization chart and decide to promote another area manager (Area 2 Manager) to manage both teams rather than trying to find a replacement, thereby producing the 'Revised' chart showing Area managers 1 and 2's new roles. What might the relationship and process implications of this structural change be?

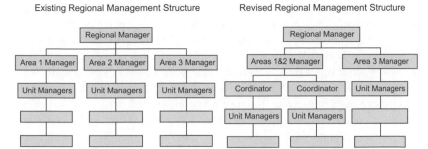

FIGURE 3.3 All reorganizations can upset organizational and human dynamics if not carefully managed.

The management process itself could change simply because the Area 1 & 2 Manager could decide to manage the two teams as one, holding joint meetings and setting joint targets. However, the 'bond' between Manager Area 1 & 2 and his original team (the Area 1 team) has been diluted because he has, in effect, been elevated through a promotion and might even nominate a senior team member, in each team, to adopt a coordinating role that he no longer has time for (because his geographical area has doubled in size). Also notice the lack of symmetry in the 'Revised' chart with the Area 3 manager role remaining unchanged. It looks like one of the 'legs of the stool' is shorter than the others resulting in the whole structure being lopsided.

It is important to reiterate that any change in structure will have an implication for process and vice versa. Trying to change one without the other will result in the weakening or undermining of the whole edifice. This can best be exemplified in Fig. 3.2 by considering the implications of putting the sales manager in charge of credit control (a structural change). This would mean them telling their area representatives that they must speak to customers more specifically about payment and credit terms during the sales process; probably not the most positive way to win sales. It would also mean the area representative having to fulfil the credit control part of the process (a process change) by chasing up their own bad debts. If both changes did not happen simultaneously, then the sales manager would be responsible for credit control without having anyone in their team carrying out this function: the 'stool' starts to topple over.

We could also look again at the new 'coordinators' in the revised structure in Fig. 3.3. They have been given greater responsibility – coordination – and might not have the additional skills required of this role. Also, they might want to compare notes with each other and how well they do this will depend as much on their relationship with each other as their position in the structure or the process. Strong and weak relationships can easily be represented on organization charts by drawing various gradations of connecting lines; the thicker the line the stronger the relationship. All organization design is dynamic though, and the HR-business strategist will do everything they can to ensure the dynamism is value adding, not value sapping.

One typical job for the HR department is to help clear up any mess caused by such changes. They rewrite job descriptions, change personal contracts and re-grade where necessary. When this is performed professionally it supports the operation, but it is still primarily work of an administrative nature. It is not strategic, even if it is a direct result of a change in business strategy. HR would be strategic if it had taken the initiative in the first place in highlighting for the CEO where weaknesses in the organization existed and how a different configuration could result in greater value. In other words, they could have informed and shaped the business strategy rather than followed and supported it: these are two very different roles. The most capable organization designers in your organization could already be HR professionals but if they are not you need to appoint someone who is qualified for this type of work. It requires skills of the highest order and can add huge value. Conversely, it will cost you dearly when your organization is badly designed, or alternatively, is constantly redesigned for no good reason. Above everything else the organization must *learn* how to change for the better; change for the sake of it is worthless.

A STRATEGIC HR-BUSINESS REQUIRES STRATEGIC LEARNING

Of all the human systems one can design the most important is a learning system. Why? Because learning is a self-perpetuating system, a self-reinforcing, virtuous cycle that builds up its own momentum and continuously generates ever-greater value. Some would go further and argue that learning is so important it demands a strategy all of its own, a learning strategy. This makes no sense when HR-business strategy is already totally integrated and has to include a learning system developed from a strategic view of how the organization needs to learn. Nevertheless, it certainly warrants some very special attention.

Many organizations think they give it special attention by calling them-selves a 'learning organization'; a phrase that must vie for the title of 'most overhyped' management speak of the last century. There is a wealth of liter-ature devoted to this subject since it was popularized in the 1980s and one of the early proponents of organizational learning, as a concept, was Arie de Geus who worked for Shell for many years. It is ironic, therefore, that as recently as 18 January 2004, when Shell was having problems with overstating its oil reserves, *The Observer* described the company's management style as having a 'history of cumbersome bureaucracy, opaque governance, lacklustre financial performance and prickliness to outsiders'. If this is an example of a learning organization then what does a non-learning organization look like?

The HR-business strategist will always look to create a culture of learning where knowledge is highly valued and an eagerness to learn and innovate is palpable. Shell's overstated reserves could be viewed as an isolated incident or symptomatic of something darker going on in the bowels of the organi-zation. Either the reserves were mistakenly overstated, in which case the basic competence of Shell comes into question, or Shell knew exactly what its reserves were and yet was afraid to declare them honestly, because it knew it would have a disastrous effect on their share price and investor confidence. Whichever is closer to the truth, their failure to face up to and deal with such a fundamental issue tells us a great deal about weaknesses in both management thinking and culture at Shell, never mind the failure of its control systems.

'The learning organization' has become such a misused and abused term that it has lost all meaning. So let us consider what the opposite, a non-learning organization, looks and feels like; viewing the negative can often be very revealing. When you think this way for a moment you have to conclude that any individual or organization that fails to learn must be stupid. Let us be clear what we are saying here. Many management decisions can turn out badly even though the original decision was 'right' (GM's original decision to concentrate on producing SUVs eventually looked like the wrong decision). Also some decisions can only be deemed to be 'wrong' with the benefit of hindsight (Sony's Betamax video format). Neither of these would qualify as stupid decisions. We might not even call an organization stupid if some of its decisions were wrong right from the outset: they might appear to be illogical, defy common sense or simply fail to collect the best information available. Such decisions might be more accurately described as foolhardy, reckless or ill-informed but a really stupid organization can be defined as one that

Fully acknowledges its mistakes and then repeatedly fails to learn from them

There can be no more distressing example of this phenomenon than the UK Department for Children, Schools and Families. In 2000 there was a public outcry over the case of Victoria Climbié, a little girl unlawfully killed by her 'carers', despite the earlier involvement of several professional agencies who were well aware of her being at risk. This led to a public inquiry led by Lord Laming. Eight years later another child died in similarly awful circumstances – the 'Baby P' case. So what was the response from the Secretary for Children, Schools and Families, to fire the local authority's head of social services and set up another inquiry by Lord Laming, even though he readily admits his first inquiry did not resolve the problem. http://www.timesonline.co.uk/tol/news/politics/article5898114.ece

Ambitious politicians have no peers when it comes to creating really stupid organizations. Ed Balls was Gordon Brown's top adviser at the Treasury for the decade prior to the collapse of the UK's financial system in 2007. Having then both received their 'promotions' they were only too willing to espouse the principle of 'not rewarding failure' when the banks collapsed.

Honda, on the other hand, has a policy that tends to encourage mistakes because they know that progress and innovation are synonymous and the relentless pursuit of improvement will mean mistakes are inevitable. It does not tolerate making the same mistake twice though, because that is unforgivable. Rather than keep firing people though it puts in place a learning system, not an external inquiry, which is specifically designed for the purpose. Ed Balls and all other politicians take note.

A very simple way to distinguish between organizations that pretend they are learning organizations and those that are the real thing is to demand 'show us your learning system'. If you ask this of many heads of training and development they point to a computer screen and proudly reveal data showing how many people logged on to the e-learning site this morning, or went on the fire-walking course yesterday (and how many are absent today with blisters on their feet). They have no understanding of the concept of either *organisational learning* or systems and, even if they did, the prerequisite of installing a culture of learning would be beyond their capabilities. They could do a great deal worse though than to start by installing the two main, albeit mechanical, elements of an effective learning *system*:

1. Quality assurance – instilling the discipline imposed by the Plan-Do-Check-Act cycle (known as PDCA) where all problems have to be resolved systematically, starting with a measure of the 'problem' and ending with checking the problem has been resolved by using the same measure
2. Double-loop learning – always insisting that all potential variables and possible root causes of the problem have been explored before any action is taken.

Let us look at a very simple example of what happens when such a rudimentary learning system is put in place.

You are the new CEO of a hotel chain and you notice from a customer satisfaction (or mystery shopper) survey that there has been a significant drop (say 25%) in customer satisfaction ratings. A reactive approach to this problem would be to call in the head of operations and tell them to 'sort it out' (or fire them like Ed Balls). A systematic approach, however, would first ensure there was at least one, overall 'owner' of the problem and the objective will always be 'what can we learn from solving this problem?' not 'who can we blame?' The actual satisfaction score would be looked at in some detail to find out which area needed the most immediate attention, following the Pareto, 80:20 principle (e.g. room service, restaurant, reception?). Let us further assume that 'unsatisfactory room cleaning' appeared to be where the biggest dip occurred.

The LEARNING SYSTEM would demand that

- Step 1 - problem DEFINITION and BASELINE MEASUREMENT - is always the first step.
- Everyone should view the problem as a learning opportunity – no one would be seeking to blame.
- Those responsible for cleaning rooms (at every level) are made fully aware of the scores and asked immediately for their reactions and views.
- The problem would be looked at by everyone involved in the complete process chain (including external suppliers of laundry and cleaning products if necessary).

- Everyone has already been taught a common approach to problem solving, including cause and effect analysis (or root cause analysis).
- The desired 'effect' is articulated as a measure (the 25% of rooms not satisfactorily cleaned has to be reduced by half).
- All of the likely causes are identified and dealt with in a sequence, based on the Pareto/size of impact rule again, and from a DOUBLE LOOP perspective (see Chris Argyris below for a more detailed explanation).
- The causes would be considered from a structure and process perspective, for example, who is responsible for cleaning and did someone try to short-circuit the cleaning process?.
- A PLAN would be produced to improve the BASELINE situation.
- After DOing something the BASELINE measure would be re-CHECKed to see if it was improving (this would be best done by the in-house people themselves, if you can trust them).
- Whether things had changed or not there would be a REVIEW process to decide whether to carry on as planned or to come up with an alternative solution.
- Once resolved, lessons would be captured and made available for future managers to learn (perhaps using an intranet knowledge base?).
- The SYSTEM is iterative – so having solved one problem those involved move on to another targeted area for improvement and the CYCLE continues. They would not wait for another 'problem' to arise.
- Everyone involved will be encouraged to look for any other opportunities that could be subjected to the system in the same way.
- Although all ideas are encouraged and welcomed the system will check all innovations for their potential value and likelihood of success before progressing.

This might seem to be an oversimplified example, but the same principles and sequence could equally be applied to more complex problems such as project management overruns, introducing new IT systems or reorganizations. Only this time an assessment of lost value would be included in the initial measurement stage, especially when IT projects can cost many millions.

There is absolutely nothing new in this approach or any of the individual steps and any organization that really understands total quality management (TQM) will easily recognize this sort of sequence. What most organizations find difficult though is moving on from the mechanics of problem solving to a much higher state of organizational mentality, SYSTEMS THINKING. This is a concept espoused by another learning organization 'guru', Peter Senge in The Fifth Discipline: The Art & Practice of The Learning Organization (Doubleday Business, 2006). Having covered the concepts Senge's team then followed with a practical manual, *The Fifth Discipline Fieldbook*, and his co-authors expressed their amazement at just

> ... *how closely our work on learning organisations dovetails with the 'Total Quality' movement....organisations seriously committed to quality management are uniquely prepared to study the 'learning disciplines'*

This is a fascinating quote. Obviously it never dawned on the authors that the concept of the 'Fifth Discipline' (systems thinking) was really spawned many years earlier by companies like Toyota whose intelligent adherence to the philosophy and methodology of Deming (an American) became known as TQM. The timescales involved might be decades rather than years, but intelligent proponents of the philosophy of TQM (not those who focus just on 'lean' or 'six sigma' tools) are bound to reach the same conclusion that *if the whole system is not right the whole system fails*, not just part of it. Leaving aside any intellectual arrogance expressed by these authors, that they can teach the TQM gurus something they did not already know, it is ironic that it was the Americans who despatched Deming to Japan after World War II, to help their industries get back on their feet, where he received a much warmer welcome and appetite for his teaching than he ever did in the USA. Yet, here we see his ideas repackaged, reheated and served up as 'TV dinner' for a new generation. Becoming a learning organization is often a case of having to unlearn and relearn very old lessons.

Right at the heart of a true learning organization, both the theory and the practice, is a very simple yet profound idea from Chris Argyris – double-loop learning. He explains the concept using a thermostat control as an example of 'single-loop' learning, where the thermostat control can only respond to one variable – temperature. Double-loop learning occurs when the organization is aware of and responds to all the 'governing variables' – this could include telling someone to shut or open the windows, taking into account how many people there are in the room and whether the sun is shining outside. Some learning specialists even suggest there is a 'triple loop', but creating an organizational learning system is difficult enough as it is without overcomplicating it. It will take many years before it is fully established and becomes *the* overriding management system that drives the organization's eagerness to learn. Stupid, political decisions notwithstanding, the challenge for the HR-business strategist is to be able to articulate what a learning system means, make a public declaration that they intend to become a real learning organization and produce some evidence that this is actually happening.

THE LEARNING MATURITY SCALE

If you thought you were already a learning organization you probably have to start again, from scratch. You have to be ready to unlearn. Whether your organization is ready for such a revolution depends on how mature it is in the way it perceives notions such as training, development and whether it fully understands the difference between the inputs and the output of applied learning. The Learning Maturity Scale shown in Fig. 3.4 offers a continuum of the stages of development and evolution for a learning organization. The breakthrough in thinking required is represented here as the Evaluation Hurdle

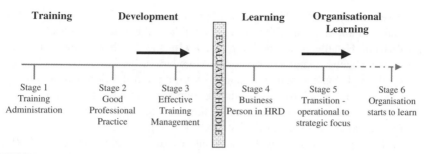

FIGURE 3.4   The Learning Maturity Scale – only applied learning counts towards value creation.

(For more detail see 'Evaluating the ROI from Learning', by Paul Kearns, CIPD, 2005). In very simple terms, this means that unless you attach a value to all training and development, *before* you embark on it, then the probability that it will add any value is minimal. So for example if you have just sent some senior managers away on a 'leadership course', and they did not know how it was supposed to be adding measurable value in their area of operations, then they attended with no pre-agreed, business purpose: a damning indictment of another missed 'learning' opportunity. This should not only make you want to revisit your own views on learning but to ask yourself some serious questions about how your training department is spending your money.

The Learning Maturity Scale is very simple. If your organization is on the bottom (left) side of the scale at

Stage 1 – all you have is a training administration department. It runs a menu of courses, in a sheep-dipping fashion, and the only thing you are interested in is the number of bums on seats and the average cost of training per head. This is a very immature and low-value view of what training has to offer and the concept of learning is not even on the agenda.

Stage 2 – you at least employ professional training staff who set a slightly higher standard by asking questions about training objectives and the suitability of candidates for particular courses, but there is still a very immature perception that 'training means courses'. These courses are not even delivered systematically at Stage 2 because any senior manager can overrule the training team if they wish, even if they are not professionally qualified to do so.

Do not be fooled by the term e-learning either. Most e-learning is actually just e-training; the technology available just transfers classroom teaching online and has no more automatic validity than a book doing the same thing. Many organizations spending huge sums on e-learning are wasting a great deal of money because their organization is still at Stage 1.

Stage 3 – you start to value the expertise of better training and development staff and employ some who are confident enough to stand up to senior management wish-lists, move away from running 'courses' and introduce systems (e.g. no development takes place without a systematic analysis of individual, development needs). You cannot progress past Stage 3 though, unless and until you and the rest of your executive address the evaluation hurdle.

Evaluation Hurdle – has nothing to do with the number of days training, 'happy sheets' completed by course-attenders or the bureaucracy of qualifications. It simply demands that all training and development activity is founded on clear business needs. No one goes on any programme unless they can articulate how they think the learning might create more value (but see also the '3 Box Priority System' in Chapter 5).

Stage 4 – requires you to develop a human resource development team (HRD) that work as partners with business managers to ensure this happens. They will only speak the same language as the business, not touchy-feely gobble-dygook, and on occasions they will put some really hard numbers on the benefits of training. This might only be an initial learning hypothesis such as 'what would a 1% uptake on store cards be worth, in $'s, if we trained all our checkout operators to sell them for us?' and, depending on the answer, they would calculate the cost and net return on investment or ROI. Learning is always best when anchored by a well-conceived business case. When the penny drops for you and your executives you will be mature enough to pass through this hurdle.

Stage 5 – the transition phase – is eventually reached where the maturity level of the whole organization has reached a point where everyone realizes that the only thing that matters is learning that is applied to the business and results in value. Now the organization is becoming so mature in its perception of learning that it will automatically and inevitably progress to the highest state possible.

Stage 6 – the true, whole system, learning organization. A genuine learning organization fully accepts that honest feedback on organizational issues is not just legitimized but positively welcomed and reinforced. Negative feedback and criticism are seen as equally important and any reference to 'whistle blowing' is a clear indicator of a non-learning culture. Another contraindicator might be sending everyone on a customer service or customer care course when complaints increase. An indicator of a stupid organization is doing the same thing again and again when you know it is not solving the problem.

Hopefully you can see that this type of deep, organizational analysis cuts through the superficial appearance that most organizations want to create about how they manage their people. We are now starting to ask many tough questions about 'people management' that you are probably struggling to answer. Worse still, all of these questions are based on simple, pretty obvious, common sense. So, you might be wondering to yourself, how come we have been getting the basics so wrong for so long? Maybe you need to retrace your steps, go back to square one and ask just what 'people management' theories you have been working to?

Chapter 4

So What is the Best Theory on Managing People?

HOW DO *YOU* MANAGE PEOPLE?

Anyone who has had to manage people for more than a few weeks will know what it feels like to have to make the multitude of mini-judgements necessary to balance the needs of the company with the needs of each employee. Poor people managers see their job simplistically as task management, either because that is just how they perceive the role or, more likely, they just find managing unique, human beings just incredibly difficult. Of course they are right in one sense – it is very difficult trying to balance the natural, human inclinations of not wanting to be bored, stressed or pressurised with the need to get the job done. There are the added layers of complexity as well that human beings tend to come with a desire for job satisfaction and recognition whilst also harbouring many conflicting hopes and fears of their own. What is a manager to do? Being too soft on people or over-empathetic can be just as counter-productive as being too hard. The standard rule-of-thumb for this classic, everyday, 'man' management dilemma is to try and be 'firm but fair' which, like all nostrums, is great at telling you what you need to be without actually showing you how to do it.

We are often left, therefore, with our own assumptions and preconceptions about what makes people tick and then compound this crime by treating *necessary* conditions (e.g. employees need to be motivated) as though they were *sufficient* (i.e. 'happy' employees will do a good job - won't they?). What we should do is test all our people management assumptions, professionally, in the cauldron that is the working environment. So do the most motivated employees perform the best? Not necessarily. We have all encountered the eager beavers and company apostles who actually need very tight controls to stop them doing damage through overexuberance. The popular notion in HR theory of the 'engaged employee' is often misread as the 'happiest'. Some of the worst performing might be the happiest (as opposed to engaged) simply because no one expects too much from them. Conversely, the employees with the greatest potential could be the most disengaged because they are frustrated at not being able to contribute more or they believe they are not valued. This is such a tricky subject and does not lend itself to simplistic, Magic Pill, practices of annual employee engagement, satisfaction or attitude surveys.

One of the reasons simplistic approaches still persist is that one of the most popular HR 'gurus' in HR departments, Dave Ulrich, has been promoting the concept of HR as the 'employee champion' since 1997 (Human Resource Champions, Harvard Business School Press). In his more recent writing ('Reporting on employee surveys' – Creelman Research/RBL 2007) he argues that there is a causal connection between engagement and performance and that this can be picked up by employee surveys -

Employee surveys are the killer app(lication) of human capital measurement and reporting …. Companies with good employee survey results will, in general, outperform companies with poor results

In his report's league table it comments that '*GM also deserves a mention because while the absolute numbers are probably not good, there is a significant upward trend.*' This seems to fly in the face of all the available evidence of GM's performance. It would be very difficult in 2009 to convince anyone that GM had any upward trends (other then unemployment), engagement or valuewise. Any *single* indicator, correlative or causal, is a very dangerous premise on which to assess an organization's overall, long-term performance.

In the same report Wells Fargo bank is singled out for excellent performance and excellent employee satisfaction. We now know this probably had something to do with this bank not copying its rivals and instead sticking to its principles and managing to steer clear of most toxic debt. Let us also consider this whole question of employee engagement further by considering what two diametrically opposed sectors, health and tobacco, can learn from each other.

SMOKING KILLS! – LESSONS IN EMPLOYEE ENGAGEMENT

Employee engagement is not as obvious or as straightforward a proposition as you might think.

Tobacco Companies

According to the warnings that tobacco companies put on packets of cigarettes 'Smoking Kills'. This is a declaration that they fully accept the causal connection between smoking their products and premature death. This must therefore mean that if a cigarette manufacturer wants to increase its sales it will have to have a strategy of killing as many people as possible! Of course, you will not find any tobacco company with this as a mission statement. Nevertheless, it poses a very interesting, strategic, HR dilemma because it means these companies have to engage their employees with this purpose. That, in turn, means the employees have to share the values of the organization.

This does not seem to present tobacco companies with any particular problem in finding enough people to work for them though. Their employees know perfectly well the sort of business they are engaged in. Each individual will reconcile their own need to earn a living with the means to do so. The most engaged employees in tobacco companies are likely to be those who are already smokers themselves and believe in the absolute freedom of the individual to make their own choices knowing the risks involved.

So if employing people, whose values some of us might consider abhorrent, presents no practical management or engagement problems what about organizations where we might expect the most laudable values?

The National Health Service

The UK's NHS employs 1.3 million people and one would assume that most of them work there because they believe it is a very good cause. Yet, the annual survey of staff by the Healthcare Commission shows nothing can be taken for granted in employee engagement.

http://www.healthcarecommission.org.uk/guidanceforhealthcarestaff/nhsstaff/nhsstaffandpatientsurveys/staffsurveys/staffsurveys2007.cfm

Job Satisfaction and Staff Engagement

The survey revealed that while job satisfaction remains high, the results for engagement were mixed. Most staff knew their objectives and responsibilities, but only a quarter felt their work was valued by the trust.

This led to a headline in *The Times* on 9 April 2008:

More than half of NHS staff feel patient care is not the priority

which took data from the survey showing that -

One in four (surveyed NHS staff) does not believe that health trusts see patient care as their most important issue.

How can this be so? Political pressure and the imposition of targets can distort an organization's objectives and managers can so easily lose sight of why they are there, thereby squandering high, innate, levels of employee engagement and motivation.

The stories above should be a salutary lesson to anyone thinking engagement is a simple, one-way system. Perhaps there is very little that we can say with absolute certainty when it comes to our own pet theories about how to manage people. So, for now anyway, we are going to make two broad assumptions without apology, accepting them for the sweeping generalizations they are.

First, people have to be managed. We cannot be left to our own devices or expected to manage ourselves. Some years ago the concept of 'self-managed teams' was very popular and while some might exist they are hardly ubiquitous. Second, most employees want their work to be seen as important and valued and they want their contribution to be recognized and appreciated. These will be regarded as two of the most fundamental tenets of both people management theory and HR-business strategy.

HR-business strategy is not just a new coat of paint applied to old and peeling woodwork though; it will not adhere if the substrate is flaky. So to test the solidity of your most cherished people management theories and practices we need to dig quite deep and revisit what most organizations take for granted, the fact that employees turn up every day and actually do some useful work. In doing so we will question the very meaning of terms such as 'man management'. However, there is not much point trying to discuss HR-business strategy or how to manage people if the people you are trying to manage keep changing.

EMPLOYEE RETENTION IS A VALUE PROPOSITION

In the global recession of 2009 many organizations are considering redundancies rather than recruitment drives. Companies like Honda are shutting down production lines for a few months and sending their people home on basic salary until things pick up. They realize just how valuable fully trained and committed their workers are, so they want to retain them. This is another one of those balancing acts that HR-business strategists have to contend with but some businesses, such as construction and contracting, rarely have the luxury of continuous employment for their employees. So what sort of HR-business strategy can they hope to adopt? This is not as difficult an issue as it appears.

In Chapter 1 Machiavelli was invoked to show that employing mercenaries was not a particularly good idea for a warmongering Prince or an embattled CEO. Effective organizations are dependent on achieving as high a level of stability in their human capital as possible. Retention is one of those subjects that tends to waxes and wane though. There have been scare stories in the past about 'demographic time bombs' and 'downsizing' and plenty of hype in the supposed 'war for talent'. Peaks and troughs will always occur in the labour market, so perhaps the best way to deal with this issue is to just own up to it. No organization can guarantee the one thing that the majority of employees want – security of employment. However, there is a world of difference between sending a signal to employees that 'life is tough – get used to it' rather than one that suggests 'we do value you and will do everything we can to keep you in employment'.

As always, the only criterion for choosing a particular approach is does it offer the most value, not which is the most 'ethical'. In a capitalist economy organizations do not exist to provide jobs; employment and careers are a by-product of the system, not its purpose. Hitachi and many other Japanese companies had to learn this lesson in earlier recessions of the 1980's and 1990's and release people they could no longer afford. Honda's policy today of trying to hold onto its employees is no more ethical than any other employer's; they are doing it primarily for sound business reasons. They believe they can run their business better than their competitors because they have already invested a great deal of time, money and culture in their employees. Nevertheless, it will stop this practice as soon as it stops making business sense to them.

Some of Honda's UK employees, however, decided that their best interests actually lay elsewhere and decided to leave rather than accept several months without full pay. The employment relationship is founded on self-interest, it will always be a case of each side deciding what is in their own best interests. Ethics, if they are part of this equation at all, are a secondary issue. Machiavelli realized this and probably also accepted that voicing such 'truths' would not make him very popular.

What matters most of all though, is not *your* perception of the situation but that of your employees. If they value loyalty and you do not, then there is a serious mismatch in values. They will feel undervalued and therefore be less inclined to give you loyalty. Loyalty can be misplaced though, and there is no guarantee that a loyal servant is a productive one. So the relationship with the employee needs to be made perfectly clear, or as clear as humanly possible. The sample letter below tries to send just such a simple message without making any promises you cannot keep.

A welcome letter from the CEO

"We would like to offer you a very warm welcome to ABC Incorporated and hope that you will see this letter as a clear statement of the commitment we are prepared to offer you as one of our employees. However, in return for our commitment to you we expect a corresponding commitment from you.

We believe that ABC is a great company and are proud of the fact that our customers continue to choose us. We hope this will continue and put every effort into trying to make that happen. However, with the best will in the world, we cannot guarantee that it will. We face relentless competition in a tough market and we will have to constantly look for ways not only to hold onto our existing customers but also to attract new customers in the face of such fierce competition. We hope you will help us in this challenge. We cannot afford to become complacent or stand still for one moment.

From the moment you responded to the advertisement for your position you may not have realised it but we knew exactly the type of people we were trying to attract. You have successfully completed a selection process that tells us we have found the right match. You have been selected for your knowledge, experience, brainpower, creativity, innovative thinking and other capabilities that match our needs. We want people who like continuous challenge. We also need people who are prepared to challenge our way of doing things. That means we recruit people who think for themselves and behave in a way that brings about constant change.

If we fail you fail. If you fail we fail. We are totally interdependent.

Our belief is that the happiest and most effective employees are those who are allowed to make their maximum contribution in a well-organised and focused business. We will endeavour to create an environment in which we can both excel but you have to tell us if we become ineffective or lose focus. If you cannot express your opinions openly and freely then you should contact me immediately.

We are a results based organisation. No one is interested in how many hours you work or the quality of your presentations. Only results count. We do not tolerate under-performance or complacency but those who get results are well rewarded.

Continued

If you believe your own opportunities for personal development are lacking tell us. We will actively support any developmental actions that are mutually beneficial. We do not subscribe to education without an anticipated organisational benefit.

We cannot make our own commitment and the commitment we expect any clearer. If we have made the right decision, you have made the right decision.

Welcome on board.

John Smith, CEO."

In low-skilled and what might be termed 'commodity' labour markets, globalization has resulted in multinational corporations being prepared to open and shut plants according to cold calculations of labour costs and efficiencies. In such instances they show apparently little regard for the other, less tangible but equally important, benefits often associated with employee retention (e.g. experienced workers have a higher performance level). Other organizations may take the view that they want to maintain high retention rates, but they are not prepared to do so at any price. Consequently, trade-offs will have to be made and establishing the value of those trade-offs is a key task for an HR-business strategist.

Most businesses will obviously try to minimize the extra recruitment and training costs and disruption caused by high staff turnover. Regardless of how high these costs may be though, the true HR-business strategist sees every HR proposition as a *value* proposition, not a cost consideration. The eyes of the HR-business strategist see the opportunity costs of losing experienced, committed employees in terms of

- Lower productivity
- Less operational efficiency
- Deteriorating customer satisfaction
- Increased exposure to risk
- Lack of innovation
- Failure to achieve premium prices for a premium product or service.

All of this can add up to enormous amounts of lost value so it is easy to make the business case for producing an employee retention strategy. Admittedly staff retention policies will, to a great extent, be dictated by the relevant labour market conditions. So, in a fast-food business, where employee turnover is notoriously high, it might be very difficult for any player to adopt an HR-business strategy that aims to promote a significantly higher level of employee retention. It is no accident that McDonalds had a system of gold stars for their serving staff. They needed something to help keep them motivated for the short time that most of them were likely to be with the company. Now their strategy includes helping their workers get qualifications they missed out on at school. Even in high turnover businesses, like fast foods, retention can be managed better and become part of a competitive strategy.

TGI Friday's in the UK used to suffer staff turnover rates as high as 100%+ per annum and their store managers came to accept this as the norm. Strenuous efforts were made by senior management to keep a focus on the high costs associated with this turnover and they constantly exhorted managers to try and reduce this figure. However the managers, quite rightly, were always more concerned with day-to-day operational targets and felt that nothing much could be done about a problem that they had become inured to. They just regarded it as part and parcel of the way the business was structured and operated. Only when a clear, causal connection was made between revenue per customer and the average length of staff service did they sit up and take notice. Staff turnover was no longer seen as a percentage of people leaving the business but as a significant, percentage drop in revenue and margin. This, in itself, created more value but it also stopped managers seeing staff turnover as a given and encouraged them to take much more of an interest in how new recruits were looked after in their stores. Being a 'caring' manager was no longer deemed to be 'pink and fluffy' or inappropriate but rather a much more enlightened and effective form of management.

STRUCTURAL STAFF TURNOVER AND RETENTION

Regardless of whether a strategy is in place or not, actual levels of retention are inextricably bound up with culture and the way an organization is structured. A company's attitude to staff retention, whether explicit or implicit, automatically starts to become part of the way it operates. If it does not really commit itself to retention then it pays less attention to the need to get the employment relationship right and inevitably gets its just deserts.

Staff turnover and retention is something that is actually built into the fabric of the organization; sometimes consciously but more likely by default. Some of the most obvious examples of the former are to be found in those Japanese organizations where lifetime employment and the culture of the 'salaryman' conspire to ensure maximum employee retention. In the face of more open markets and increasing globalization this type of HR strategy is becoming increasingly difficult to sustain.

Staff turnover will inevitably turn into a vicious cycle in immature organizations where no coherent strategy exists. Call centres tend to have high levels of staff turnover and when operational managers are crying out for replacement staff they will do anything to procure people. This can undermine workplace discipline for fear of losing them again. To make matters worse, the same managers, when interviewing new candidates, often tend to paint a very rosy picture of what life is like in the company, in a vain attempt to attract more staff. This sets up false expectations in the minds of new recruits that inevitably lead to disillusionment after a few weeks of experiencing the reality. The vicious cycle continues.

So what level of turnover would suit your organization? If your first stab at an answer is 'zero' then maybe you need to think again. Without fresh ideas or new blood coming into the organization, you are in danger of breeding a culture of complacency that can lead to organizational atrophy. At the other extreme, a 100% replacement rate is equally undesirable. You would not have to produce any figures to support this argument; it would be self-evident that it would lead to serious organizational difficulties and unnecessarily high costs. So between these two extremes there has to be an optimal level of employee retention for your organization.

A restaurant chain may be very happy with a 75% staff turnover rate, especially if its competitors suffer 90% plus. A target of 5% might be a much more appropriate figure for a nuclear power plant. Choosing the right level for you is never going to be an exact science, but the HR-business strategist will definitely want to agree a goal and be very clear what sort of turnover is required. The aim is to have the level of staff turnover that you planned to have, this becomes the purpose behind your new staff retention *system*.

An HR-business strategist will already have calculated how big the salary bill is and what the costs of selection and training will be to run the organization effectively at that level of turnover. Organizations that want to develop high value, knowledge workers cannot do so if their people keep changing. If staff turnover or stability is not close to what you want it to be it means something is fundamentally wrong with your HR-business strategy. If the turnover problem cannot be resolved then the HR-business strategy itself has to change.

A SIMPLE MODEL OF PEOPLE MANAGEMENT

Even if we assume that you already have a high retention rate we still have to ask how productive and innovative these employees are. This leads us to take

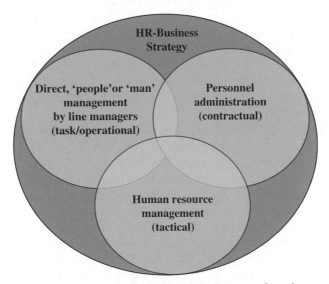

FIGURE 4.1 HR-business strategy is the glue that binds all aspects of people management into one, holistic approach.

a fresh look at what 'managing people' really means and we will do this using the simple 'Venn' Diagram in Fig. 4.1.

Without an all encompassing HR-business strategy (the large outer circle) the way we consciously manage people can be seen as three distinct forces:

Personnel administration – we issue contracts, terms and conditions, job descriptions, pay scales etc. This hopefully provides a sound basis for a new recruit to be happy enough working for the company.

Direct 'man' management – we have supervisors and managers whose job it is to make sure the employee completes the tasks they are assigned. Good managers do this well and aid the motivation and job satisfaction of the individual. Poor managers become simply 'task managers' and the worst are 'hard-task managers'.

Human resource management – this is tactical in the sense that the company introduces schemes and ideas to try and help the performance of the employee so this would include training programmes, appraisals, career development plans and the like. If these are all the result of disjointed policies in the absence of an overarching strategy then they add little value.

The interrelationship between the three inner forces is best illustrated when things go wrong. An employee is unhappy about a task that they are asked to carry out (e.g. working at heights, working a weekend, doing a particularly dirty job) so the manager checks their contract to see that it is within their job description and then involves an HR adviser to help resolve the matter; with union representation present if necessary.

So what difference would the HR-business strategy make to this relatively simple dynamic? Well, the psychological contract would outweigh anything on paper. A solid relationship between manager and employee will mean they do not resort to the disciplinary or grievance procedure as a first resort. There would be give and take and a more flexible approach. The 'unexpected' task would be a very rare occurrence not a regular feature. There would be voluntarism rather than coercion.

Another example might be how the employee receives training. The contract might specify 5 days training a year, the immature training manager would already have a menu of courses available (e.g. Six Sigma) and the manager might happily allow their staff to attend, as long as it fits around work schedules. All of this would be operational and tactical though. An HR-business strategy would not see training as a series of courses. The focus would be on outputs and outcomes and then training analysis would be applied specifically to deal with issues in a focused, planned way. Learning would be taking place in a conscious manner, but in an environment where it is most easily assimilated. It would be part of a continuous learning process, not in an ad hoc or piecemeal fashion.

If the three inner circles loosely match what already happens in your organization, then all we need to do now is look at what constructing the outer ring, the all-encompassing HR-business strategy, requires. To do this properly we need an underpinning theory that binds all these circles together and this presents us with a problem – there is no 'General Theory' of HR strategy. What exists instead is a collection, some might say a mishmash, of individual theories. Here is a highly simplified list of some of the most common ones that are deployed, to a greater or lesser extent, by most HR departments:

- **Competence theory** – people can be developed according to a template of common competencies for any required role.
- **Engagement theory** – we can only expect employees to give of their best if they are engaged with the objectives of the organization.
- **Diversity theory** – equal opportunities should mean access to the widest, potential talent pool (an alternative, 'ethical' version of this theory is based on individual rights and sometimes the two theories are combined into one).
- **Talent management and succession planning theory** – talent has to be identified, acquired, developed and retained for organizational growth and development.
- **Reward and recognition theory** – people do not work just for money and want a well-structured career path, preferably job graded.
- **Appraisal theory** – all employees need regular opportunities to have their development reviewed at a personal development planning or review session.
- **Performance management theory** – individual performance has to be reviewed on a regular basis.
- **Learning theory** – how people learn will affect how they and the organization perform.
- **Organization development theory** – probably the least developed of all these theories and usually coalesces with others, typically learning and succession planning theories, OD specialists often struggle to articulate precisely what their role is.
- **Organizational behaviour theory** – people behave differently in a work environment and the organization needs to understand this in order to encourage the right behaviours.
- **Organization design theory** – how you structure the organization and the processes you use influence how effective and efficient it is.
- **Leadership theory** – better leadership means better organizational performance
- **Systems theory** – all organizations use systems for control but whole, human systems are the only way forward.

We have already dipped into several of these topics as we have proceeded but it is amazing, when you see a much fuller list that no one has actually managed to mould them all into a single, coherent General Theory. So it is time they were tested. Our definition of HR-business strategy suggests that they all have to be tested against the simple criterion of 'do they offer, singularly or in combination, a means for gaining sustainable competitive advantage and creating value?'

TESTING HR THEORIES

Let us apply this simple test to the theory of competence. Presumably, the theory suggests that if we improve the competence of a manager it must surely make them perform better than a similar manager would in a company without competence development? If you are part of a large, multinational organization these days the chances are that all of your competitors have all been reading the same text books on their MBA programmes and so have copied each other with identical concepts, similar competence frameworks and identical management development modules. It therefore fails this test, even if competence theory 'works'. If the theory does not work .... Well perhaps we do not need to go there. So, at best, competence theory might have a neutral effect in the sense that if everyone is doing it, it must be having the same effect everywhere.

So let us try applying the 'negative' test again. Is the negative of 'competent' what we might call 'incompetent'? This begs the next question of whether 'competence' is a binary concept, does it have to be either on or off, or is there a halfway house called semi-competent? How would you like to hear the captain of your next business flight announcing that they were only a 'semi-competent' pilot or to be operated on by a semi-competent surgeon? These sound rather worrying possibilities don't they? Yet, if competence is to mean anything, it has to mean 'qualified to do the job to the required standard' and this is exactly how the dictionary defines competent. Anything less than qualified is deemed incompetent. We will not fly or be operated on by anyone without a licence, or under very close and strict supervision from a competent person while they are learning.

Yet, we allow managers to do exactly that every day of the week: knowing full well that no manager is perfectly competent and there is no widely accepted 'managerial licence' that qualifies anyone to operate without supervision. A business degree and an MBA provide no such guarantees. So competence theory, like any other management theory, has to recognize the harsh realities of organizational life. Human beings are not hamburgers, you cannot decide whether you want pickle, mayonnaise or lettuce. They come as a complete package. It is a bit like asking top sportspeople, someone like the former captain of the England rugby team, Martin Johnson, to be super-competitive but at the same time to control his emotions in the heat of battle. Well, these two aspects of his behaviour are inseparably linked and indivisible. You either want him to charge into a ruck with absolute determination or you want him to stand back objectively and weigh up all the potential implications of his actions. Ideally we do want the perfect combination but if we pull one lever we might have to release another. If we want him to be determined to win at all costs then maybe we have to accept the odd transgression of the rules?

This line of argument was proposed in the first edition of this book and Marcus Buckingham and Curt Coffman's book 'First, Break all the rules' was invoked in support.

They (competencies) lump together, haphazardly, some characteristics that can be taught with others that cannot.... even though designed with clarity in mind they can wind up

confusing everybody. Managers soon find themselves sending people off to training classes
to learn such 'competencies' as strategic thinking or attention to detail or innovation. But
these aren't competencies. These are talents. They cannot be taught.

This time around it is worth looking at how these debates have developed in the light of more recent and fully informed experience of competencies. Garry Platt, a highly experienced and very knowledgeable training and development consultant had this to say in a piece entitled 'Competence Frameworks: The Bubonic Plague of Training?' in August 2008:

> *There are so many negative things that I have encountered in relation to competency frameworks that have led me to believe they are one of the great white elephants in the HR and training community.*

> http://www.trainingzone.co.uk/cgi-bin/item.cgi?id=187188

If this makes you want to throw your present competence framework out the window you had better make sure you have something to replace it.

We will not look at all of the other theories listed in the same detail, but suffice it to say that any theory purporting to tell us something about human capability or behaviour is never going to be based on an exact science. First, the laboratory conditions in which to test and develop watertight theories about people just do not exist. Second, every organization is a different conglomeration of context and circumstances and should be regarded as a unique set of 'laboratory conditions'. The only valid advice therefore is to treat all HR theories with extreme caution before using them as a foundation for practice and if they fail the simplest tests then they have failed, full stop. No wonder solid theory is so often discarded by HR and learning directors and the Executives they serve.

'MAGIC' PILLS AND HR 'HOMEOPATHY'

It is unlikely that many CEOs have the time or the inclination to delve too deeply into HR theories, but it is time you stopped taking what your HR or learning specialists have told you at face value. Doctors have the same dilemma every day. Sometimes they cannot find what is ailing a particular patient, other times they know that a patient will respond just as well to a placebo. Unscrupulous doctors are writing out the prescription before the patient has even sat down. In the world of HR the shelves are overflowing with ready-made answers to all your people problems – these are touted as silver bullet answers or Magic HR Pills just like the bottle in Fig. 4.2, although in reality they are more likely to look like a book cover with a title such as the 'The 101 habits of the most incredibly brilliant CEOs in the world ever, ever, ever' or 'The One Minute Genius'.

The field of HR is especially prone to the use of potions, lotions and even alchemy because it is very difficult to diagnose either the precise nature of the 'disease' (e.g. 'poor customer service') or its likely causes (is it the product or the service?). HR 'Magic Pills' can come in many forms from employee

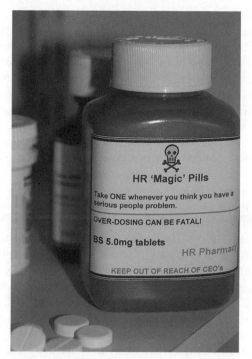

FIGURE 4.2   HR 'Magic' Pills can be very dangerous!

engagement or attitude surveys to personality assessments and training courses (some years ago Marks & Spencer put 20,000 employees through the same customer intimacy programme without a single business objective identified), team-building exercises and 360-degree feedback instruments (to force everyone to give feedback whether they want to or not). Some of these 'drugs' are well-known, proprietary brands (Q12, Myers Briggs etc.) and others have a 'seal of approval' from a business school or popular academic (e.g. Robert Kaplan at Harvard?). None of them can guarantee any efficacy and the worst are no better than homeopathic remedies, with absolutely no science to support their claims, inexact or otherwise.

Then there are the generic variants, which in the case of psychometric tests can amount to literally thousands of different varieties of personality instruments and aptitude tests on the market. You might think that none of this matters too much, that even if they do not do any good they will not do any harm. Unfortunately, this same simplistic and dangerous belief causes some individuals to pop vitamin pills on a daily basis as though they were sweets. Yet even vitamin pills can be dangerous in the wrong doses and if you have tried to cure your organizational or managerial 'cancer' with homeopathic remedies by the time you find out it has not worked it is probably too late to try a more conventional treatment.

It is relatively easy to see why any busy CEO would want a quick-fix solution to a people problem though. Large banks, when not paying inflated salaries, are happy to pay out huge sums to settle sexual harassment and discrimination cases rather than address a really intractable, usually macho, culture issue. Lehman Brothers had their own head of diversity in Canary Wharf in London, but no one ever made any connection between her role and the performance of the bank and she could not articulate why she was there for any business, or ethical, reason. The cynic would say that she was there for PR purposes only. Certainly the Chief Executive, Dick Fuld, known on Wall Street as the 'Gorilla', probably made his own personal views on diversity very apparent every minute of every day of the week in his behaviour and dealings with colleagues. Diversity was certainly not part of an overarching HR strategy and had nothing to do with Lehman's performance. Perhaps a bit more diversity among its management group might have saved the bank if it had been taken seriously?

For any dedicated, senior HR professional the attitude of some senior executives can be exasperating because they put absolutely no time or effort into managing their human resources effectively and yet, when they suddenly realize that change is required, they want behaviours to change instantaneously. Hence they reach for the bottle of Magic Pills every time, usually in the form of a new policy or initiative, be it competence or diversity, leadership courses or bonus schemes.

One particular area of reactivity likely to result in a triumph of hope over experience is training and development. Organizations need good leaders so what do they do? – at a click of their fingers they send their top people on leadership development programmes. When they return there is an assumption that these managers have developed some leadership capability that they did not previously possess. In other words, *physically attending the programme* is deemed to indicate an improvement in leadership capability. The same argument would suggest that anyone who watches a premier league football or baseball game is going to learn how to be a great player, without having ever kicked a ball or picked up a bat.

Of course, if no one asks too many questions about whether the pills are working or not, leadership course providers can just blithely carry on with absolutely no accountability. Fortunately, more and more questions are now being asked about such programmes. In particular, finance directors have never been happy spending money on activity with no declared outcome and have been trying to apply their usual return on investment (ROI) criteria to such expenditure. This explains why those who run leadership programmes now feel they have to defend their actions. Here is one such response from Mike Sweeney, Managing Director, UBS Leadership Institute, in 2005 and note the choice of the word 'Institute' to offer a more official, quasi-academic credibility.

> *The assignment of business value to development is a tough job in general. Measures like ROI and other monetary results cannot be directly attributed to the work of the Institute. There is no formula. However, while 'bottom line' metrics are certainly valuable, perhaps the business impact can also be demonstrated daily in the fabric of the organisation, and*

the ways in which senior management are aligned with leadership development. …. The
Institute has tried to resist the temptation…(of allowing) 'making the metrics' …distract
from delivering added value to the organisation.

(published in Conference Board Research Report R-1361-05-RR)

With the best will in the world one could hardly say that Mr. Sweeney is warmly embracing the concept of ROI in leadership development but any calculations he might have made would have been overshadowed by the story reported by the BBC in August 2008 how UBS's involvement in the US subprime mortgage fiasco:

… has turned a bank which just 12 months ago was showing healthy profits, into an
institution which has lost over 12 billion dollars, and written off a staggering 42 billion.

http://news.bbc.co.uk/1/hi/business/7556976.stm

The 'leaders' (sic) at UBS were making exactly the same mistakes as every other large bank. Perhaps they should have renamed their 'Institute' the UBS Lemmings Institute? It appears that it is still in existence today, presumably because no one is making a connection between its activities and the business's results? But then again, it was never intended to be linked to hard, ROI-type results in the first place. So now that Mr Sweeney is in a position to reap the full benefit of his hindsight what might he have done differently to develop leadership at UBS? Would he have asked the simple question – how will this add value? Sometimes Magic Leadership Pills can be incredibly expensive and yet incredibly noxious.

These same mistakes are not exceptional or rare, they are the norm in learning departments and leadership schools because the prevailing 'wisdom' is that you run the programme first and ask (as few as possible) questions afterwards. Here is a quote from somebody working for Panasonic who was asking other 'development professionals' using the UK-HRD website (19 March 2004) for advice about developing leadership competence (notice the combination of two theories here):

The modus operandi of the programme is that we will produce pools of future leaders from
which the best candidates will be selected when the role becomes vacant. A lot of work has
already been done around producing the required competences for future leaders and
scoping out the required development, so I am happy that we have this covered. However,
there are a couple of characteristics that we believe are key to the success of the pro-
gramme that we still have to tie down. These are:

1. How we select the best candidates? …….

This development manager is working to a competence theory that can be traced back to the academic Richard Boyatzis (*The Competent Manager: A Model for Effective Performance*, Wiley, 1982) whose theory implied that managers and leaders can be replicated, according to a predetermined blueprint. This theory does not demand that any particular business problem be defined before development activity starts because it is treated like a mini 'general theory' with universal applicability. If Panasonic had bothered to do an organizational performance analysis first though they would already have identified the 'best candidates' by linking their development to specific and very relevant business needs. The managers getting the best performance should have been first on the list for consideration of leadership potential. Panasonic would also do well to treat managers as unique individuals rather than pill-popping automatons.

Both of these examples are easy to ridicule and are crass enough to deserve it. They are an awfully long way away from being part of an HR-business strategy, despite the fact that both companies have been very successful businesses in the past. Organizations that are really serious about ensuring they have the right quality of leadership have career development *systems,* not just leadership programmes. They aim to assure future leadership over a very long period. Any attendance on a formal, classroom-based leadership programme, assuming it is well designed, is only one infinitesimal element in a continuous process. Such organizations tend not to have to advertise externally for their next CEO. So, while many organizations may have the same wish to grow their own talent, not all of them get the strategic bit right. They might look like they are doing the right things (sending senior managers to Harvard or Insead) but there is no real substance behind their style. This is a key indicator of the distinctions to be made between genuine HR-business strategy and mere HR activity but what is even more interesting is how often such activities can have exactly the opposite effect to the one desired.

THE HR 'CATCH-22'

Take the subject of staff appraisal or personal development plans. These are often self-defeating. Good managers generally do not need them and bad managers do not really want them. Good managers always appraise their staff regularly, informally and quite naturally. Bad managers do not and so HR people, who were taught that appraisal is good practice, create a paper-based or even online process (not a system, because a system would actually guarantee performance improvements) to ensure that they sit down with their staff, at least once a year, and go through the motions of appraisal. This could be described as a classic case of a Catch-22, an HR policy that cannot win.

The good managers, who do not actually need appraisal forms because they naturally make time to appraise their staff on a regular basis, are the only ones that complete the forms by virtue of their good management principles. The target audience, however, the poor people managers, are those who do not possess the natural skills of talking to their staff openly and giving and receiving critical feedback constructively. They are the ones for whom the forms were originally designed and are the very people least likely to use them effectively because they just highlight and reinforce their own inadequacies.

You might be surprised just how endemic HR Catch-22's are: almost a law of nature. Some years ago an HR director confided that he had just finished piloting a senior management, 360° feedback scheme. The theory of 360° feedback is that you can never have too much feedback, despite plenty of evidence that many people find it very hard to give or receive open, honest feedback. This was borne out by his observation that 'the good managers loved it and the bad managers hated it'. The ones who really needed it, who were unapproachable, insecure, afraid to accept any criticism and perpetuated a blame culture, were the same ones who did not learn anything from the exercise or modify their behaviour as a result of it.

When you know what an HR Catch-22 is you can spot them everywhere. The employees who make use of company learning centres or online resources are the same ones who used to borrow management books from the library anyway. The learning centres never attracted those who were not interested in learning; the very ones who needed to learn new ways of working. Those avidly using the new HR intranet are the ones who were good anyway at using the old manual system. The people who never miss a day's training are the ones who need it least and the ones that do not turn up need it most. The employees who complain about lack of communication are the same ones who never read company magazines or circulars. The companies that want accreditation so badly (Investors in People, Best Company to Work For, Gallup Q12) for the public relations 'badge' do not have any evidence that it is good for business. The ones that do not bother to apply for such schemes do not need external approval or recognition for their management effectiveness. The list is endless.

If this is a truism, a fundamental of human nature and organizational behaviour, what lessons can we draw from this that can be used to our advantage in strategic HR thinking? Home truths, like honest feedback, are often difficult to swallow but at some stage we have to acknowledge them and address the issues they raise and the tough questions they pose.

In spite of what has been said above though, no self-respecting HR director would choose *not* to have an appraisal scheme of one sort or another and would not say no to winning an award for it. Partly because they would regard this as a widely accepted, good HR practice but also because, if they do not have an appraisal scheme, what would they replace it with? There has to be some process for reviewing individual performance and training needs. With this mindset in operation it is relatively easy to see why HR directors are much more concerned about ensuring an activity takes place than they are with asking too many questions about whether it works or not. They regard many HR practices as a given and therefore not in need of any justification or fresh reappraisal. Hopefully one of the benefits of the present recession will give them the jolt they need.

Performance management schemes are certainly part of that dogma and as a generic HR practice it has been transferred directly from commercial companies to the public sector; on the very shaky assumption that it works. Yet when it fails to work rarely is anyone held to account. Some years ago, one HR director in an NHS hospital declared, in a very defensive tone, that it was not his fault that the new performance management system was not working properly. He had introduced and developed the process, following what he believed to be best practice, but that is precisely where he saw his responsibility end. It was up to the managers themselves to make the best use of it. If they chose not to that was their fault, not his. Worryingly, this same person now holds a very senior post in the NHS.

Now we may all understand and have sympathy with his views, but it does not alter the fact that HR initiatives without impact become a waste of everyone's time and energy, regardless of whom we try to pin the blame on. Worse still, they build up resistance and defensive attitudes to future initiatives that could actually be very well designed. This is the fundamental problem with HR theories and most of the academics who espouse them. What is the point of developing theories, or the systems to implement them, if the organizational groundwork has not been prepared to ensure they take root? One of the primary tasks of an HR-business strategy is to prepare the ground. In this case, the hospital needed a performance culture before it needed a performance process and it needed a holistic performance system not bits of paper - a system that managers welcome and will work with, rather than against. A human system designed by human beings for human beings.

This is yet another, common sense test of HR practice. Ask any HR director why they have job evaluation or competence based pay systems and they will start explaining the theoretical underpinnings of consistent and felt-fair reward systems. They will also mention legislation regarding equal pay for work of equal value and the need to demonstrate this to the authorities. In effect, the rigid system of evaluation has taken over and ignores the fact that every one of their employees is a unique individual with a unique pattern of motivation and personal circumstances. The dogmatic theory and practice have become blind to the human beings involved. This is one reason why new job evaluation schemes are usually very expensive to introduce because they increase pay where necessary but red circle, for employee relations reasons, those cases requiring a drop in pay. Even on the rare occasions when pay cuts are to be implemented the piecemeal approach to pay and grading, rather than a completely new HR-business strategy, results in very adverse reactions. Here is what happened at Birmingham City Council (UK) in 2008 when trying to equalize its pay and grading structure:

http://www.personneltoday.com/articles/2008/01/18/44020/birmingham-city-council-defends-hr-role-in-equal-pay-dispute.html

'The council admitted earlier this month that it was drawing up emergency plans to deal with strikes that have been threatened over its pay equalisation plans. More than 80 workers at the UK's biggest local authority face pay cuts in excess of £16,000 per year....'
and the leader of the opposition Labour party said 'People are very unhappy with how HR has dealt with this situation. They have not communicated well, and not followed up on staff queries. They have treated staff appallingly.'

Needless to say, no one suggested that anyone in HR, or any other department, should have been fired for previously paying these same 80 staff £16,000 per year more than they were worth for many years. Obviously the old grading scheme was a disaster just waiting to happen. Neither was there any mention of how such people could help to finance their own pay by working smarter or harder (a point that the unions at GM do not currently accept either). In the end, the council decided that the workers who were to have their pay reduced would not suffer any reduction for 3 years. This is an easy decision to make when you have a captive audience of taxpayers who have to pick up the bill but a terrible indictment of poor council leadership and strategic management. It would probably not be too wide of the mark to describe this whole episode as a colossal case of HR mismanagement and one that has been repeated, to a greater or lesser extent, across many local authorities in the UK.

Of course, there must have been some very good reasons for needing to address the pay and grading issues. Women were being unfairly paid in relation to their male colleagues and there is absolutely no justification for that, but what lies at the heart of all major organizational upheavals is a need for change and change is always likely to hurt somebody. So one of the purposes of HR-business strategy is to bring about the desired or necessary changes with the minimum of disruption or loss. This raises the perennial debate about one of the most fundamental questions in managing people – can people change? It is time to consult our master, Machiavelli, once more.

THE MYTH OF 'CHANGE MANAGEMENT'

> *There is nothing more difficult to handle, more doubtful of success, and more dangerous to carry through, than initiating changes in a state's constitution. Because the innovator makes enemies of all those who prospered under the old order; and only lukewarm support is forth coming from those who would prosper under the new. Their support is lukewarm partly from fear of their adversaries, who have the existing laws on their side, and partly because men are generally incredulous, never really trusting new things unless they have tested them by experience.*

Machiavelli, *The Prince*, 6

Machiavelli still gets a very bad press for someone whose genius lay in his profound understanding and yet simple exposition of the universal, enduring truths about human nature. In this short paragraph he shows why most attempts at change are doomed to fail before they start. This, of course, has to be read also as a call for strong leadership, precisely why Machiavelli was writing for his Prince.

Change management and HR-business strategy are synonymous. Without the need for change there is no need to produce an HR-business strategy. Business as usual just requires an operating plan and more of the same. If the main purpose of HR-business strategy is to create a competitive advantage through people it implies that you have to change the way you manage those people. That does not necessarily mean, however, that the people themselves have to change. It may well just mean bringing in new people. Either way we need to be clear what we mean by change. There may be more than a grain of truth in statements such as 'we need to be more customer focused', or 'we need people with a "can-do" attitude' or even 'a knowledge sharing culture' but any observer would have to admit that the words used are very non-specific, nebulous, generalizations. It would be difficult to say exactly *who* was not very customer focused and, most important of all, none of them suggest what the solution to these problems might be.

This is why change is both open to so much debate and yet produces such little positive progress. Problems that are ill-defined will always lead to misdiagnosis, but the temptation of generic change programmes is that no one has to admit that they, personally, have to change their ways and no one can be held responsible because there are no measures in place. This is why, despite all the talk of change, there is little evidence that anything changes when it comes to human nature or organizational behaviour.

Any student of social and economic history will readily acknowledge that societies have always been through fundamental change. No doubt cave dwellers thought twice about building a simple hut and their co-cave-dwellers waited to see if they survived before they joined them. Societies have changed in terms of all the outward signs of material wealth, but have the needs and desires of the people themselves changed?

Think of anyone you have known well for say 20 years and ask yourself whether they have changed in any significant way at all? They got older and hopefully wiser but, as a rule, their personality has been one of the most constant things in their lives. There are bound to be exceptions to this rule, but there may have been exceptional circumstances. Whether you agree with this generalization or not we all tend to hold close to our own views as to whether people can or cannot change. What matters is that *your* view of the world influences how *you* deal with people. If your belief is that people do not change, then you will not attempt to change them. Also, think how you would respond now if someone told you – 'you're going to have to change your attitude!' It is not very likely to make any real difference to you is it when your attitudes have been shaped and hardened over many years?

Everyone has their own opinions on the subjects of people and change and those views will probably be as unshakeable as yours. Our attitudes are like the trees you see on cliff tops by the sea. In the face of many years of buffeting they have learned to lean backwards in the direction of the wind to survive, yet in doing so they become twisted and distorted. You would never be able to make them grow upright again but if you tried it would probably take the same time with the wind blowing in the opposite direction to undo the damage.

In the brilliant film 'The Candidate' (Directed by Michael Ritchie, 1972) Bill McKay (Robert Redford) is a clean-living, campaigning liberal lawyer who abhors conventional politics but reluctantly enters the race to become a senator when offered the candidacy by Machiavellian, political fixer, Marvin Lucas (Peter Boyle). In trying to convince McKay to stand Lucas offers McKay a guarantee, scrawled on a book of matches, which just says 'You lose'. By the end of the film McKay, having been seduced by power, wins the election after compromising his principles, alienating his friends, learning how to go for the jugular, uttering endless platitudes and cheating on his wife. In the final scene he stumbles across the book of matches, only to realise too late what Lucas knew all along, that this was a Faustian pact in which he would lose everything that he had previously held dear. Not only is it a brilliant film, as sharp and relevant in 2009 as it was in 1972, it shows how and why climbing the greasy pole often results in distortions and perversions that go with a quest for power (and is therefore mandatory viewing for any students of HR-business strategy).

Why is this so relevant? Because if leadership means anything it means tapping into peoples' belief systems and often the 'goodness' that an organization could achieve will so easily be traduced by CEOs forgetting that they probably started out on their journey to the top genuinely caring about what they were trying to achieve but lost sight of it along the way. Why else do so many millionaires want to give so much of their wealth to charity? If they can keep what they care about uppermost in their minds then maybe they can get their employees to care about it as well.

So what are the attitudes of the people who work in your organization now? Do they care what you are trying to achieve or is it just a job? How willing are they to follow you into your strategic battle? To help you answer this question there is a model shown in Fig. 4.3 that divides people into four categories.

Terrorists are those employees who feel they have been so badly treated by their organization that they are capable of doing damage. They are the ones who readily voice their negative views in public, or worst still, in front of customers – 'Yes, I've been telling my boss that for months and he hasn't done a thing about it.'

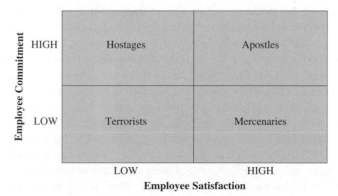

FIGURE 4.3   Make sure you employ 'apostles' not 'terrorists'.

Mercenaries might be all right while they are on your side (although Machiavelli called military mercenaries 'useless and dangerous') but they are likely to desert when offered a better deal.

Hostages, on the other hand, may not actually create havoc but they certainly feel trapped. They are usually those who started out loyal, but when their career has plateau-ed or they have barely survived a reorganization they lose heart. Often it is only their pension that keeps them there.

Apostles are ideally what you want. They are totally committed to the cause and will gladly spread the word of how wonderful the organization is.

So the challenge for an HR strategist is simply to create an environment where people feel their working life is part of something much bigger than their day-to-day task. Whether they are sweeping the floor, making nuts and bolts, building jet aircraft, arranging foster homes for children or giving an elderly patient a cup of tea, they will know that their work is a small but important contribution to the way a good society functions and one they are very proud to be part of.

One thing absolutely guaranteed to get you on the wrong side of your employees is to suggest to them that their behaviour needs to change. Most of us are reasonably comfortable with who we are. We are painfully aware of our shortcomings and we have probably spent many years trying to make our way through life within our own constraints and limitations. The last thing we need is to have to fundamentally change our behaviour patterns, especially those that have been sculpted out of hard-won experience. Even if we wanted to try and change we might be better off finding an organization where we fit in, rather than try to adapt to one where we do not.

For example, some people might regard banking as a soulless enterprise, even if their brain tells them that banks nevertheless perform a very important function in society (or used to). They would not feel comfortable working in such an environment though, because it does not match their own most cherished beliefs and values. The aim of a good HR-business strategy is to ensure that the organization has the right people doing the right things to deliver business strategy. If you are running a restaurant chain do you try to *train* staff to be nice to the customer or do you employ people who naturally enjoy working with the public and have a talent for pleasing customers? You want the innate behaviour of those who have a natural warmth, an eagerness to please and give good service. You do not intentionally recruit awkward, unfriendly and aggressive staff and then try to change them to suit to you, even though we have all been in restaurants where this appears to be the recruitment policy.

This problem should normally be resolved at the recruitment stage, but what do you do with existing employees who have been with the company for some time? In 2005 it was reported that Stuart Rose, the new CEO of retailer Marks & Spencer (M&S), decided that if he was to turn the company around (after a steep drop in profits and many board changes in recent years) he would have to 'rip up' the contracts of his 66,000 shop floor staff (*Personnel Today* 7 June 2005). Probably the only thing that stopped him was his HR/legal advice that this would be very difficult and probably costly. He did not pursue the idea but it does not alter the fact that he obviously felt that M&S needed to change its ways to win more customers and its staff would have to follow suit.

The organization they had originally joined needed fundamental change because the world around it had changed. There was now much more direct competition for M&S customers, so what other options did he have? One possibility would be to base the HR-business strategy on finding those in the organization that were already responding to and welcoming change. This would be a minority initially who probably stood out like a sore thumb in the old M&S culture, but over time such a group can be fostered without falling foul of the 'old guard'.

In the event Stuart Rose managed to turn M&S's performance around during the boom years that followed by introducing new lines and having an ambitious store revamp, albeit leaving M&S with long-term borrowing standing at £2 billion in February 2009. He did not choose an HR-business strategy that changed the people, probably because he did not have an HR-business strategist on board who could have helped him change 60,000 contracts for the better. Walk into any M&S store today and you are just as likely to meet an old style attitude as a new one. They are certainly not winning any more customers through changing staff attitudes and are suffering the downturn just as much, if not more than other retailers.

It is easy to understand why a CEO would feel hidebound by employment legislation in such circumstances and might conclude that the only other option is to reach for a bottle of Magic Pills, sending everyone on training courses in customer service. However, if any other retailer comes along to challenge M&S with a radically different approach to HR-business strategy then even a CEO as well respected and successful as Stuart Rose will have to revisit his original, preferred idea. In fact one of Rose's predecessors was the one responsible for sending 20,000 M&S employees on a 'customer intimacy' programme after the first big drop in profits. The programme was about developing a different relationship with their customers. This was a classic 'Magic Pill'. No connection had been made between the training course and sales or profit and it was wholly inappropriate for the majority of staff who did not particularly want to get 'intimate' with anyone, especially customers.

This is the reality of 'change' programmes in many organizations., the universal, sheep dipping of staff, whether they have 'ticks and fleas' or not. Apart from the stigma of being plunged into the same trough with everyone else, regardless of their own standards of personal 'hygiene', commitment or performance this is tantamount to an open admission of strategic HR failure. No HR-business strategist in their right mind would treat 20,000 employees as a homogeneous group, even if they were aiming to create a common culture.

Change management continues to bedevil organizations and there is a never-ending stream of academic and charlatan literature produced each year ('change management' produces 84 million hits on Google). Yet, all this attention would be pointless if someone produced a theory of human psychology that said adult human beings just do not change in any meaningful sense. Freud contended that after the age of about 6 or 7, or even earlier, there is virtually a nil chance of fundamentally or significantly changing someone's personality. By the time someone reaches the age of employment their behaviour patterns are very well established. So an HR-business strategist will accept, as a given, that they cannot change their employees in an organizational context and just concentrate on getting as much value from each individual, whatever that takes.

INDIVIDUALLY CENTRED HR-BUSINESS STRATEGIES

Our earlier discussion about HR-business strategy being a new, generic, strategic option might not have struck you as a genuinely new development. After all, everything presented in this text is meant to be, at least on one level, simple common sense mixed with an understanding of the most predictable aspects of human behaviour. So let us just briefly reconsider whether any people strategy can be generic when every single one of the 6 billion-plus humans on this planet is uniquely different, with their own unique DNA.

The problem with seeing people as homogeneous is that it encourages managers to adopt a one-size-fits-all approach. The many psychological assessment tools and psychometric tests available that purport to categorize people into well-defined groups reinforce this thinking. One of the most popular, well respected and widely used is the Myers–Briggs Type Inventory (based on Jungian rather than Freudian thinking). Regardless of the research that underpins this instrument, and its claims to scientific validity, it has one very obvious flaw for the pragmatic HR-business strategist; it is predicated on a model that only allows for 16 types of personality (or more accurately personality preferences) for the whole of mankind, all 6 billion varieties. This would suggest, therefore, that it must be more akin to a very rough and ready guide rather than an accurate predictor of human behaviour.

As with any model or technique though, if it does not work well we should not blame the tools but the person handling them. As organizations are prone to reach for the bottle of Magic Pills whenever they can we should not be surprised to see such instruments used in a similar fashion. The cautionary note for any CEO here is – make sure any HR or psychological tool is used intelligently. This is a general principle applicable to any management tool.

Job evaluation is one tool that might be used as part of an overall reward policy and, as we have seen with Birmingham City Council, it is still common in many organizations. This could be described as a generic solution to pay and grading issues because the system is applied to all employees (with the exception of CEOs). The focus of job evaluation though is the *job* itself, not the jobholder or individual employee per se. This tends to mean that all employees with the same job title, let us say section head, will be given the same job evaluation score and grading; with some leeway allowed for slight variations such as greater experience being required. In other words, job evaluation produces uniformity in job classification and, where the gradings have to be agreed with union representatives, encourages inflexibility that takes no account of the individual's efforts, performance or willingness to take on other tasks or a wider role. Moreover, without being combined with an effective performance management system it can be a recipe for organizational stasis, not dynamism. It plays to the wishes of the mediocre and the union member wanting to protect their position and militates against the release of individual potential and value. So one of the most common tools used by HR departments, all over the world, can actually work against the very tenets of a high-value HR-business strategy.

A more flexible HR-business strategy could eschew job evaluation in favour of rewarding section heads on a totally individual, performance-related basis. This could be a key element in an individually centred, HR-business strategy and the decision of which route to choose is absolutely critical. Usually no clear or explicit decision is made about choosing the generic or individual options. Things tend to just happen by default and in a reactive, non-strategic way, as in Birmingham; no one addressed the issue of unfair payment of men and women until the legislation forced them to. What does this tell us about the real values of the good Councillors of Birmingham? Those taking the initiative though will always define the strategy and individually centred strategies will always be looking for bespoke solutions, not off-the-shelf bottles of generic medicines.

This cannot be any better illustrated than by reference again to the sort of training courses run in organizations. Pre-prepared menus of management courses, with no clear link to any personal, specific, organizational objectives are the epitome of a one-size-fits-all, people management mentality. The HR-business strategy driven organization may well still have some standard courses but its performance management system will be integrated with its training system to make sure they work in tandem and harmony. There will also be a whole range of other learning opportunities, some formal and some informal, but all guided by the single principle that they have to be linked, in some way, to the creation of value. Even those employees who receive coaching or mentoring on a one-to-one basis will be asked what difference it is making to organizational outcomes. They will not regard this as odd or unusual because every other aspect of this holistic HR-business strategy would have already been sending clear, consistent signals that this is the way the organization is moving. It would have managed out those who find this too challenging. An individually centred, HR-business strategy values each individual and does not tar everyone with the same brush. This is a recipe designed for personal initiative and potential to flourish.

There is no reason for any employee to fear HR-business strategy because it is only aiming to help them to get the best out of themselves. If it cannot, then it will help them decide whether their own interests could be better served elsewhere. The only employees who are likely to fear the new world of HR-business strategy are those still trying to promote unfocused, unproven and often value-destroying HR management methods that do not work. Some of those already reside in your

HR department, but others will be operational managers who do not really want to manage the full value potential of their people. They see that as a threat to their own position and status. You will have to face up to both of these groups if you want to move forward. They have a lot of growing up to do if they are to find a place in your organization as it reaches maturity.

Chapter 5

Are You Mature Enough for HR-Business Strategy?

JUST A MINUTE BEFORE YOU RUSH OFF

If the earlier chapters have achieved their aim of whetting your appetite for HR-business strategy then you might want to rush off straight away and start working on it. That would be a big mistake. HR-business strategy is not a rush job or a quick fix, even though there should be plenty of opportunities for some early gains. It has to be a holistic approach, involving everybody, and this takes time and careful planning. It will also involve changing the way employees perceive the organization and helping them to choose how to behave differently; HR-strategy has to be based on the principle of voluntarism.

As with all solid principles, we will never stick to this one 100%. You will lose some people when developing an HR-business strategy and there is always the business to run, so people have to do things they would not always choose to do. Nevertheless, in order to help everyone cope with this change we are going to look at where you are starting from and where you need to get to. This should help you communicate your plans openly and educate people enough for them to want to make this journey with you. They need to be going into this with their minds and their eyes wide open. An HR-business strategy should also show sophisticated organisations how to keep things very simple; yet another paradox. So what does that mean and how should it feel to be part of such an entity? Well, first we need to change the way you view the HR function.

"WHATEVER PEOPLE SAY HR IS – THAT'S WHAT IT'S NOT"

Hopefully you already appreciate what your HR department does for you, but you would not be the first CEO to either have serious doubts about HR people or be unsure exactly what their role is. Take these comments from entrepreneur and venture capitalist Luke Johnson in a diatribe he launched in the *Financial Times* (29 January 2008):

> HR is like many parts of modern businesses: a simple expense, and a burden on the backs of the productive workers .... Managers too often think their company isn't grown up unless it has all these important-sounding departments.

… and it continues in much the same vein.

Luke Johnson, as a private equity entrepreneur himself, should be very careful about what burdens are placed on the backs of productive workers. Many private equity deals add no value whatsoever, but still make profits by increasing the burden of debt. Nevertheless, his assessment of the 'HR' people he has met echoes many similar comments in surveys over the years asking CEOs what they expect from 'HR'. But he is wrong to think that this represents real HR. One survey of senior business executives in particular was Deloitte's 'Aligned at the top' in 2007 that found that '63% never consulted HR leaders on mergers and acquisitions', only '19% saw people management as valuable to the ambitions of the business' and a mere '5% described the HR function as "highly effective" in addressing business needs' (*Personnel Today* 19 June 2007).

Most 'HR' departments of today might look modern but they are really just old style personnel departments with a new name. They do lots of new activities (psychometrics, 360 feedback, assessment centres, employee surveys etc.) but none of these activities have much, if any, value because they are not part of a strategy. At the same time the costs of personnel work have increased significantly in line with employment legislation and the ever-increasing rights granted to employees and no business likes to see an increase in overheads from something they already perceive to be a necessary evil.

Whether Luke Johnson needs any HR expertise or not one question that he and other private equity partnerships might like to ask themselves is why on earth anyone, who does not have any equity in the business, would want to work for them? What's in it for the ordinary employee? If private equity partners were as interested in societal value as they were in profit then they should get on fine with a real HR-business strategist. Luke Johnson would have to take his blinkers off though, to understand that there is much more to real HR-business strategy than the sort of number crunching 'management' beloved of private equity partnerships and hedge funds. They might like to think they make better managers than the ones they have just bought out but they are not known for their people-management skills and, if private equity firm Candover is anything to go by, even their financial management skills are seriously in question. When Candover's share price slumped by 88% John Waples, Business Editor of *The Sunday Times* Business section (1 March 2009) remarked that although Candover had convinced 'investors they could drive superior returns of at least 25% a year, run companies more efficiently and still grow them. ... They were often no better at running companies than the people they replaced.' So if private equity people like Luke Johnson want to become great all round managers they have to be more than financial managers, they have to be great people managers.

So why do hard nosed CEO's still employ HR departments? One possible reason is they help to keep employees onside in what can often be a tough commercial environment. Paul Walsh, Group CEO at drinks giant Diageo was reported in *Personnel Today* (1 December 2008) at the annual CBI (Confederation of British Industry) conference as saying 'HR's role is inclusion and communication: getting everyone ... to understand what's going on and the role they play as we navigate through these troubled times' adding that 'We will expect more from our employees (in terms of) nimbleness, creativity and agility'. So what can we learn from these differing views on HR's role and performance?

Well, Luke Johnson's suggestion to get rid of HR is only considering one small part of the value equation, cost. As long as the legalities of employment are fully covered and the organization is not leaving itself open to unnecessary risk then that might be fine, but he offers no way of adding value through better people management. Paul Walsh, on the other hand, appears to be suggesting a more positive role for HR (probably because he employs so many of them), but his words sound vague and unfocused: much more unfocused probably than the words he would use to discuss margins on a bottle of Scotch. Has he really made any commercial connection in his own mind between the strategic management of people at Diageo and hard margins?

Both Johnson and Walsh have exactly the same problem as anyone else trying to get to grips with this subject and that includes all HR professionals; they do not have any means for articulating, other than as a pure act of faith, whether they see any explicit value in HR management or not. What exactly does Paul Walsh mean by 'nimbleness, creativity and agility'. For a 'hard-nosed' CEO he can certainly sound very touchy-feely. An HR director can do nothing with this type of nebulous and indeterminate brief, although that does not stop them reaching for a bottle of Magic Pills called the 'Nimbleness, Creativity and Agility Course' as they know there will be plenty of dealers out there only too willing to supply. Usually though they will just pass this brief on to the head of learning and development (L&D) to put together a course themselves, safe in the knowledge that most L&D specialists would see nothing wrong in doing so without bothering to stop for one moment to ask 'why?'

Of course asking a CEO 'why?' all the time can be very career limiting in many organizations. Are you a CEO who always welcomes being asked 'why?' Or do you expect people to just do what you tell them? It is the simplest, most obvious question and yet the scariest when the person you are asking does not have a clue what the answer is. Sir Fred Goodwin, the former chief of collapsed, and now nationalized bank, Royal Bank of Scotland (RBS) at a an executive 'away-day' in 2001 was told by his executives (through feedback from discussion groups) that the biggest problem facing the bank was a 'culture of fear' (reported under the heading 'How Fred shredded RBS' in *The Sunday Times* 8 February 2009). So it takes executives with guts to ask the CEO 'why' and even more guts to suggest they might be taking a wrong turn.

We are not questioning the sincerity of Paul Walsh's views, nor are we challenging their validity. He obviously knows his own organization very well and presumably has an intuitive understanding of what might be holding Diageo back but every strategic need has to be articulated using the common language of hard value. If he waved a magic wand and 'nimbleness' improved by 10% which hard indicator in the business would he expect to improve: sales revenue, volumes, margins, market share or what? By the way we are not going to suggest for one moment that he should try and measure nimbleness, even though a consultancy somewhere is probably working on developing a 'Nimbleness Inventory' as we speak.

The only thing we can say for certain is that any CEO that criticizes their HR function, for failing to add value, is damned by their own comments. If they genuinely believe that HR does not add any value at all then they should not be employing them. Except that they know there are some of their services (e.g. dealing with employment legislation and regulations) that just cannot be dispensed with. In effect, HR departments are employed for their necessary work but criticized for not doing more, even though most CEOs still struggle to explain exactly what 'more' looks like. This might sound like an impasse until you realize there is an extremely simple way that any CEO can get out of this. It is called the three-box priority system and is shown in Fig. 5.1.

THE THREE-BOX PRIORITY SYSTEM

The three-box system has several purposes, which are to ensure

- All management activity contributes value
- Risks are minimized
- As many resources as possible are devoted to value creation (Box 2)

Using the system is extremely simple. You just list every activity you can think of and then allocate them to one of the three boxes.

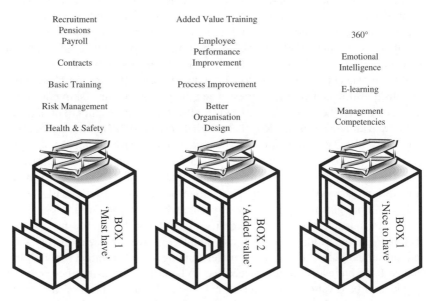

FIGURE 5.1   All management activity can be categorized into three boxes.

Box 1 – '*Must have*' activities keep the organization running, that is all. This includes all personnel administration (including pay and contracts), recruiting and training people to a minimum standard and managing risk (i.e. legal, health and safety requirements).

Box 2 – '*Added value*' activities enhance employees' performance through such things as performance management, higher skills training and development and redesigning their roles. What marks out Box 2 activities is a direct line of sight to a measurable business improvement – for example, 'agility' here would mean responding to customer needs more readily and this would increase cash flow in £'s.

Box 3 – '*Nice to have*' activities are usually the 'touchy–feely' or 'pink-and-fluffy' stuff associated with many HR, training and organizational development teams. Take emotional intelligence as one example. It is a nice notion that managers should be alive and responsive to the human, emotional needs of employees. So someone in HR (or learning and development) might want to undertake emotional intelligence assessments and attempt to develop these attributes in managers who do not already possess them. Yes, it is a nice idea but while it is in Box 3 it is unlikely to work, because Box 3 does not 'have to' happen and no one knows what its 'added value' is so it is not taken very seriously. Activities that are not taken seriously do not result in advantageous behaviour change.

Luke Johnson only sees Box 1 activities for HR and is primarily concerned with cost. He should be careful though that Box 1 work is monitored to make sure it is done well (e.g. no one is employed without the correct safety certification etc.). Box 1 is normally straightforward, but when it goes wrong it tends to go very wrong – the employee has an accident and the company is sued or fined and its reputation seriously damaged. Box 1 should be regarded as a hygiene box. Cadbury's had a salmonella outbreak at one of its plants in the UK in 2006 that cost it £25 million in lost production and product recalls. Someone had failed to get the basics right.

Paul Walsh, of Diageo, is probably thinking of the rest of HR work as something indefinable or intangible as in Box 3. If it is really important though, he can move it into Box 2, where it becomes very valuable, by articulating what he wants in hard, measurable outcomes.

HR teams can only be as good as the CEOs that employ them. HR has a very long history of bad press (often well deserved) but if executive teams find themselves always holding a sceptical or critical view of HR then it behoves them to demand a better service from HR or replace them with a better alternative. Real HR-business strategy demands much greater people-management consideration and skill from all executives, a challenge that many do not want or are incapable of mastering. It is often easier for CEOs to retain HR as a scapegoat for their own poor people-management skills but truly professional HR people would not allow this to happen.

GETTING HR STRUCK OFF

Of course, all of this begs the question – how professional is your HR team? Are HR people just the lackeys of your executive? Do they not have minds of their own and are they incapable of defending their methods? Hopefully not, but do not ask too many questions about what HR 'professionalism' means because it seems to have no foundation at all.

The best analogy for the role of HR is a medical doctor. Every organization has ills and diseases that the HR 'GP' has to accurately diagnose before offering a prescription. Any 'pills' they prescribe should have had their efficacy checked through proper, evidence-based trials. If you went to any HR 'surgery' you should expect them all to subscribe to a common methodology and uniformly high standards of practice. Unfortunately, this is not the case in the world of HR and learning specialists.

The acid test for professional standards is the existence of a strong professional institution with the power to strike charlatans and incompetents off the professional register. Doctors, lawyers, accountants and teachers can be struck off; HR people cannot because there is no recognized register for them. So any CEO should be advised that when it comes to buying HR expertise *caveat emptor* (let the buyer beware); you could end up with someone doing a great deal of damage. The examples from the AA, UBS and Birmingham City Council in Chapter 4 should be a salutary lesson.

If any institution were to take on the task of establishing a register you would expect it to be an organization that purports to act as the 'professional' body, like the Chartered Institute of Personnel and Development (CIPD) in the UK or possibly SHRM (Society for Human Resource Management) in the US. This proposition was put to the CIPD's institute secretary some years ago and the reply was quite unequivocal. They simply do not see it as part of their remit to uphold professional standards.

> *Since we are not an exclusive closed shop, we have no powers to formally debar a member from practising nor to directly remove his or her livelihood if they are found wanting.*

http://www.personneltoday.com/articles/article.aspx?liarticleid=9780&printerfriendly=true

So we are all left in a professional limbo. This means that you have to judge your HR function's professionalism for yourself, but on what basis can you do that? Are you even sure what role you want them to play? Are they even on your 'side' or do they see their main role being the champion of the employee? Perhaps they are really just 'industrial social workers' or should they really be talent spotters and gold miners? Are these roles mutually exclusive and contradictory or can they both be reconciled with the common goal of value? The answers to all of these questions lie in a better under-standing of the full range of roles that HR can fulfil and to look at this we need a benchmarking scale very similar to the Learning Maturity Scale in Chapter 3 (Fig. 3.4).

THE HR MATURITY SCALE

As an employer, have you ever stopped to imagine what it must have been like to be a worker in one of the 'dark satanic mills' at the beginning of the industrial revolution in the early nineteenth century? The hours would have been long, the conditions dangerous and dirty and the rewards a meagre subsistence level. It was probably not much fun: about as rewarding as working in the type of sweatshops that are still in operation in different parts of the world today, including the UK, where some companies try to stay in operation without paying the legal minimum wage.

Some economists and business people still argue that free markets are the only way to run an economy and that labour markets are no different. Yet, in developed economies, an ever-increasing raft of legislation has been introduced to protect the rights of workers and make it more difficult for employers to hire and fire at will. Whether this is a good thing or not might remain a moot point, but these are the competing forces that confront the HR-business strategist. Do you take a cold, clinical, hard-nosed approach to the value of people or does management have to factor in notions of fair treatment and a minimum level of dignity afforded to all human beings? Is this a classic dichotomy of mutually exclusive aims or are we talking about a continuum of gradual evolution?

Let us think the unthinkable for a moment and adopt the most inhuman business case possible – a return to the use of slave labour as the most profitable way to exploit people. If you think this is just hypothetical though, you might be surprised to find that slavery still exists today (see http://www.antislavery.org/). You might be even more surprised to find that someone has already tested such a hypothesis (see M. Spoerer: Profitierten Unternehmen von KZ-Arbeit? Eine kritische Analyse der Literatur, Historische Zeitschrift (HZ) 268/1, 1999). In a table of data entitled 'The economics of slave labour' Spoerer compares the profitability, during the Second World War, of a German company using 'normal German labour' with the use of 'concentration camp (slave) labourers'. Fortunately, for mankind, Spoerer's findings demonstrate that enslaving people does not make good business sense. If we go much further back, to the building of the Pyramids in Egypt, we also now know that slaves were not used then either, for the same obvious reason that slavery is not the most productive way to use people.

A little further up the scale, away from these dark recesses of management thinking, you could consider the proposition of sweatshops. So are they a good way to run a business? What does the evidence tell us? If they are such a great commercial proposition then why are they not the predominant type of business organization in the world today? Moreover, why does the UN International Labour Organization (ILO) have a global mandate to promote 'decent work'? Simply because we all know that sweatshops are neither desirable nor sustainable, even though they continue to exist, for now. Sweatshops tend to be the type of production method used only in simple, low-value goods, the sort that can only be produced by highly labour-intensive methods, in low-wage economies, outside the usual tax and regulatory regime. Many textile and shoe businesses still operate this way.

You would not choose to buy your prescription drugs or your brake pads for your car from such a supplier because you would not expect any safety or reliability guarantees. Quality systems would be unlikely and the producers of such goods may not be around very long to deal with any returns, defective goods or subpoenas. Those who work in sweatshops probably do so out of necessity and probably do just enough to avoid upsetting their boss. This is not an environment in which we might discuss the possibilities of maximizing employee value so we will not be looking at slave camp or sweatshop HR strategies. Both would be oxymorons, a contradiction in terms.

If slavery and sweatshops are off the scale then presumably large, global businesses are at the top, strategic, human capital end? They are in highly competitive, mature markets employing thousands of people, using sophisticated marketing and production techniques. Yes, but do they have the HRM techniques to match? Attracting the right calibre of people and making best use of them is more likely to be a crucial issue in such organizations.

In between these two extremes, there must be a whole range of different enterprises and employers from small, family-owned businesses to medium-sized public companies, as well as a full array of public sector and third sector entities. So where would all of these organizations be placed on this scale? We could call such a scale the Human Resource Management Maturity Scale, as shown in Fig. 5.2. This is a framework designed specifically for you, the CEO,

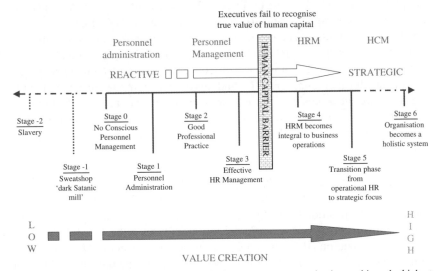

FIGURE 5.2 The HRM Maturity Scale – only the most mature organizations achieve the highest value status.

to understand where your organization is now, what the strategic implications of that position are and what stage you need to get to if you are to have the best chance of becoming a high-value organization.

Before we explore each aspect of the Maturity Scale in more detail the general idea is that you, each of your executives, every manager and every single employee have their own perceptions of how seriously the organization takes the subject of HRM. Their perspectives will include: -

- How much the company 'cares' about its people?
- Whether it offers opportunities as well as a wage?
- How professionally it manages career development?
- How fair it is in selection and succession planning?
- Whether it fosters working relationships that are mutually beneficial?
- Does it have a culture of trust and openness?
- Does it make the best use of everyone's brain power?
- Is it an organization that wants to continually learn how to improve and grow?

This is an evolutionary journey that involves moving carefully through each of the developmental stages shown. We will assume that you are not at stage -2 or -1 but after that all bets are off. Do not be surprised if you are not as mature an organization as you might like to think you are. The Maturity Scale is intended to be the toughest organizational test available and you should relish the challenge this represents if you want to be one of the best CEO's.

THE STAGES OF THE HR MATURITY SCALE
Low Value Versus High Value

The most obvious element of the whole scale, its whole purpose, is to assess your organization's current value against its potential value. The low end (left) of the scale means low in value and the high end means you are getting as much value as possible. Making huge profits does not automatically qualify you to reach stage 6. The question that needs to be answered to get to stage 6 is – are you getting as much value *out of your human capital* as possible? This will only happen if you are mature enough to acknowledge that you do not get the best out of people by treating them as overheads, like children or failing to let them flourish. You also do not get the best out of them by giving them everything they want – there lies the road to the prima donna; ask any football coach or investment bank.

The further to the left of the scale, the lower the value you unleash. One very good example of this key element of the Scale is Microsoft, which still makes a lot of profit but is only between stages 1 and 2 in terms of its maturity. So what indicator suggests such a lowly position? Look at this comment from a story in *Business Week* (ominously entitled 'How to make a Microserf smile' – 10 September 2007),

"Steven A. Ballmer (CEO) had an epic morale problem. Microsoft Corp.'s stock had been drifting sideways for years and Google envy was rampant.... The chronically delayed Vista was irking the Microserfs and blackening their outlook. Ballmer decided he needed a new HR chief, someone to help him improve the mood".

It is not just the magazine's playful reference to 'serfs' (which would put Microsoft close to slavery at Stage -2?) that sets off an immediate alarm. Neither is it the fact that Ballmer appointed someone who had no previous HR experience. Nor even that what she deemed to be her priorities (recruiting practices, flexible workplaces and company perks) did not seem to be directly addressing any business priorities (e.g. Vista delays). No, the loudest alarm bell was triggered by Ballmer, thinking he had a 'morale' objective rather than a 'stock' price problem and that no one made a direct, causal connection between the two. Even the author of this piece assumed the new HR chief could not '... do anything about the stock price', which just reveals the HR immaturity of business journalists. It appears Microsoft is an organization that has disconnected the way it manages its people from the necessities of its business; that is why it is so low on the Maturity Scale. A shrewd HR-business strategist will see straight through the morale-focused, motherhood and apple pie, 'feel-good' hype beloved of such executives.

Reactive or Strategic

The second major shift along the spectrum of the scale is from reactive to strategic approaches to human resources issues. Reactive means everyone goes on a diversity awareness course because the company has just been sued for sex discrimination. Strategic means diversity is a crucial talent pool issue, not a legal requirement. 'Reactive' also means piecemeal and ad hoc, where nothing is planned as part of a coherent and cohesive whole. While at the far right of the scale 'strategic' means that every part of the strategy has to be working in harmony, a whole system organization (see Chapter 3 on human systems).

Now let us look at each evolutionary stage in a little more detail.

Stage -2 'Slavery' and Stage -1 'Sweatshops'

We have already defined what these are and need not dwell here any longer except to say that some 'state-of-the-art' call centres of the twenty-first century have been unfavourably compared to the dark Satanic mills of yesteryear.

(http://news.bbc.co.uk/1/hi/business/3376803.stm) This should be a salutary lesson to us all that improving the technology or the workspace is no indicator that we have improved our attitudes to the way we expect people to work.

As both of these stages are on the negative part of the scale, we should really move on quickly but there is one more stage before there is any positive approach to HRM.

Stage 0 – No Conscious Personnel Management

Stage 0 is not actually on the positive part of the scale because there is no sense here at all that any form of HRM is taking place. For an example of stage 0 we could envisage a small contract catering company that recruits casual workers for occasional catering contracts, such as a wedding or party. There is no real selection process and the temporary workers are paid in cash at the end of the event with no records kept. Based on this description there should be very few organizations still around at stage 0.

It is not just companies in low pay sectors that tend to be at stage 0 though. A hedge fund that only pays according to individual returns would also be at stage 0. There is no conscious attempt to manage people at this stage and so no value is added to them or by them. Stage 0 companies tend to try and ignore any legal or statutory employment legislation. That is why high-profile litigation by women employed in the City or Wall Street is a typical indicator of a stage 0 organization.

Stage 1 – Personnel Administration

Stage 1 is the first point at which some conscious, albeit minimal, effort is made to manage and control people costs. In the case of the catering company it would progress to stage 1 by keeping basic records of previous recruits and will contact the same people for the next contract. By now everything is being done in accordance with the most basic stipulations of employment law and the tax authorities and so a proper payroll system is in place. The company can tell the tax authorities how many people it employed and how much they were paid.

Any CEO satisfied that stage 1 is all they need to cover off 'human resource management' has a very immature, Luke Johnson-type, view of what HR is, regardless of whether they choose to call it Personnel or HR administration. There is no dedicated, professional, HR person; it is more likely to be the CEO's PA. The name given to the function dealing with people issues and the titles of those who work there, provide absolutely no clues as to their professionalism, role, effectiveness or value.

Stage 1 organizations tend to be command and control cultures. The CEO does not see any intrinsic value in people and neither do their managers (remember the principle that bad people drive out good). The word 'management' is taken to mean controlling staff, making sure the job gets done and dealing with any immediate disciplinary matters; usually in a rigid rather than enlightened way (the employee is always wrong and the manager is always right). Employment tribunals occur regularly because management is undertaken by catering managers or supervisors who have no expertise in employment law and only turn to an employment lawyer or professional adviser in extremis.

This is still a very immature organization that would not recognize anything other than reactive, operational management. Crisis management and an ability to fight fires are viewed as management strengths, rather than weaknesses.

Stage 2 – Good Professional Practice

From having the bare minimum personnel records at stage 1 to developing a personnel approach at stage 2 the company has to start seeing that there is more to people management than just operational 'man' management. It starts to grow up and realize that good, professional personnel management practices can make a difference. It might even decide to employ someone with a CIPD qualification. So the personnel records used for payroll purposes are used to record rudimentary performance comments from the supervisor. These are then used, as part of the next recruitment exercise, to contact only those ex-employees who previously did a good job.

It is worth noting that this is a basic, minimum level of professionalism and it does not necessitate the setting up of a personnel department as such. The supervisors could quite easily carry out this function. So the HR maturity scale makes no specific prescription for employing a team of HR professionals. However, a professionally qualified personnel practitioner is more likely to be aware of other tools and techniques that are available and be trained in their use. They may well introduce simple psychometric questionnaires to gauge an applicant's suitability for catering work, which could result in a better selection of candidates, a better quality of customer service and less waste through staff turnover. They will probably be better at interviewing candidates as well because they do it more often than a line manager and have been trained in interviewing techniques.

There is nothing particularly difficult about reaching stage 2. All it requires is a belief by the management team that 'personnel management' disciplines bring something to the operation that good man-management skills, on their own, do not. Hiring your first HR manager should make a noticeable difference simply because they start to install professional procedures and policies. The only word of caution is that they will be installing what they believe to best HR practice; that means copying what every other HR professional is doing. They will not be questioning their methods and they would not dream of providing any evidence to support them. If you are not careful they will produce very cumbersome and bureaucratic processes such as competence frameworks, job evaluation and appraisals. They will also treat everyone the same, as a 'grade' or 'job group', rather than the unique individuals that they are. Stage 2 is a very rigid, static stage. Moving up the scale to higher stages is desirable but much more problematic and the timescales involved can be considerable. When an organization does reach stage 3 it will signify a big shift forward in both management thinking and maturity levels.

Stage 3 – Effective HR Management

If a name is to mean anything then stage 3 marks the point when 'HR' will be preferred to 'Personnel'. Not because it is the latest, sexiest title but because people are finally being seen by the organization's executive as important resources. Stage 3 will not happen by chance though; it has to be a conscious move towards a systematic and structured approach to managing this important resource. Real HR professionalism will now be a mandatory requirement because the executive realizes that an amateurish approach will not suffice if it is to grow a respected business.

In the catering company, some benefits will already have been gained at stage 2, from the rudimentary recruitment and performance systems being put in place. As time moves on it finds, in a very tight market, that some of its competitors are winning more contracts on price. So the CEO wants more effort put into cost controls and efficient ways of working. He or she decides that some supervisors have no understanding of portion control and levels of wastage are unacceptably high. So the standard of supervision needs to be raised by assessing their skills and providing training where necessary. However, the business is too big now for the CEO to manage this so she decides to hire in someone who does – an HR and/or training professional.

The HR professional quickly establishes that some of the older supervisors will never make the grade in the new, leaner company and advise the CEO to bring in some new blood. They simultaneously increase salaries to attract a higher calibre of supervisor and institute a structured training programme. At stage 3 this is as far as their professionalism will stretch. Stage 3 HR professionals have not yet learnt how to make a direct connection between profitability and supervisor skills so the CEO is asked to accept their advice more on the basis of 'trust us we're the professionals' rather than any hard evidence. Very quickly, the CEO sees wastage figures, staff costs and turnover tumble simply because they are now the focus of a great deal of effort. She decides she can now drop her prices accordingly and win more contracts whilst still making a healthy margin. She really starts to value what she now perceives as effective HRM and sees the important contribution to her ambitious business strategy of moving the company into bigger volume, more profitable, catering contracts.

While all of this is going on some of the longer-serving supervisors, the ones who managed to keep their jobs in the last clear out, have found the transition quite difficult. Nevertheless, they have raised their game and started to improve their own people management skills because they have been stretched and supported with development. This is reinforced by the new, formal personal development process, introduced by the HR manager with the blessing of the CEO. Every employee, on every contract, now has to have a formal assessment on file. Those who do not reach the required standard are managed out of the business. The whole culture and atmosphere of the business is gradually changing, sometimes imperceptibly. This could now be described as a well-managed business. It does not carry passengers and, crucially, the workforce have started to grow up as well and are now mature enough to view that as a positive development. We start to see the young shoots of a performance *culture* breaking through to the light.

Before we move on to consider stage 4 we should stop for a second and ask whether an organization has to move, sequentially, through each of the stages on the maturity scale? There is probably a two-pronged answer to this. In an existing organization, at stage 0, a decision could be taken by a new CEO to bring in an HR manager in order to fasttrack the organization to stage 3. While there is nothing to stop them doing so, it raises many questions about how line managers would cope with suddenly having an 'HR expert' sticking their nose in, so to speak, and 'telling them how to do their job'. Of course, a sensitive HR professional would not want to get on the wrong side of the manager but the Maturity Scale is primarily about perceptions and HR-business strategists accept that 'perception is reality'. If a line manger holds a negative perception of what HR management is about then that is their reality and they will react accordingly.

In general terms, if an organization wants to short-circuit the natural, evolutionary, organizational development cycle that underpins the Maturity Scale, then maybe tougher decisions have to be made. This can be self-defeating though, if the overall impression held by the workforce is that this is brutal or hard nosed. The message you would want them to hear, and fully understand, is that this is the best way forward for the business and them, in turns of job security and development opportunities. Nevertheless, the further you move up the scale the more resistance you are likely to encounter. Change is perceived by most people as painful, even if it is not likely to be as painful as they anticipate. The group that are likely to feel the most pain, initially, are the Executive team themselves.

Crossing the Barrier

Now we have reached the biggest hurdle of all. A barrier represented by a brick wall in Fig. 5.2 with the label "Executives fail to recognise true value of human capital". You might be the most sophisticated, experienced and enlightened CEO in the entire world but if you were asked the question 'what is the value of your human capital' the chances are that you would not know how to provide a convincing answer. It is highly unlikely, without being patronizing, that you would even know what human capital is and why we are suddenly talking about human 'capital' instead of human 'resource'. You do not have to see this as a personal failing because you would not be alone. This is a topic that has moved on apace in academic circles and the practicalities have yet to catch up. This is what happens when we are right out at the edge of innovative, sophisticated management thinking. We think the unthinkable, pose more and more questions and then try to work out how to provide answers. Some answers will be provided in Chapter 9 but for now you are just asked to open your mind and be prepared to have it awakened to new possibilities.

In order to help you mentally prepare consider these points

Question 1. How does the cost of your human capital reveal itself in the accounts?

Answer 1. Probably just as salaries/wages in overheads or direct/indirect costs?

Q2. How is the return on that cost calculated or amortised?

A2. It probably isn't. Except maybe in some ratio or average such as 'sales per employee'?

Q3. If you increased the value of your human capital by 1% – say, increase average productivity by 1% – what would that be worth in pre-tax profit? (or patients treated, or customers served if you are a not-for-profit organization)

A3. At least 1% off your total wage bill, presumably, with a consequent impact on profit?

Q4. Where would your finance director show that amount in your profit and loss account?

A4. It would probably show up as a reduced cost, assuming productivity is not included in the P&L?

Q5. If you asked your FD to come up with better answers to these questions what else might have to change?

A5. The whole of accounting conventions, budgeting, performance manage-ment, and company reporting, just for a start!

This is why this is such a huge and seemingly impenetrable barrier. The way we run organizations are predicated on measuring performance, success and value to suit very old-fashioned, accounting conventions: not up-to-date human capital reporting principles. Do not forget, the Accounting for People Taskforce (see Chapter 2) found that no one has come up with a better way of doing it but that does not mean you should not try. There are many benefits to be gained from asking your executives to think differently. It is their attitude and willingness to learn that will remove this barrier, not suddenly inventing new accounting or reporting procedures. No executive should be condemned for not knowing the latest thinking about human capital (well, not yet anyway) but they can justifiably be condemned for not wanting to help the organization create greater value. You, as CEO, will not make much progress towards HR-business strategy until all executives receive this message, loudly and clearly.

This is not a naïve suggestion. Executives who have clawed their way up the greasy pole of fame and ambition; trampled all over their rivals and honed their political skills to a very sharp, stiletto tip will not all rush to embrace what HR-business strategy has to offer. Some of them will welcome this development for their career ambitions: others will see it as an impediment. HR-business strategy has to deal with both and inroads will have to be made into their domains, fiefdoms or whatever other phrases are used to describe the territory they may wish to protect. This wall has to come down, one way or another, if you want to get to stage 4: Ford and GM never got past this wall in over 100 years of existence.

Stage 4 – HRM Becomes Integral to Operations

At stage 3, before the barrier comes down, your organization will feel very much as it does now. The only noticeable difference would be the relationship between line managers and the HR function. To be at stage 3 you need effective HR management and that will come from a combination of line managers working closely with business focused HR professionals. A simple example could be recruitment. Up until stage 3 line managers would be telling the HR department how many vacancies they have. At stage 3 the number of vacancies would be agreed with the HR team after discussions about the wider implications of vacancies (e.g. succession planning, seconding staff from other departments, changing requirements due to reorganization).

Stage 4 feels very different. For a start a new role has emerged for HR that most HR people would call 'HR business partner'. The name itself means nothing as plenty of conventional HR people have given themselves shiny new titles with absolutely zero difference to their modus operandi. Someone undertaking this key role properly will not be sitting on the sidelines; they will be highly proactive, knocking on managers doors relentlessly with ideas for improving value. This could not happen at stage 3 because you and your line managers would still be too immature to appreciate this approach by HR. By the time you get through the barrier to stage 4 you will have fully understood why they are adopting this role and will welcome it, as will the line managers.

One very noticeable difference will be the changing nature of management information available. In our ongoing catering business example, budgeted staff turnover figures for the coming year will dictate how much money is available for recruitment and training. Managers that do not manage staff turnover well will be struggling to find the funds to shore up any level of turnover that is higher than planned. The HR business partner will present data that tells them how well people are being trained and link this directly to operational performance. This will not be just more courses; the managers with the best portion control are now taking time out to coach, advise and train the worst. This inevitably stretches line managers to a higher degree of management capability because their people measures become part of their overall performance data. The best and worst people managers will start to be highlighted. Fortunately, the maturity level at stage 4 is such that this forms the basis for discussing how to achieve further improvements, not the witch-hunt that would predominate in an organization stuck at stage 1 or 2.

These indicators, in isolation, do not mean that the organization has reached stage 4. There needs to be a whole collection of indicators to earn this position. Stage 4 sets a very demanding standard in terms of HR thinking and action. Other 'people measures', as opposed to conventional financial and operational measures, could include the annual employee opinion survey, but only if it closely correlates employee views and attitudes with actual business performance. Managers who get good employee opinion ratings and are performing well in the business start to become the role models.

The whole organization's management information system starts to be regarded as an employee performance measurement system. Someone actually measures project lead times and identifies who was running and sitting on the project teams that were the best and the worst; this forms part of their 'track record' file. When choices for new project team leaders are made these measures are used as the basis for such decisions. Similarly, in an R&D environment, each phase of the product development cycle is closely monitored so that staff who deliver, on time, can be distinguished from others who seem less effective. None of this type of data lends itself to snapshots (e.g. whose project is doing worst at the moment?) and so the creation of trend data on people becomes crucial. The negative management principle that 'you are only as good as your last job' used to write people off, this is now replaced with a much more mature attitude that the best managers can only be judged over time and a range of projects. This reduces the number of 'one-minute wonders' and 'flashes in the pan' that often irk and undermine steady but highly valuable competent managers.

Another significant shift that has to happen is that line managers must value HRM expertise because they can no longer do their jobs effectively without it. At stage 3 they could actually choose whether to include HR considerations in their management decision making, now they do not have that option but they would not choose it anyway, they value this input. They are not able to restructure their team or develop new roles (or even decide on new job titles) unless this fits with the HR-business strategy. They must also actively engage in developing and coaching their staff to meet the needs of the business. Coaching is no longer a 'nice-to-have'; managers without coaching skills no longer work for the company.

Stage 5 – Transition – from Operational HR to Strategic Focus

While the organization is developing a much more strategic perspective on HR, and ensuring that line management follows suit, the emphasis still tends to be on existing business objectives and targets. An organization at stage 4 is very well *managed* but somewhere along this continuum it needs to move away from thinking that organizational success is all down to improving operations. The control freaks have already left the company by now because their behaviour was seen as increasingly bizarre and it gradually dawns on most senior managers that the best form of 'management' is to treat employees as adults and to let them bring their brains to work. This would not have been possible before the barrier came down. The mistrust in the organization would not encourage employees to use their own initiative and the control freaks would not allow ideas to be suggested. There would have been no way of finding out who was generating the best ideas and who had a great track record.

The other obvious difference between stages 4 and 5 is that conventional business strategies *tell* employees exactly what needs to happen. An HR-business strategy expects employees to take the basic strategy and move it on to greater heights, to pick up the ball themselves and run with it. This would be a very scary thing to do in an organization that had not adequately prepared the ground. The organization will start to enter into a different state, one where everyone in the organization is focused not only on delivering performance today, but is thinking about their performance tomorrow. The production line manager who managed to reduce wastage or scrap parts yesterday is trained, as are his team and they set about redesigning the production process to move on to another level of performance entirely. Their colleagues, in other areas, do not stand in their way or try to protect their 'turf' because the redesign will have been handled in a highly systematic, structured way that involves all the relevant parties, who are also equally well trained. They are all still with the company because they are adaptable and welcome change. It is this fundamental shift in attitudes, which has taken a long time, that signifies when the organization has reached stage 5.

'Stage 5' might be a slight misnomer though, because it is a transitional phase. At the far left of this maturity model are organizations that are very tightly controlled. There is no freedom to act and decision making only takes place at the highest levels. In the middle are the well-managed organizations of today. On the far right are organizations where only the strategic direction is set and everyone in the organization translates that into both their day-to-day behaviour and their forward thinking.

As with all personal journeys though, they have to pass through phases, in this case stages 5 to 6. They have to experience it for themselves and know what it feels like before they become totally committed to this way of working. There has to be a period of general enlightenment and the reins have to be completely loosened. Teamwork is absolutely critical if the extremely high levels of performance that can be achieved are to become a reality (have another look at the league table in Chapter 1 to see how far Toyota has moved away from all of their competitors). While the organization might look like it is conventionally structured, showing functional silos and reporting lines, the reality is a much more fluid organization. It will be a much friendlier and less frustrating place to work. Individual managers will not have to get agreement from their own boss every time they are asked for assistance by another section or project team. The relationships will be much more mature than that. This is an organization for grown-ups.

You will probably have noticed that as we explore what the indicators are for each of the higher stages it becomes much more difficult to define and articulate exactly what it means to travel along this continuum. This is not surprising when we are talking about the difference between a personnel administration activity, such as writing a simple (but rigid) job description at stage 1, and the concept of fluid roles at stage 6. There is a real danger here that such language can be dismissed by sceptical CEOs as 'touchy–feely' or 'pink and fluffy' and such criticisms are often levelled at HR and training professionals. We now know that CEOs like Peter Walsh at Diageo are equally 'guilty' of using such language. As you move from stage 1 to stage 6 the organization does not become populated with 'luvvies', despite a worrying trend to use actors in development exercises. In fact, entirely the opposite happens, everyone in the organization becomes hyper-focused, even obsessed, with creating value and of all the obsessions we might become slaves to we could do a lot worse than to choose value: it demands the use of our most acute, intellectual capabilities. There will be no room here for fuzzy thinking; everything is being done for a very clear purpose, value. Only when you realize this will you understand what stage 6 has to offer.

Stage 6 – The Organization Becomes a Whole System

Can you remember when you stopped being a teenager and became an adult? Or what about when you moved from being a graduate trainee to being regarded by your peers as a fully experienced, rounded, professional? These may seem like valid questions, but there was never a single point in time when you were transformed from one state to another. Your own developmental journey was not even a straightforward continuum, no matter how well you planned your career. When looking for your first job you would have been expected to act like an adult during the interview, but later the same day you may well have reverted back to acting like a typical teenager when out with friends. Or, despite being professionally qualified, say as a lawyer, whenever you were faced with a completely new case you knew only too well what it felt like to be a 'beginner' again. Progress often necessitates taking steps backwards in order to move forwards.

Our own development can seem quite schizophrenic, particularly when we become more senior and have to consider a wider set of issues and responsibilities, many of which might appear to conflict. The most obvious example would be the conflict between working efficiently and working safely, a classic dilemma that BP had to face on its Alaskan pipelines. Does it pay the huge cost necessary to reduce internal corrosion or does it save maintenance costs and just hope that it holds? The experienced manager has to bring judgement to bear; there are no black and white answers until the worst happens and the pipeline leaks. The company needs to portray a public image that looks safe, secure and environmentally friendly (BP's green 'flower' logo) while internally there is often fear, crises and panic. These are the occasions when we receive the most accurate impressions of how organizations manage the latent inconsistencies in the whole value equation.

Let us now paint another scenario to provide real insights into what stage 6 might *feel* like if you worked in such an organization. For a start, you cannot use your present mindset or frame of reference because you have not experienced what a stage 6 organization is like (unless you worked for Toyota) and it is perfectly understandable if you find this extremely difficult. So this might require a leap of faith but then, as we discussed in Chapter 1, all ambitious strategies are exactly that, a leap into the unknown with no guarantees. Maybe the first insight into this world, the first fresh perspective, would come from considering whom you report to and who reports to you? You see, even the word 'report' might be inappropriate.

By the time you reach stage 6 this will not be foreign or strange because it will have become the natural way for you to think and for the organization to behave. There is no need here to try and spell out in every detail what might happen at stage 6. The rest of the book will put more flesh on these bare bones. However, a collection of key indicators is shown in Table 5.1, for each stage of the HR Maturity Scale. This is not intended to be a complete or exhaustive list by any means.

ORGANIZATIONAL INDICATORS OF MATURITY

We can also look at the evolution of maturity from the angle of how it influences the development of HR policies. Let us follow one thread on rewards policy.

Stage 0

The 'boss' follows an unwritten 'policy' of paying as little as possible and offering few additional benefits. The payroll is managed by the accounts team overseen by the head of finance. Inconsistencies arise frequently due to a range of unforeseen circumstances such as

- Good employees threaten to leave unless they get a better package
- Rewards are kept secret and employees threatened with dismissal if they divulge details
- While recruiting new employees the company reacts to market rates while existing employees, who are not aware of internal rates, slip behind
- A new recruit accidentally lets slip what they are being paid, which causes uproar among colleagues
- Managers under pressure agree ad hoc payments to try and placate the best people
- Favoured employees start to move ahead, in pay terms, for all the wrong reasons

Obsessive secrecy about salaries can lead to employees leaving unnecessarily because the company did not recognize, or react quickly enough, to their genuine complaint. The company's salary bill is not well aligned with the relative performances of its employees.

TABLE 5.1 Indicators to Assess Where You Are on the HR Maturity Scale

Maturity level	Organizational indicators
Level −2	You own slaves – 'tote that barge, lift that bale'
Level −1	You run a sweatshop – '...employee rights? What employee rights?'
Level 0	There is no conscious approach to personnel management
	Accountability rests only with senior managers
	Little decision making allowed below the top level
	A command and control mindset fosters a blame culture
	Intuitive, gut reactions supersede conscious, systematic management decisions
Level 1	Personnel administration acknowledges legal requirements
	Basic administration tasks performed (payroll, advertising vacancies) but no professional approach adopted
Level 2	Conscious decision taken that a professional approach is required, which in turn requires line management to accept the need to take professional advice
	Recruitment and selection procedures operated professionally
	Appraisal and personal reviews take place but in a perfunctory manner
	Training and development tends to be menus of courses, programmes and initiatives
	Not evidence based, as professionals follow what they deem to be 'best practice', but bottles of HR Magic Pills are filling the shelves
Level 3	HRM systems have teeth, so managers cannot use seniority to override them. Better people management processes are evident (full assessments of candidates)
	The relationship between HR professionals and the line starts to become more integrated with line accepting more involvement from HR
	Appraisal starts to look more like a performance management system
	The value of 'Magic Pill', generic solutions is questioned and more convincing evidence sought
	Simple evaluation/feedback systems are put in place (e.g. training courses have clear objectives and feedback is given on the outcome)

Continued

TABLE 5.1 Indicators to Assess Where You Are on the HR Maturity
Scale—cont'd

Maturity level	Organizational indicators
Level 4	HR 'business partners', or equivalents, work proactively and closely with line managers after raising issues in anticipation of future problems
	Performance management system starts to include clear business measures
	Levels of personal accountability increase significantly and rapidly at all levels
	Underperformance is not tolerated and is managed effectively
	Tailored solutions (e.g. bespoke development) start to replace generic and off-the-shelf activities
Level 5	Individual accountabilities are superseded by team and project accountabilities as the value chain is fully understood
	Performance measurement becomes a value measurement system that crosses increasingly flexible, departmental boundaries
	Reporting lines stay clear but flexible, there is a more adaptable culture blossoming
	Organization is restructured around core processes that are designed to maximize customer satisfaction
	The concept of 'training and development' is replaced by a clearly understood concept of applied learning
Level 6	All activities in the organization have a line of sight to strategic objectives.
	All employees own strategic objectives
	Every employee can articulate how he or she contributes to value
	A 'not-seeking-to-blame' culture exists, there is little fear holding back innovation
	The 'initiative' approach to continuous improvement is replaced by a natural, systemic and dynamic obsession with improvement
	Adversarial unionization does not exist because of absolute trust between employer and employee

Stage 1

In a stage 1 organization pay rates are monitored and so glaring discrepancies and inconsistencies are inevitably highlighted. This tends to generate more moderating and less reactive actions by management (e.g. a favoured employee who threatens to leave only gets a pay rise that can be justified). Employees realize that inconsistencies are less likely to occur so their expectations are managed accordingly. The salary bill tends to be better directed to where it should be spent.

Stage 2

At stage 2 the basic payroll and salary records are founded on a formal, job evaluated, grading system. This is much more systematic but it is also very restricting. No one can get a salary increase without going through a mechanistic process of re-evaluating their job. Managers do not have much leeway to reward staff, who are nominally in the same job, but are performing much better than their colleagues.

Reward policy and employee relations policy obviously go hand in hand. A unionized environment, with collective bargaining, tends to lead to rigidly controlled pay scales. A professional, employee relations specialist is employed to deal with this but all they can do is perform a holding operation.

Stage 3

Strict adherence to the job evaluation system is causing the organization to stagnate so the broader concepts of performance management and broad banding are gradually introduced in an attempt to free things up. Simple performance measures start to highlight the high performers and the importance of 'recognition' grows. Reward becomes part of a larger, integrated system made up of base salaries, linked to the grading system, but topped up by a simple performance element in the total package. Managers start to use the combined system to ensure that rewards are targeted at the right people: the ones who really make a difference.

Stage 4

The organization has started to realize just how much difference the good performers make. The best project leaders and their teams are rewarded for delivering on time. This is a difficult stage to get to because others, who are not as effective, start to question the validity of performance targets. Individual accountability is increasing sharply and rapidly and some employees react to this by being defensive and making excuses as to why their performance is dependent on the performance of others.

At stage 4 the importance of looking at processes and the value chain becomes a serious issue. Some organizations fail to address this so never get past stage 4. Where this is anticipated, as part of the HR-business strategy, there has already been a process of managing out of the organization those who will not accept personal accountability. Strenuous efforts are also made to free up the organization structure with cross-functional, performance objectives in place.

Stage 5

Stage 5 is the transition period during which the organization moves from a good performance to a high-performing organization. It can take some time as it enters into unknown territory. How will different departments work with each other to achieve common goals and how much will turf wars and egos get in the way of progress? Only very strong leadership will crack heads together when necessary and be brave enough to avoid the inevitable drift backwards, towards a blame culture, when things are not going according to plan.

Reward structures and systems are becoming infinitely flexible with interim management and ad hoc specialists employed as needs arise.

Stage 6

It is very difficult to resist the temptation of describing stage 6 as some kind of organizational Nirvana. Everyone feels they are earning what they deserve and work well together. The departmental and functional boundaries, drawn on paper, are almost non-existent in reality. Transparency is the rule of the day. The organization is now really tapping into the intellectual capability of its human capital as knowledge and ideas are exchanged freely and innovation and creativity start to move the organization well ahead of its competitors who are still mired in rigid hierarchies based on functional silos. Those who are generating the highest value ideas are being extremely well rewarded to ensure they do not leave or get poached by the opposition.

We could run through a similar scenario depicting other aspects of HR policies and you might be reading this thinking that all big employers auto-matically gravitate towards the right-hand side of the scale but this is not the case. Very few businesses, if any, will survive if they are stuck at stage 0 or even stage 1, but there is precious little evidence, today, that any have even reached as far as stage 4. The first academic research study based on the HR Maturity Scale was undertaken by Reykjavik Business School in 2005, which had taken part in the Cranet HR Survey for some years (see http://www.cranet. org/about/about.htm). Their findings from 118 organizations ('Diagnosing the maturity of HRM in the organization'. Presented by Ásta Bjarnadóttir and Finnur Oddsson at the annual conference of the Society for Industrial/Organizational

Psychology, April 2005), showed a spread of organizations along the scale:

- Stage 1 – 65.3%
- Stage 2 – 26.3%
- Stage 3 – 5.9%
- Stage 4 – 2.5%
- Stage 5 – 0%
- Stage 6 – 0%

The lack of any companies at stages 5 and 6 was only to be expected because it is a challenging scale. However, they did suggest a 'clear linkage' between the presence of an HR director and higher levels of HR maturity and a 'clear connection between the financial outcomes (profit, turnover, profits as % of turnover) and the HR maturity stage of the company'.

This research supports the view that the reality of 'HR' is not living up to the rhetoric, and why should this be so, because the conventional wisdom in HR is predicated on untested and unproven theories.

CALL THAT AN HR-BUSINESS STRATEGY?

If you employ an HR director go and ask them now whether they have an HR strategy? Be careful though, because this is a trick question. If you do not know the answer to this question then you were obviously not involved in any 'HR strategy' they might have dreamed up. Remember the VP of HR at Verizon in Chapter 2, who got everything the wrong way round? Most HR directors will genuinely believe that their list of HR theories and policies constitute a strategy. Imagine asking any parent whether they believe that their children have been brought up well or not; what answer would you expect?

A much better question is have you, as CEO, got an HR-business strategy? If not then you had better find someone who can help but an HR-business strategy has to be designed to change the very fabric and mentality of the organization otherwise it will not be worthy of the title. So who can you start to learn from? Unlikely as it might sound, you could do a lot worse than to learn from organizations that have failed miserably.

HR-business strategy has to be as consistent and as coherent as possible. Always aim for perfection but never expect to achieve it, because you are embarking on a journey with no end. Now let us look at one particular example of a very large organization, in a very competitive market, trying to put together some coherent HR policies. In 2000 the Ford automotive company announced that it was thinking of shutting its Dagenham production plant in the UK (something it had been threatening to do for many years). Almost simultaneously it announced a new policy of encouraging all its employees to learn at home, using personal computers that Ford would provide. Meanwhile, its 'white-collar' workers (notice the divisive nomenclature) were discussing

strike action for the first time in years. Maybe the timing of their announce-
ments was just very unfortunate. Perhaps they would not expect anybody to be
watching closely enough to spot the irony of the situation. Regardless of how
these policies came about, the HR-business strategist would suggest that they
do not form part of a coherent whole.

More recently, in 2008, General Motors, which blames its high employee
health care and pensions costs for its loss of competitive advantage, have tried
many initiatives over the years including something called ChangeFast! (GM is
offered as a management exemplar in *Why the Bottom Line Isn't* by Dave
Ulrich and Norm Smallwood, Wiley, 2003) that included 'seven critical success
factors to ensure that work happens faster'.

The very odd title of this book has been proven to be highly prescient. Any
CEO might have thought the one unambiguous thing they can cling to is the
bottom line. Apparently not. General Motors were obviously basing their
business strategy on a different bottom line, one that said the US Government
would always be its bottom line, always being prepared to bail out such a huge
American employer. Perhaps instead of promoting 'faster' working they should
have focused their employees on working 'more valuably'? Health care and
pension costs, regardless of why they were originally conceded in union
negotiations, are still costs that have to be passed onto customers. Working
faster will do nothing to remove these 'production' costs and companies and
unions that fail to face up to reality in their HR strategies are jointly writing
their own 'death warrants'.

HR-BUSINESS STRATEGY MUST ENGAGE THE BUSINESS, NOT THE LATEST FAD

The other key word that keeps cropping up in HR departments, engagement, is
another very tricky one; we can all be engaged on different levels. We can
choose to shop in a local supermarket either because it is conveniently located,
because its prices are low, because we think it represents good value or because
we want to support it for other reasons (e.g. it is 'green'). These are all very
different motivators. The first two appeal to our simple economic assessment of
the proposition on offer (time and money), the third is a more rounded
assessment (value for money) but the fourth is on a much deeper level. The
local supermarket might satisfy all of the first three criteria and yet its policy on,
say, intensive farming methods will mean we travel further afield to shop at
a more 'ethical' store. In short, as customers, we are more likely to be
personally engaged with any company that shares our personal values.

This same principle of shared values applies equally to our decisions about
who we choose as an employer and this logic has driven two very popular HR
practices, employee engagement surveys and efforts to become an 'employer of
choice', otherwise known as employer branding. There is absolutely nothing

wrong with this line of thinking, in theory, as long as when they are put into practice they form part of a holistic strategy. Without a coherent HR-business strategy though, they just become more disjointed, disconnected, Magic Pills. Let us look at one product in particular that any HR director can buy off-the-shelf and ask whether it delivers what it says on the packaging? A typical candidate would be Gallup's popular Q12 engagement survey (see www.gallup.com), which, according to their advertising, claims that Gallup's research

> *... has shown that engaged employees are more productive employees. The research also proves that engaged employees are more profitable, more customer-focused.*

We will come to question in Chapter 9 whether research in HR is ever able to 'prove' any such thing but for now we can garner much simpler and immediate evidence to challenge Gallup's claims by looking at the experience of one of their own major clients, B&Q, a large home improvement retail chain with operations around the world and part of the Kingfisher Group, which has been popping these particular pills for some years.

On 9 May 2008 *Personnel Today* magazine reported that

> *B&Q was the only UK employer to receive a prestigious award for employee engagement last week – as a survey laid bare the poor state of staff commitment in this country. B&Q scooped the Gallup Great Workplace Award, created to honour businesses with high employee engagement, for the second year running.... The HR director at B&Q, said: 'We are delighted to receive this award as it really recognises the huge strides we have taken to put employee engagement at the heart of our business. Our people are the key to success in the current economic market'.*

This has to be contrasted with another story about B&Q in *The Times*, less than 1 month later (5 June 2008), under the banner headline 'Kingfisher chief Ian Cheshire predicts worse to come as B&Q falters'. This reported

> *A trading statement yesterday showed that like-for-like sales at its B&Q chain tumbled 8.1 per cent in the three months to May 3.*

So, while the HR Director was collecting the award, the business was in serious decline. An impartial observer might feel compelled to ask Gallup whether this disproves their research, but an HR-business strategist would be more interested in what the CEO's complete strategy for the future is, rather than become bogged down in a quagmire of statistical semantics. Conventional sales/margin/profit figures will only ever tell part of the story and disconnected HR initiatives only serve to confuse the picture further.

The only way to make sense of this, from an HR-business strategy perspective, is to do what Gallup already says it does, directly connect employee engagement to business performance. However, B&Q and Gallup had already committed the cardinal sin of placing the emphasis on the powers of their Magic Pills rather than undertaking a proper analysis of what ails B&Q. Q12 is used as a 'vitamin' pill in the belief that it is bound to help and never hinder. This is putting the cart before the horse. One key plank of B&Q's

original business strategy, in the very early days, was choosing the best store locations. A business model based on having stores available in the best locations is much more likely to be the key contributor in B&Q's earlier domination of the DIY market. Now that market itself has changed and employee engagement might not even be a priority in formulating a new business strategy.

Any CEO facing problems of poor business performance should always ensure a through analysis of people issues is part and parcel of the formulation of any nascent business strategy. Any 'HR prescriptions' should then be seen as an integrated element of the complete course of treatment, not a disjointed collection of pill bottles and unguents.

In B&Q's case we get some clues as to what this nascent strategy looks like from the same *Times* article:

> *Mr Cheshire, who headed B&Q before taking the top job at Kingfisher five months ago, added that managers were being set higher investment return targets in a bid to boost margins across the business. Gross margins in the UK rose by 300 basis points in the first quarter. …. Mr Cheshire stands to make as much as £16 million over the next four years in salary and bonuses if he achieves a turnaround at Kingfisher, long seen as a potential takeover target for Home Depot, its American rival.*

If you were one of the employees at B&Q, proud to be receiving the Great Workplace Award, would you be further motivated by trying to help Mr Cheshire become a multimillionaire? Some years ago a painter and decorator in a building company, having just seen the CEO's new top-end-of-the-range executive limousine, quickly worked out how many walls he would have to paint to pay for it. Employees always personalize things and will become very demotivated if their own level of engagement is wafer thin. This is why, when the CEOs of Ford, GM and Chrysler (Mulally, Wagoner and Nardelli) turned up in their separate executive jets to a Congressional hearing in November 2008, to ask for a $25 billion bail-out, it sent all the wrong messages to both taxpayers and their employees.

The danger here is that any CEO can produce good short-term figures (were those margin improvements at B&Q achieved from cutting corners?) to impress the City. In this respect Mr Cheshire certainly achieved his goal because here is the response from the City in July of the same year, when Kingfisher group published its results -

> *City analysts have welcomed Kingfisher's latest results and the surprise sales uplift seen by B&Q, which helped the Kingfisher share price shoot up 6.5% on the London exchange. (July 24).*

http://www.diyweek.net/news/news.asp?id=11456

But would the same analysts be able to discern whether what was going at B&Q was strengthening or undermining its long-term viability and profitability? Was anyone asking about the management of all its human capital or would a Gallup Great Workplace Award be a good enough measure for them?

We could easily get lost in such labyrinthine analysis and it would serve no purpose. The HR-business strategist will always critique the value creating potential of any organization using a range of indicators and measures, which will always include the current and historical financial performance. The only relevant question here is – has the CEO of B&Q developed a business strategy that gives the company its best chance of creating the most sustainable value? That is exactly the same question as any long-term shareholder or investment analyst would ask.

Of course now we have arrived at the whole question of executive reward packages; at a time when they are being more closely scrutinized and criticized than ever before. If CEOs can become multimillionaires through get-rich-quick, performance (sic) bonus or share option schemes related to short-term, risky, corner-cutting tactics, then we should not be surprised if all they want from 'HR' is a shiny badge to burnish their image. However, if the goal is long-term value then only an HR-business strategy that deals with the substantive, underlying issues will be appropriate. These two alternatives do not have to be mutually exclusive. HR-business strategy also requires 'quick wins' to aid its progress. So here are some practical suggestions about how to make sure this nascent business strategy could move towards becoming an HR-business strategy.

(1) If improving margins is a key, strategic objective then every single employee is already having an impact by dint of the fact their wages influence margin. So every employee needs to be asked what they can do to reduce costs.

(2) The other main variable in margin of course is revenue. Obviously the sales staff have a direct influence here but so should every other employee. Asking each one of them how they might influence revenue might elicit a more puzzled response. For example, how does a fork lift driver in the loading bay influence revenue? Have they ever been asked this question? Perhaps they have some ideas that the executives never considered? Does asking them such questions make them more engaged or less? Well, who knows, but let us at least put that question on the agenda. Executives do not know all the answers to their own questions and they will not be speaking directly to the customers that the forklift driver meets every day. It could even be these types of relationships with customers that keeps them spending with B&Q.

(3) If they do have any ideas about cost or revenue how would they be welcomed? How do innovations become assimilated into the business so that they are translated into actual value, in hard £'s?

We could look at numerous other practical suggestions but this will all be a pipe dream if we cannot find someone to help develop a proper HR-business strategy.

Summary of key lessons on HR Maturity analysis

- Any analysis of business performance and success is, at best, an inexact science and, at worst, intentionally misleading. The best analyses use as many meaningful indicators as possible, combined with clear-headed, sharp-eyed judgement. Just as many lessons can be learned from organisations that fail as from the 'success' stories that hit the headlines.
- Correlations between performance measures and people management are easy to make and never provide proof. Causation is needed to provide the right solutions for the right problems.
- The various banners under which HR departments operate should not fool us – the titles used are, in themselves, meaningless. The Maturity Scale reveals whether an organisation is taking the value of employee potential seriously or not.
- While some HR professionals could have a very important role to play, their contribution to value will ultimately be restricted or unleashed by how they handle the 'barriers'. HR-business strategy can only do as good a job as it is allowed to.
- The efficacy of HR practices and tools cannot be assessed in isolation and they do not have automatic, generic applicability. Their effectiveness is dependent on being part of a coherent strategy for a specific context.
- The only HR practices that are worthy of the title 'best practice' are the ones that help a particular organisation, at a particular time, to achieve its strategic objectives, measured in value terms (see Chapter 6 – So what exactly is value? for further detail).
- Any discussion of organisational, people matters is plagued with loose and ill-defined language. This usually means the real issues are often under-estimated or even ignored. Concepts such as 'engagement' can become very powerful building blocks in HR-business strategy but the phrase 'engagement' (as with culture, empowerment, commitment) has to mean on a very deep, personal level. It also has to mean engaged with the clear goal of value. Engaged employees are not just 'happy' or innocent bystanders, they have to accept greater levels of personal responsibility and accountability.

Chapter 6

Who Will Develop the HR-Business Strategy?

DO CEOs MAKE GOOD HR-BUSINESS STRATEGISTS?

Conventional thinking in HR circles has taken the view that the purpose of HR strategy is to *support* your business strategy. The approach recommended here is for the business strategy and HR strategy to be totally entwined. So who will make this happen? The first choice has to be you, the CEO, if you understand how to integrate HR strategic thinking into your own business strategy. Alternatively, the job is likely to be left to your HR director or you will have to delegate the job to someone else who can be developed for this specific role. This person could be a senior manager, but it has to be someone who always had a natural interest in the human side of organizations. What follows is their training manual.

Jack Welch, formerly CEO at American giant GE, like many successful business leaders who write their memoirs, will allude to the ways in which they have learnt to harness the talents of their employees. He became famous for many aspects of his business career; not least of which was his strategy that required all GE businesses to hold the number 1 or number 2 position in their chosen markets. However, it was his philosophy on the best way to manage people, what he called the 'vitality curve', that is of most interest here.

If you measure employee performance, using a rating scale of 1 to 10, the chances are you are going to produce something like the normal, bell-shaped distribution curve in Fig. 6.1. Then we just need to add two 'goalposts' for the 'unacceptables' (3 and below) and 'superiors' (8 and above). Jack Welch used this theory to introduce a policy of 'forced ranking', or forced distribution, always forcing 10% of managers into the unacceptable range. Once there, they would either be fired or moved into a more suitable job. In each subsequent year he would repeat this process. Obviously, in this system no one can become complacent about his or her own performance, so it is designed to produce the sort of 'vitality' that Welch was seeking; although vitality is probably not the word most of us would choose.

One example of an organization copying this approach (among many) was the Bank of England whose new HR Director in 2004 joined from Glaxo SmithKline (now GSK) and brought with her the flavour-of-the-month idea of forced ranking, which aimed to remove the bottom 5% of their

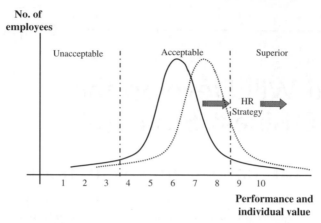

FIGURE 6.1   Working with the reality of 'people' performance.

1800 employees. One response from a highly qualified Bank employee, (quoted in the *Daily Telegraph* 13 October 2005) reveals how this move was perceived:

> *There is a feeling here among the economists that we came here for respect, job security, pensions and peer relationships. If we are going to get arbitrarily fired, we may as well go off and treble our salaries at a merchant bank*

Whether this should be seen as a clash of cultures or a particularly bad batch of poisonous Magic Pills we should only judge any such HR initiative by results and outcomes. One wonders now, in the light of the ensuing banking fiasco, and Sir John Gieve's tenure as head of financial stability (see Chapter 3), whether forced ranking removed the wrong 5%? Reduced financial stability might also have been due, in part, to the restructuring that axed 20% of their Financial Stability department. As we said earlier, the wrong strategy will always prove disastrous; it is just a matter of time before all is revealed. Needless to say, the HR director did not find herself in the bottom 5% and is still in post (as at 1 January 2009).

THE PERFORMANCE OR 'VITALITY' CURVE

So having raised doubts about the sainted Jack's management methods in the first edition perhaps we should now revisit Welch's vitality theory once again. Figure 6.1 represents what some educationalists regard as the infamous, bell-shaped curve that has provided a theoretical foundation for many social policies; not all of them successful by any means. Yet there is nothing unsound about the mathematical and statistical methods used to produce this curve. It is predicated on a very solid piece of theory, the theory of probability, and one that we use to assess human attributes and predict human behaviour. If we measured employee height or shoe sizes the likelihood is that we would produce a curve like this. If we split the shoe size group into men and women we would have two curves like the ones in Fig. 6.1, with the male curve to the right of the female (men will have larger feet on average). At each end of these curves there would be a few with very big feet (relative to their own group) and a few with relatively small feet and the majority, in the middle, would wear 'average' sized shoes. The bell curve is just a simple, graphical representation of what we can see with our own eyes. It is a truism, an unfortunate law of nature that whilst we might all be equal in the eyes of god some of us are more equal than others in the talents we possess and our ability to produce value. When we generalize, as we all do, this is a very quick test of whether we really mean what we say. For example, do you believe that most people are decent human beings? How many people do you personally know who fail your test of being decent, 'acceptable', human beings? Would those who do not pass this test be the minority at the bottom of the curve?

This might start to sound like a very one-sided view of what human beings are capable of. In reality, if you put any single variable on the X-axis, say entrepreneurship, we can see with our own eyes many successful entrepreneurs, who make fortunes, many more who make losses (the vast majority of business start-ups fail) and many who do not have an entrepreneurial bone in their body. The distribution curve does not take a particular view on this; it just reflects your reality. Moreover, the curve is always relative, in the sense that if you had a skewed curve or one shifted to the right, then there are still two discrete groups who are low/high on the scale relative to the whole population. When used for HR-business strategy purposes though, it should be emphasized that meritocracy always rules – you want everyone to give their best, but you certainly want the best from the best.

So now consider what other variables on the X-axis we might use to measure the population. While we are doing so let us look at the two goalposts in more detail. These goalposts are the dividing lines between what are acceptable attitudes, attributes or behaviour and what could be regarded as superior, or extraordinary. How about

- Honesty?
- Integrity?
- Fairness?
- Commitment?
- Effort?
- Leadership capability?
- Criminality?
- Politicality?

Let us take honesty first; do you see yourself as a 10 out of 10? What is your view about how honest your average fellow human being is? You have already developed your own view on this, based on your personal experiences of dealing with thousands of people throughout your life so far. So your view is actually based on a pretty good sample size. What you have not done so far though is tested your experiences in a more scientific way – you are still in 'intuitive', gut reaction, non-thinking mode. Using the curve in Fig. 6.1 will not make your views any more accurate than anyone else's and they might not match those of a trained psychologist, but that does not matter. All that matters is that *your view is the one that dictates the way you try to manage the people around you*. So, if you think the 'honesty' curve is skewed to the left, with a large proportion of people being 'unacceptably' dishonest, you will not trust the majority of people you manage. You will behave in a way that always seeks to install very tight control systems, keep a close eye on everybody and have a tendency to micro-manage. This is one of the causes of control freakery.

Try the same simple exercise for each of the other headings and add some more of your own (how about 'racial prejudice' as a variable?) but this time draw an imaginary curve on the scale to represent what you really think. This should help you become more conscious of your views and hopefully more aware of how this influences your management thinking and style.

When you have done that go and ask one of your trusted colleagues to do the same for their view, overlaying their curve on top of yours. Also imagine what the perception is from any of your employees. Are they much more trusting of each other than you are, for example? This should lead you to consider the last on the list in more detail, your own leadership style. Do great leaders trust people or micro-manage them? It should also prompt you to consider how many people in your organization have a superior capability for leading others and whether they are the ones in leadership positions?

There are several other angles from which we could view what is building up to be a complete series of curves, a total picture of the people dimension. One would be your view on meritocracy. Do you always aim to ensure that the people at the top end of the curve get the most important jobs? If so, what evidence is there that this is the case? Or are you still perpetuating the old boy network or the blue-eyed-boy syndrome? Another angle would be your views on how these curves would differ between men and women?

What you cannot escape though is the fact that this curve is always likely to apply. No matter what you do to ensure you have only people above the minimum acceptable level there will always be some who fall below that standard. Take a company like Goldman Sachs, which had a reputation for making many of its staff into millionaires; you would think that must mean it only employs top-quality people (or at least you might have done until recent events) but the curve is *always* relative within an organization. If you can afford really good people then some of your employees, who may well be in the top group in another firm, will fall into the bottom category when compared to their own, equally highly qualified, peer group. This is something that Jack Welch fully understood. Jack Welch was convinced that this curve applies to how people perform and used it to help him achieve some spectacular results at GE (although the market capitalization of GE has dropped by over 50% since). So whether his approach was sustainable, or had any useful momentum after he had left, is another matter.

The final angle we need to consider here is whether individual performance always, automatically, creates organizational value? One only has to think of subprime mortgage salespeople, and the hefty bonuses they earned, to realize that they were deemed to have performed well, but actually destroyed huge amounts of value (huge long-term debt defaults). That is why our graph in Fig. 6.1 has the X-axis showing 'performance and individual value' as the measure that needs to be used, not just a narrow definition of performance per se.

We will return to this crucial distinction again later in this chapter (see 'So what exactly is value?' below) and explore all the implications it has for HR-business strategy, but let us now establish another fundamental principle – performance management is only as good as the measures and management disciplines that underpin it. Poor data, or measures, will produce poor performance. *Performance management will not add value unless the measures used are added value measures.* The principle that Michael Porter established (see Chapter 2) also needs to be repeated here. If you are going to copy a technique then you have probably already got it wrong. You have to copy everything, every aspect of the whole system, if you are to have any chance of making it work. The probability that the Bank of England could copy everything else that Jack Welch did at GE is so low as to be negligible. It was the wrong prescription for the wrong organization. Nevertheless, if you still think forced ranking is a good idea, then at least consider the practicalities of it before you embark on what could be a very risky endeavour.

Imagine you have 100 managers and you use a forced ranking system to get rid of the worst 10. You then have to replace these managers either from within your own ranks or from outside. Either way, the replacement managers are untested in your organization. Following the forced ranking philosophy you have to cull another 10% in 12 months's time and some of these, newly appointed managers might fall into this group. In fact, you could find that they perform even worse than some of their predecessors; who you ousted 12 months earlier. Yet, if you insist on replacing this batch as well you are susceptible to repeating the same problem again and again (this is starting to sound like a stupid organization). If you hang on to them though, in the hope that they will improve, then your forced ranking system is actually accepting a lower performance this year than it did last year (definitely a stupid organization). So the theory may not be as simple or watertight as it might at first appear. Perhaps we can come at this from another angle?

LEADERS, BACKBONE, DEAD WOOD AND THE DANGER ZONE

The major concern with forced ranking is illustrated in Fig. 6.2. showing a typical four-quadrant matrix plotting ambition against talent. If ambition always equalled talent and if academic qualifications equalled managerial intelligence there would not be a problem. But ambition does not equal

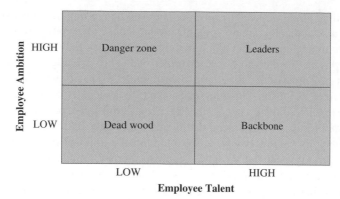

FIGURE 6.2 Every organization needs effective leadership with a strong backbone.

talent; just look at the ambitions of the thousands of politicians, wannabe pop stars and movie actors whose 'talents' reside only in their own heads. More important, having an MBA does not guarantee intelligent decision making; many MBA-qualified executives have ruined perfectly sound businesses.

There are two good quadrants and two bad quadrants here. Ideally, we want the most ambitious and genuinely talented people to become our leaders, but they are always up against their Machiavellian counterparts who just play the system. They will make sure they get good scores, any way they can (e.g. the Permanent Secretary keeps his nose clean).

Ambitious people who possess no special talent fall into the 'Danger Zone' in the chart. They will cause untold damage in their determination to reach the top. Organizations have a tendency to become blinded by someone's raw ambition, falling for their self-publicity material while failing to see that there is insufficient talent in support. Hence they promote these people into positions well beyond their capabilities – the Peter Principle is exactly that, a universal principle. Enron had a well-publicized, even respected, talent management strategy that obviously found plenty of ambition, but little if any valuable talent. The HR-business strategist that wants to depopulate the 'danger zone' had better start reading their Machiavelli again. This is called the Danger Zone for a very good reason. One HR director involved in many mergers and acquisitions (M&A) used to blow the metaphorical smoke from the end of his 'gun' after a hard day's culling.

Of course, all organizations need good leaders, but no organization can handle too many of them. Large companies like GE and Tesco lose excellent senior people simply because there is never enough room for them all at the pinnacle of the pyramid. Losing such people should not be seen as a failure of HR-business strategy. Those who lost out when Jack Welch was appointed CEO at GE were too ambitious to accept second place and went on to higher office elsewhere. Interestingly, some of Welch's protégés also moved on eventually and applied similar techniques in their new roles without the same degree of success (see 'Do They Know Jack? Jack Welch's disciples have gone forth to preach his gospel. So far, most of them are failing'. http://www.slate.com/id/2079650/). One of these, Robert Nardelli (see Chapter 5), is currently the CEO at Chrysler asking for government money. All this just keeps reinforcing the message that business strategy, never mind HR-business strategy, does not migrate well between organizations. The 'HR' in HR-business strategy should make sure of more 'happy marriages' than 'divorces' in the world of M&A.

The core of the workforce should be in the 'backbone' quadrant. These are the people who come to work every day, work hard and do their best to help the organization. They are competent and most of the organization's knowledge and expertise resides here. They might not be spectacular but they are very valuable and you disrupt them at your peril. These are the ones who suffer most when a new CEO brings along a new broom. They should always be recognised for their important contribution (see the recognition system in Chapter 3).

On a more negative note, the HR-business strategy will have to include a system for clearing out the 'dead wood'. There is nothing wrong with a performance management system that roots out dead wood if the majority who stay perceive it to be a valid and fair system. Forced ranking, as a philosophy, will always struggle against these criteria and is more likely to be feasible only in organizations that are already doing reasonably well. What do you do when the whole organization is underperforming as markets collapse?

Perhaps the most worrying aspect of forced ranking is what sort of relationship does it foster between employees and employer? What chance is there of getting employees to innovate if the risk of innovation might be a low score? Is this a relationship of trust and loyalty or more that of the mercenary who joins the army that just happens to be currently paying the highest wages? Welch's 'vitality' curve might just improve overall performance, but it is worth asking whether it truly maximizes the full, potential value of all employees, in a sustainable way, for the long term? Against this standard, the highest standard set by HR-business strategy, it fails on all counts.

So whatever plaudits Jack Welch won from his business peers did he institute the sort of HR-business strategy we are promoting here? If not, can we expect any CEO to master this complex task? We might like to believe that CEOs, like yourself, are supreme managers, fully thinking through everything you do before you act: that you are totally systematic in what you do and everything is well ordered and structured. Certainly if you have an MBA, from any respectable business school, you will have learnt a number of textbook models and management techniques. One problem with an MBA though is it cannot put you in the hot seat of today's real world. It can only teach you a range of disciplines that you, as a CEO, have to combine into a holistic approach in your own mind. Even Harvard, set up in 1908 to provide financial and management skills and arguably the most famous business school of all, is willing to admit they have not found a satisfactory solution yet.

PROFESSIONAL MANAGEMENT AND
HR-BUSINESS STRATEGISTS

None of the current staff or the most high profile alumni of Harvard Business School predicted the 2008 banking crisis or did anything to prevent it. They include Henry 'Hank' Paulson (US Treasury Secretary), Christopher Cox (Chairman Securities and Exchange Commission) and several more who became CEOs at big banks like Merrill Lynch, JP Morgan and Barclays Capital. When Jay Light, the Dean of Harvard Business School, was asked how this could happen he replied

> ... academics did pick up on the individual pieces ... but nobody had put all the pieces together. We just didn't understand how interwoven the different elements were and how we would get this conflagration. None of us really realised that this course of events would expose such a fragile structure.
>
> The Times 13 October 2008

So what do they teach at Harvard about how organizations need to handle their people? Especially the ones who can do so much damage? More to the point, what management skills do they teach there that makes management a profession?

This is a question that two Harvard professors of business administration, Rakesh Khurana and Nitin Nohria, have been asking themselves. In a Soapbox article in the *Financial Times* (20 October 2008) they say that when the present financial crisis is over

> ... longer term, it is essential to restore legitimacy to and trust in the practice and profession of management.

and suggest a code (from their Harvard Business review article of the same month entitled 'It's time to make management a true profession'), which includes enhancing

> the value of the enterprise to create wealth for society in the long term,

with

> judgements based on the best knowledge available

and presenting

> the company's performance accurately and transparently.

This seems like it makes eminent common sense; why would any ordinary citizen or employee want to disagree with it? The only thing we might add to the code is a reminder that the best value can only come from the best management of people: which brings us right back to our question of who is going to be the best HR-business strategist?

One might assume that this should be human resource management (HRM) professionals. Yet if we consider all the large business failures that have happened around the world in the last decade we see companies like Enron replete with such HR people. They did no more to prevent failure than the Harvard academics. This is primarily due to their lack of both strategic capability and board level credibility, echoed in a report by the UK's professional body the Chartered Institute of Personnel and Development (CIPD) whose research in 2007, with the Institute of Employment Studies, concluded

> With respect to the competencies of HR staff, the biggest challenges that lie ahead are considered to be in developing influencing skills and strategic thinking. Business knowledge, leadership skills, willingness to innovate and, to a lesser extent, being able to deliver against targets are also commonly noted to be a challenge.
>
> The Changing HR Function – Survey Report 2007, CIPD

Even Dave Ulrich, who has promoted the development of HR business partners for many years since his 1997 book *Human Resource Champions*, and whose ideas are cited by many HR directors as their route map, had to admit in 2008 (Ulrich's model defence, *Personnel Today* 15 April 2008) that

> HR has been woeful at knowing the business well enough. We still have people in HR that cannot talk to board members when they start talking about cashflow or (financial) numbers.

As someone who has advised Rick Waggoner, the CEO of GM, it would appear that maybe Ulrich himself did not know the business well enough when he was using it as one of his best practice case studies. So if we cannot look to CEOs themselves and to the top HR academics then maybe we need to start developing a very new type of manager, one that will match the code suggested by Khurana and Nohria?

Following this train of thought perhaps we can prescribe what is required of this new, hybrid, breed of senior managers. They will probably already be highly capable operational managers, who are already 'professional' both in terms of their knowledge of management literature and tools as well as having high personal standards. They will also have an innate, humanistic mindset and they will be eager to learn new, unconventional tools and techniques for assessing how well human capital is being managed. In the first edition of this book we were still holding a flickering candle for the best HR practitioners around to rise to this challenge. This flame has now spluttered into extinction. Most of those who work in HR have been happy enough with their main role, personnel administration (stage 1) so they are unlikely to metamorphose into top-notch HR-business strategists.

HR-BUSINESS STRATEGISTS ARE GREAT FORECASTERS

Strategists do not have to possess superhuman powers. They are at the mercy of the vicissitudes of life just as much as any other mere mortals. The essence of a good strategist is in their ability to cope with the vagaries of life by anticipating them and producing a plan that gives them a much higher probability of defying the odds; especially when compared to those who just take life as it comes.

The weather provides a very simple illustration of the distinction between a strategist and someone who just copes with whatever they have to. Weather forecasters have a whole armoury of techniques and technology to help them predict weather patterns, but the weather is determined by such a huge range of variables that they can still get it wrong. The further into the future they try to look the higher the probability of inaccuracy and error. At some point in the future, say more than 3 months, the forecast will only be as valid as any ordinary citizen's guess; based on nothing more than their own experience of the seasons.

One other technique that meteorologists are not so famous for is something called hindcasting; that is, the opposite of forecasting. If a ship sinks, hindcasting considers what weather conditions were like at the time, draws inferences as to how the ship got into trouble and also tries to learn some lessons to avoid it happening again. All this is very useful information, but one thing meteorologists cannot do, regardless of their forecasting or hindcasting skills, is to actually change the weather (cloud seeding being the exception that proves the rule). They can only tell you to pack an umbrella. A strategist, however, tries to make things happen the way they have planned or want them to happen. They are definitely not victims, passive bystanders or impotent observers. They will do their best to collect enough evidence to make the future happen the way they want it to.

EVIDENCE-BASED HUMAN CAPITAL MANAGEMENT (HCM)

It is an incredible claim to have to make, in a twenty-first-century management book, that management over the preceding centuries has never been predominantly evidence based. Yet, it is a view held by some of the most respected business management academics in the world. Two of the foremost proponents of a move towards a more evidence-based approach are Jeffrey Pfeffer & Robert Sutton (*Hard Facts, Dangerous Half-Truths & Total Nonsense*, 2006, HBS Press) who regard evidence-based management as

> *First and foremost, … a way of seeing the world and thinking about the craft of management….. Evidence-based management is based on the belief that facing the hard facts about what works and what doesn't …will help organizations perform better.*

So this is as much about a completely different management attitude as it is about collecting better evidence. It is a conscious move away from intuitive, gut-feel management. It is directly analgous to the medical profession, which is probably the profession most dedicated to the cause of evidence-based analysis and decision making. Yet, even the medical profession includes many practices that do not stand up to a rigorous test of evidence. Take the whole field of homeopathy and 'complementary' medicine. In 2008 it was reported (*The Times* 30 January – 'NHS homeopathy in sharp decline') that

the Royal London Homeopathic Hospital was fighting for survival after eight (NHS) trusts cancelled contracts over the past year and a further six reduced referrals.

Even mainstream clinical problems, such as the incidence of 'superbugs' or the bacteria MRSA (Methicillin-resistant staphylococcus aureus), required a more robust, evidence-based approach before serious inroads were made. University College Hospital, London, cut infection rates by 40% after it finally realised that patients could be bringing the bug into hospital on admission. So they tested patients on arrival, using nasal swabs and found 850 carried the MRSA bug (reported in *The Times* 19 December 2007). So an evidence-based approach will usually mean not only challenging assumptions (many hospitals just installed hand cleansers to deal with the same problem) but also having to fundamentally change the way the organization operates (new admission procedures) and managing a customer's expectations.

Another leading advocate of evidence based management, Denise Rousseau, Professor of Organizational Behaviour at Carnegie-Mellon University, former President of the American Academy of Management (2004–2005) and a founder of the Evidence-Based Management Collaborative (see https://wpweb2.tepper.cmu.edu/evite/ebm_conf/index.html) has been working in this field for some time. In January 2009 she remarked that -

Evidence-Based Management (EBMgt) means making organizational decisions based on scientific and practice-informed facts, in conjunction with professional judgment and ethics. For practitioners, it involves learning how to obtain and use the best available evidence to inform their decisions and develop effective organizational practices. For educators, it entails building courses and a broader curriculum around up-to-date scientific knowledge, emphasizing validated principles rather than war stories, conventional wisdom, or management research's version of Piltdown Man, Maslow's hierarchy of needs. It means preparing students for the activities required of them throughout their careers to master evidence-based principles and to keep their knowledge current as new scientific developments emerge. For scholars, it means working with practitioners and educators to identify critical questions and conduct systematic reviews to assemble the full body of relevant research in order to provide evidence-based answers and guides to implementation.

This is no quick fix, sticking plaster being suggested and it applies to all aspects of management, not just HR management, although it is HR managers who will probably find it the most difficult to adjust because of their failure to embrace rigorous measures of their own efficacy. Take this extract from an interview headed 'Tried and attested' in *People Management* magazine, the official journal of the CIPD, on 1 November 2007, with Rob Briner, Professor of Organizational Psychology and Head of the School of Management and Organnizational Psychology at Birkbeck College, University of London:

Interviewer: What is the evidence that HR professionals don't already use evidence?

Rob Briner: Practitioners don't become evidence-based without access to appropriate resources. In the case of HRM, these do not yet exist. This alone makes it unlikely there are

many, or indeed any, evidence-based HR practitioners – although I would be delighted to
be proved wrong. Another sign that evidence isn't used a great deal is the dominance of HR
fads and fashions – the exact opposite of EBM.

These challenges to the conventional wisdom are part of a growing trend
that is picking up speed as the twenty-first century unfolds. Evidence-based
HCM is likely to be the biggest breakthrough in management thinking for over
70 years since the advent of total quality management. Assessing, managing
and reporting on human capital will be as commonplace to the twenty-second-
century manager as double-entry book-keeping was to a twentieth-century
accountant, only a great deal easier to understand and much more meaningful
as a guide to underlying organizational strengths.

PUTTING A VALUE ON HUMAN CAPITAL –
THE HCM REVOLUTION

There have been many attempts made since Gary Becker's work in the 1960s to
actually put a measurable value on human capital. Why? Because there was
a growing realization by Wall Street and in academic research that the market
value of an organization was often much greater than its book value, or the sum
of its tangible assets (look again at Table 1.1 from this perspective, comparing
Toyota and GM who produce a similar number of vehicles and probably
possess not dissimilar physical assets). Allied to recognition of this phenomenon is the acknowledgement, particularly in developed economies, that
knowledge workers are higher value workers. So we witnessed a huge interest
in the whole notion of human and intellectual capital and the potential that can
be derived from effective knowledge management.

It is these developments that have led observers to ask the question what
really accounts for the difference? Could it be the way people are managed?
This is particularly relevant in computer software and services businesses
where there are precious few tangible assets and the success of the company is
almost entirely dependent on the knowledge base and expertise that resides in
the heads of the company's employees.

Early attempts to provide better answers tended to apply conventional
accounting principles to a subject for which they were never designed and
'human asset accounting' or 'putting people on the balance sheet' were ideas
that had a relatively short shelf life. People were being referred to as human
capital but were being treated as just another type of bean that had to be
counted. There is no single definition of HCM that has gained wide acceptance,
there is no new 'general' theory of HCM to replace HRM and there have been
no HCM practices that are easily distinguished from conventional HRM. In
fact, if you ask anyone who purports to practice HCM what the differences are
it is likely to be a very fine line.

The definition we have borrowed from the Accounting for People Taskforce
(see Chapter 2) could be described as quite different to what is going on in the

TABLE 6.1 Indicators of the Paradigm shift between HCM and Conventional HRM

HCM	HRM
In HCM people are viewed as value adders not overheads or costs. (e.g. Tesco expects its checkout operators to engage customers to find out how they can give better value)	People are a significant cost and should be managed accordingly. (Tesco tries to replace people with self-scanning checkouts)
Value always means £'s and any HCM practice has to demonstrate a connection to the 4 value variables O,C,R,Q	Focus is on HR practices – competencies, 360°, job evaluation, leadership programmes, initiatives, Magic Pills
HCM is context dependent – unique to each organization	Focus on 'best-practice' HR processes regardless of the organizational context
The most important stakeholders in HCM are external – investment analysts, policy makers, shareholders	The most important stakeholders in HRM are internal – managers and employees
HCM specialists need to explain the difference between the book value and market capitalization of their organization and be comfortable with financial analysis.	HRM professionals do not see any direct connection between their work and share price or other key financial indicators.
There always has to be a line of sight to value and all employees understand why this is necessary	HR best practice is an article of faith, not evidence based
Causality (a clear cause/effect relationship between input and outcome) is a guiding principle for people management	A correlation in academic, ex-post studies is deemed to be sufficient justification for HR interventions
Business value is the only valid evidence of success	Input measures, costs and HR ratios are used to benchmark with other organizations (e.g. HR costs, staff turnover, absence)
HCM is clearly seen and respected as an integral element in the HR-business strategy by the board and Executive	HR team are seen as an operational support service to existing business plans
Value measurement and management replaces individual performance measurement and management	Performance management is the role of line managers. HR supports disciplinary and underperformance casework

Continued

TABLE 6.1 Indicators of the Paradigm shift between HCM and
Conventional HRM—cont'd

HCM	HRM
Underperformance is not tolerated	Many underperformance issues are not addressed (often because of union pressure)
HCM has to be holistic, organization wide and systems based	HR is based around the function and HR team performing a discrete and separate role from other functions
An HCM report reveals a holistic picture including underlying indicators of long-term sustainability (see Chapter 9)	HR function reports on HR issues (recruitment, training days etc.) that offer little insight into issues undermining organizational effectiveness.

majority of HR departments. Certainly the case studies in the back of the Accounting for People Report did not provide any evidence to match their definition. Nevertheless, the definition is sound and fits perfectly with the HR Maturity Scale. So why not call it the HCM scale or even the strategic HCM scale? Simply because, as we have to keep reiterating, what we call it is irrelevant. It is what happens on the ground that defines what HRM/HCM means to a particular organization. So let us not get bogged down in further definitions or pedantic issues of nomenclature. Instead let us build a set of robust and rigorous indicators that your organization treats people as human capital and creates a business strategy from it. However, nothing this good comes easily and when you realize what this brand of HCM really means you will see it demands a total revolution in management and organizational thinking. The revolution starts with some revolutionary questions.

So, first, who needs to know about HCM?

- Investment analysts and shareholders want to know whether the companies they invest in are maximizing their potential returns
- Boards of directors and executives need to be able to convince shareholders they are doing everything to maximize the value of the organization
- Anyone given the specific task of trying to get the best out of people needs to know whether they are doing a good job
- Governments need to know that each sector in the economy is using the nation's human capital as productively as it can
- Good governance needs to be manifest in accurate and meaningful reporting on every aspect of organizational health and viability including human capital reporting

Second, what do they need to know?

- How do we measure the value of our human capital?
- Are we getting as much value as possible from our human capital?
- How can we get more value from our human capital?

You will immediately notice that the common theme here, obviously, is the pursuit of value. This was set out right at the beginning of Chapter 1 as the single goal of an HR-business strategy and we have used the word 'value' over 150 times already without actually defining it. You might not even have stopped to ask yourself the question 'what sort of value are we talking about here?' because it is usually taken as read that we all know, roughly, what we mean by value or even 'added value'. Whatever loose definition you might have in your own mind we need to really pin this term down now if we are to make any real progress (and for a much more in-depth exploration of what being motivated by value really means see *The Value Motive* by Paul Kearns, Wiley, 2007).

SO WHAT EXACTLY IS VALUE?

The concepts of value and added value are extremely simple on one level and can be explained by using Figure 6.3. If we assume your company makes bars of chocolate, then its current value – 'Value of business now' - could be the amount of profit you make. If you want to add some more value all you can do is make improvements to one or more of the four variables shown. You can make more chocolate bars (**Quantity or O, for output**) per £ spent on production, or reduce the **Cost (C)** of the finished bar, get more **Revenue (R)** per bar (sell at a higher price) or improve the **Quality (or Q)** of the chocolate, assuming this leads to more sales or premium prices. Any CEO should see all the problems they face as **VALUE PROBLEMS**. Lack of market share means you need to sell more **O**. Poor branding might mean you need to improve **Q**. Poor cost consciousness means you need to reduce **C**.

You should never be fooled into thinking that any other problems exist. If you think 'leadership is poor' then you must think that it will eventually lead to poor performance in one of the value variables. If your organization is not

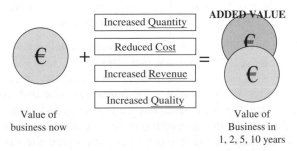

FIGURE 6.3   Value is always about money and only four variables.

'customer focused', 'responsive' or does not have a 'can do' attitude then what you are saying is it is not creating as much value as it should. You should never sanction a leadership programme, customer service course or attempt any other attitudinal change without first articulating which of these variables is likely to improve and by how much. There are no 'pink and fluffy' items on the value chart. Each of the four value variables can be measured in hard currency and they are all we need to measure the value of human capital. We do not need to invent any new measures. This is meant to be a 'light bulb' moment for you, but if you have not seen the light yet then maybe we need to explain a bit more.

We need to build this simple truth into a model that can cope with any organizational complexity that you might want to throw at it. To do this we need to make the model more sophisticated. So, instead of just putting a profit figure in the circle on the left for 'value of business now' there are other possibilities you need to consider. If you run a commercial company the answers might include

- We made a profit of £100 million last year
- We have 20% of the market
- Our share price is at an all time high of £10.50
- Our market capitalization is £5 billion
- We can produce our goods at 10% lower cost (£10 less) than our nearest competitor

All these statements are highly measurable and all have a monetary value attached to them. We will now refer to this side of the diagram as the *baseline valuation of the business* – it is a reference point for gauging *added value* because in subsequent years 2, 3, 5 or even 10 (on the right) you can ask whether the measure originally chosen has moved forward at all. For example, in year 2 the figures could be as follows:

- We made a profit of £110 million in 2005 – that is £10 million in added value
- We now have 25% of the market which is worth an extra £250 million
- Our share price is at an all time high of £11.00
- Our market capitalization is £6 billion
- We can produce our goods at 12% lower cost (£12 less) than our nearest competitor that is an added saving of £2 per product

Each of the above could be deemed to have added value. *Added* value can only be gauged by using a combination of measures of pre- and post-management intervention. So what were total sales before the new advertising campaign was launched and what were sales after? The measures have to be the same, of course, to compare like with like, but otherwise added value is no more complicated than that. Although you might be scratching your head and saying to yourself surely there is much more to organizational life than these four simple variables? Let us put that to the test and stick with our task of valuing human capital. What other variables might need to be factored into this simple equation? No doubt human brainpower, knowledge, expertise, creativity and innovation are all key factors that can make a significant difference and they do not feature at all in Fig. 6.3, so why are they not there?

THERE ARE NO INTANGIBLES IN HCM

No one has yet come up with a credible way of measuring this type of human factor so they tend to be referred to as 'intangibles'. Goodwill, a catch-all for a range of intangibles, is usually given a value in £'s by accountants when buying or selling a business; even though it defies scientific measurement. If that is good enough for many business transactions and accountants we do not need to set a more scientific standard because we are not trying to prove anything. Organizations are just too complex to separate which specific variables have an impact. However, we are going to make a radical departure from conventional thinking by declaring there is no such thing as an 'intangible' when it comes to running an organization. We need to put this proposition to the test.

Many consultants try to help organizations be more 'creative', whatever that means. You might think creativity is a perfect example of something important yet intangible. You cannot see it or touch it, it is difficult to analyse and you cannot guarantee it will still be there tomorrow. Yet, we all know that creativity, innovative ways of working, and new products and services are bound to be a source of great potential value. This sounds like a real conundrum for anyone wanting to put a value on their human capital because there is no way of measuring the total sum of 'creativity' in the workforce. The reason the word 'creativity' does not appear in Fig. 6.3 is simply because it is only worth something when it is translated into one or more of the other variables shown. Only then can it be deemed to be valuable. Having more creative employees has to mean getting more output ('hey, we've worked out a better way to treat more patients'); less cost ('he had a great idea for using less consumables on the ward'); increasing revenue ('customers are prepared to pay a premium for that enhanced service) or better quality of service or product ('patient satisfaction is increasing'). In other words, all 'intangibles' that are worth something become tangible value eventually. We can always touch the money in the bank. Whereas a new colour of paint for a car might be very 'creative', but is worthless if no customer pays for it.

Value is a very slippery concept. What if a hospital saves money by shutting a ward down? Is that added value? – Or if the car company reduces the quality of the paint job to save money? Does that add value? – The simple answer is that added value is not about 'cutting corners' or doing less. Added value means providing more per £ spent; more for less, not less for less. Value only comes from getting the balance right between all these four variables; it cannot happen if you try to rob Peter to pay Paul. It is extremely important to understand this in an HCM context and the way businesses report on their human capital performance.

So what practical use is this model? All it requires is for anyone, but particularly those working in HCM, to always ask the question 'how will this intervention, activity or project add value?' This is not a rhetorical or hypothetical question. If there is no clear line of sight to an improvement in O, C, R or Q, then there is no business justification for continuing. Conversely, where there is a clear line of sight, then there is already a reasonable probability that the project in question will eventually be translated into added value. Apply this simple test immediately to anything your organization is currently doing on leadership programmes, competence frameworks, knowledge management, corporate universities, e-learning or even e-HR. If you do not have a high confidence level that the value objectives of each of these activities was clearly articulated at the outset, using one or more of the four added value variables OCRQ, then they could be described as completely pointless.

Another quick test is to use the simple ROI (return on investment) formula in Figure 6.4. Just produce a quick and dirty, back-of-an-envelope cost of the project you are planning and then imagine what a 1% improvement (benefit) in one of the four value variables might look like in £'s. If the resulting sum looks attractive it warrants further investigation.

The reason we are spending some time discussing value in detail is because the performance curve in Fig. 6.1 was really looking at how individuals add value, not just a very narrow definition of individual performance. Individuals might be 'performing', but value only comes from the whole organization working well together. For anyone who has spent many years trying to train and develop employees, at all levels, this fact of life is probably one of the most important lessons they can learn. It is also one of the most difficult to accept. If the individual you are trying to train is highly motivated, capable and in a position to make use of what they have learnt, there are often many other factors that can come into play that can militate against that piece of training having any impact at an organizational level. This can mean the efforts of even the most professional trainers are nullified by other organizational constraints.

$$\text{ROI} = \frac{\text{GROSS BENEFIT - COST}}{\text{COST}} \times 100\%$$

$$\text{Eg. ROI} = \frac{\text{£3.7M - £1.4M}}{\text{£1.4M}} \times 100\%$$

$$\text{ROI} = \frac{\text{£2.3M}}{\text{£1.4M}} \times 100\%$$

$$\text{ROI} = 1.64 \times 100\%$$

$$\text{ROI} = 164\% \text{ in 1 year}$$

FIGURE 6.4   The simple ROI test of value – what would a 1% improvement be worth?

For example, research scientists might not be allowed to use their newly acquired skills or techniques or they might be confined to strict and rigid standard operating procedures. Or take as an example the basic training of police officers, which includes cautioning suspects, how to make an arrest, taking witness statements and collecting evidence. All this is of little or no value to society if the criminals apprehended are not successfully prosecuted. Even the most professional officers, who follow the letter of the law and are assiduous in their methods, may see their best efforts come to nought because of a legal technicality or the poor performance of a prosecuting counsel. Society only gets the true value of its investment in the policing and justice system when all parts of the system work well together. Consequently, HCM has to focus not only on the development of the individual but also, simultaneously, every other relevant factor that might influence value. If we were looking for a single, distinguishing feature between HRM and HCM this would be it. HCM, value management and holistic, systems thinking are all synonymous. This is not just another light bulb moment; this is a completely new paradigm.

THE PARADIGM SHIFT IN MANAGING PEOPLE – THE FOCUS ON VALUE

It is this obsession with value that characterizes HCM and the extent of the shift in thinking required cannot be overestimated. We are talking about a totally new management philosophy, almost a new 'religion' in management. Such a shift requires a completely fresh perspective on what managing people as capital means. It is the equivalent of Galileo telling the Pope that the earth

FIGURE 6.5 Both are women but, like Cubism, HCM provides a revolutionary perspective on people.

rotates around the sun, Einstein telling physicists in 1905 that space–time is relative or Picasso shaking up the art world with Cubism. In fact the most dramatic way of conveying this shift in perception is to view two of Picasso's works of art in Fig. 6.5.

You might be drawn to one more than the other. Certainly the blue nude is beautiful and if that represents 'HRM' then the alternative, the 'HCM' woman on the right is a very odd figure. Yet if what Picasso is trying to portray, among other things, is a three-dimensional image on a two-dimensional medium then it is an excellent analogy for the difference between thinking of HRM as administration and HCM as a multidimensional organizational representation.

If we now can get back to the practicalities we can illustrate just how this new paradigm differs so markedly from HRM conventions in Table 6.1 highlighting some of the most telling and distinguishing features.

The most noticeable change of all though will be in the way you measure success.

Chapter 7

Strategic Value Measures and Management Tools

PEOPLE MANAGEMENT CANNOT BE REDUCED TO A FORMULA

Charismatic leaders can never rely entirely on their charisma. It is said that political leaders campaign in poetry but govern in prose: the grand words have to become prosaic at some point, when they are translated into specific measures. If employees do not understand the language being used they will switch their brain off and resort to working as automatons. Another prerequisite in HR-business strategy, therefore, is constantly ensuring the language of measurement is fully understood and if any single chapter in this book had to be chosen as the most important, this is it. It challenges all of the conventional wisdom on how organizations are managed by objectives and performance indicators. The collapse of GM is probably one of the best examples available of an organization that has failed to manage itself holistically, but there are many others. The stark example it provides is just symptomatic of a long-term trend in management thinking that can only be described as 'mathematical'. When mathematics alone rules disaster will not be far behind and if any blame is to be laid at a particular door then one culprit would be the now infamous Black Scholes model (below) that is probably unintelligible to the vast majority of ordinary people, including senior banking and regulatory staff, and your author, which is why there will be no attempt made to explain what it says.

$$C(S,t) = SN(d_1) - Ke^{-r(T-t)}N(d_2)$$

This formula can be regarded as a prime contributor to the Long Term Capital Management (LTCM) debacle that nearly brought the US financial system to its knees in 1998. We do not have to go back as far as 1929 to see stupid behaviour masquerading as science. Economics Nobel Prize winner Myron Scholes was himself on LTCM's board of directors. His model promoted the use of a type of financial derivative that eventually led to the banking collapse of 2008. This serves as a nasty reminder that businesses cannot be run on cold, mathematical calculations devoid of human soul. The citizens support businesses in capitalist systems because they can see the huge benefits it brings to them. If it loses its soul it loses its moral authority. Such pure economic and mathematical theory does not factor in the human part of the equation (fear, greed, nerve, confidence). It also fails the common sense rule that if you need a degree in pure mathematics or econometrics to have any chance of understanding it then it is of no use in managing the vast majority of people. When even the traders using it do not fully understand what they are doing it is bound to be calamitous.

So rather than make measurement an even more esoteric and intellectual pursuit we are only going to focus on simple measures of value. Paradoxically, these simple measures are actually of the highest order (so you might wish to refresh your memory of what we mean by value by looking back at Chapter 6). You might also wish to reconsider your own thoughts on the principle of *you can only manage what you measure*. Many people do not accept this as a principle, never mind one of universal applicability. So let us be clear what we are saying and how it particularly applies in the context of human capital measurement.

WE ALL MEASURE EVERYTHING WE DO

Do you think your executive colleagues subscribe wholeheartedly to this principle? Ask them for one example of something they 'manage' without measuring it. How about their marriage or relationship with their partner, or even how they 'manage' their children? The way most humans react to this question though is entirely predictable. As soon as we use words to denote the value of something, like 'well' or 'not as well as I could', we have already admitted that we measure things on our own mental scale of value that presumably ranges from 'it couldn't get any worse' to 'as good as it gets'. This is a principle:

- Human beings measure (or gauge) everything they do
- They also use their own mental scale of relative measures

Now before you resist or dismiss this thought we are not trying to reveal any earth-shattering breakthrough in management thinking here. This is not intended to be a 'Blue Ocean' moment (defined here as a statement of the blindingly obvious but dressed up as something new). We are just hoping you will acknowledge that this is the way you think. We all do. It is just your realization and acceptance of this fact of life that is called for. Once you embrace this notion it should help to transform the way you manage people. Managing people to release their full potential should be a world of tangibility, something you can see, measure and touch; it is not a world of intangibles.

None of us could say what makes a perfect marriage, or a perfect working relationship, even if we believed that we had one. No professor of social science specializing in marriage could tell us either. Every relationship is different. Presumably, most happily married couples do not feel the need to have strategic planning meetings (so what's our performance target for the number of children we plan to have darling?) because they trust their relationship, based on their vows, to cope with whatever life has to throw at them; what will be, will be. The same cannot be said of organizations though; they have to be organized. They have to have very clear and agreed strategic goals because this is a 'marriage' with many partners, some of whom might perceive it to be a 'marriage of convenience' or, worse still, a very unhappy union. You will only know how successful this relationship is when the indicators and results tell you.

A happy and stable marriage is the tangible outcome of many years of building trust in a relationship. It is already positively measured in your children's success at school (broken homes produce worst results), lower divorce rates (and all of the consequential costs to both parties and the economy) and even health (married people live longer on average). Yet the word 'trust', a feeling that is probably *the* defining word for intangibility, produces probably the most valuable tangibles known to man. If you do not accept this argument at face value then consider the near total collapse of the global financial system in 2008 – entirely due to a loss of trust and therefore confidence in the system. Banks do not survive on real assets but trust that you can get your money out when you need it. A run on a bank will happen, regardless of the tangible assets it holds, if the customers lose faith in it. Re-capitalizing the banks is as much about restoring and rebuilding trust as it is about capital ratios. But if you still need convincing that 'intangibles' and measurable value are one and the same then try the simple exercise below.

SOFT AND HARD MEASURES – WHAT IS THE DIFFERENCE?

The picture in Fig. 7.1 shows two managers considering words they use every day. Now they are asked to categorize these thought bubbles according to

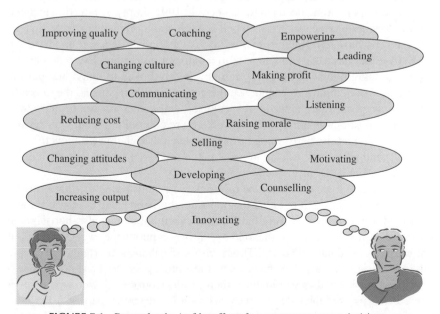

FIGURE 7.1   Do not let the 'soft' stuff confuse your management decisions.

whether they are 'soft' or 'hard'. Try writing them down yourself and use three columns if you wish – 'soft', 'hard' and 'don't know'.

The first problem you will encounter is that we have not defined our terms very clearly, but then who does when such words are bandied around the boardroom at every meeting? When we talk about 'morale' do we ever stop to consider whether we all mean the same thing? Most people use the term 'hard' to mean measurable or tangible although they often confuse this with being 'difficult' as well. 'Selling' tends to be regarded as hard and tangible as it can be measured in terms of total sales. However, we all know that 'selling' requires a very complex mix of soft skills such as 'listening' to what the customer really wants and 'communicating' what you have to offer. It can also involve personal attributes such as an ability to empathize with the customer and building rapport. So which column would they be in?

There is only one answer to this exercise, they should all result in value or they are worthless to your organization – fact. Imagine your salespeople telling their colleagues at a sales conference that they had fantastic rapport with their customers, only to learn that their sales were the worst? Of course, in real life, we have salespeople who manage to achieve excellent sales through other means. Sometimes this could have been the 'foot in the door' approach, not the 'softest' selling technique available. Some years ago one UK life insurance company, Allied Dunbar, had such a terrible reputation for intrusive sales techniques that it became known as 'Allied Crowbar'. This sounds like a 'soft' description of the culture of this business but its reputation eventually fed through into disastrous sales. In the same way that Gerald Ratner brought his own jewellery retailing business to its knees in 1991 simply by referring to some of his cheaper products as 'crap' when speaking at a private, business dinner.

The HR-business strategist makes no distinction between soft and hard, an activity either has a clear link to potential value or it does not. Every single one of the thought bubbles in Fig. 7.1 can be directly linked to individual performance. If your employees cannot see the connection then you and they need to think again. For example, we might 'counsel' employees at work because they have a domestic problem, but the reason we are counselling them is to restore them to being a fully performing employee (even though this will benefit them as well) and what does 'raising morale' mean if it is not 'going that extra mile' to produce more (O) or give a better service (Q)?

This simple logic should not be misconstrued as justifying the 'hard-nosed' disposition of many CEOs. Quite the opposite, this is intended to be warm logic not cold and heartless. A truly hard-nosed executive is innately short-sighted because hard-nosed and cold-hearted executives cannot hope to get the best out of warm blooded human beings. Those who sold subprime mortgages to people living in trailer parks must have been the epitome of the hard-nosed sales-person. They knew they would make their profits from people who would never be able to pay off their debts. They also knew they were part of a pyramid selling scam and made sure they had their exit ready in plenty of time before the inevitable crash. If you are that type of hard-nosed CEO, who can see nothing wrong in this, then you are reading the wrong book. Even 'gorillas' like Dick Fuld of Lehman Brothers failed to make his hard-nosed banking model work.

Now let us return to more positive considerations of how you might use this principle, that there is no distinction between soft and hard. Probably the most relevant thought bubble here is 'leading'. As a CEO you have to be a leader, unless, of course, you and the board think the status quo is just fine. Some of the most popular, developmental activities in business and management schools over the last 20 years have been leadership programmes. If you have ever been on one of these, or sponsor some of your own managers to attend, you now need to draw a clear line of sight between attendance on these programmes and value. Not after the event, we should hasten to add, but before you go. The very fact that the vast majority of providers and users fail to do this tells us quite clearly that many senior managers must regard their own development as either something intangible, indeterminate or incapable of being measured. Of course, it could equally be an indicator that they are not taking the whole programme seriously enough to bother thinking in this much depth. Either way, whether unfocused or apathetic, if leadership is not about adding lots of measurable value then what is it?

We need a complete paradigm shift in the way we view management by measurement. Every employee will personalize whatever measures they are set, so we need to design into our performance measurement systems the willingness of the individual to own those measures and to make the best use of them, rather than see them as an onerous burden or a punitive stick. This leads to yet another sacrosanct and closely allied principle of HR-business strategy, what gets measured gets done; our behaviour is channelled into those things that will be used to measures us.

So choosing the most appropriate measures to boost motivation, rather than diminish it, is a highly skilled job. Being aware of all the potential pitfalls of performance measurement and management will certainly help. Setting disjointed targets can easily lead to conflicting management behaviour with the VP of Sales trying to hit sales targets, while the cost-focused VP of Operations desperately tries to keep costs down leaving the VP of Customer Relationship Management picking up the pieces, dealing with complaints that were not of their own making. This is hardly a recipe for value maximization.

THE BALANCED BUSINESS SCORECARD

One answer suggested for this management conundrum is to make sure every part of the organization is pulling together, in the same direction using mutually reinforcing measures. This is the thinking behind the concept of the balanced scorecard, which tries valiantly to avoid designing competing and conflicting internal measures and replaces them with a balanced combination of different perspectives, all of which have their own set of measures. The Kaplan and Norton version of this genre, like the model shown in Fig. 7.2,

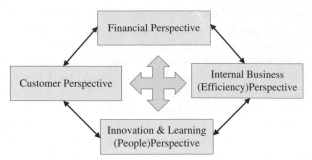

FIGURE 7.2   A balanced business scorecard yes, but is it holistic?

suggests the organization has to view performance measurement from four key perspectives:

- Financial measures
- Customer needs and satisfaction
- Internal efficiency and effectiveness (usually referred to as internal processes)
- Learning and growth (i.e. is the organization developing from continuous learning and innovation?) – but often referred to as the 'people' box

The balanced business scorecard was a serious and intelligent attempt to address many of the sorts of organizational issues raised throughout this book but does it work? Whatever performance was achieved in the boom years since their model was launched (late 1990s to 2007), the next decade will be a much tougher and truer test of management capability.

The biggest weakness in scorecards and other generic, business models is their failure to address the human capital issue correctly. Even when a need for 'people measures' is acknowledged, there are no useful measures offered. Exactly the same problem faced by the Accounting for People Taskforce when trying to produce an HCM report. These models also imply that the arrow of causation points from measurement to performance and 'success', as surely as night follows day. The HR-business strategist's perspective turns this thinking on its head, 'day' can be seen to follow 'night' when you have a different starting point. This causation question is always of paramount importance and Norton himself confessed, in a foreword to The HR Scorecard (Huselid, Becker and Ulrich, yet again HBS Press, 2001), that the 'people measures box' is the one that has always presented the most difficulties for organizations -

> the worst grades are reserved for their understanding of strategies for developing human capital. There is little consensus, little creativity, and no real framework for thinking about the subject. Worse yet, we have seen little improvement in this over the past eight years.

This is an amazing public admission by one of the original designers of the balanced scorecard. His own theory demands that all four boxes or perspectives are balanced so if the people box is not resolved satisfactorily one can only assume that Kaplan and Norton's scorecard cannot have been working at all. A 'three quarters' balanced scorecard' makes no sense at all. In fact, without the people box the balanced scorecard is just another collection of disjointed, conventional measures. The people box has to be the secret ingredient.

'The HR Scorecard' by Ulrich et al. tried to remedy this situation and Norton's foreword admits a solution was necessary to bolster their own approach but they failed to resolve the crucial issue of *causality*. As we have already seen in Chapter 4 Ulrich's own HR model is still based on the employee–customer–profit chain, predicated on a notion of employee engagement *causing* business performance. The arrow could just as easily be pointing the other way though. A well-run business, based on a sound business model with satisfied customers, is just as likely to result in a satisfying place to work. This is an issue that the famous, Sears Roebuck case study (see 'The Employee-Customer Profit Chain at Sears', *Harvard Business Review*, January–February 1998) tried to resolve. It tried to show a strong and direct correlation between employee satisfaction, customer satisfaction and business performance and claimed this relationship was *causal* to the extent of specifically linking a '5 unit increase in employee attitude' to a '0.5% increase in revenue growth'.

One obvious problem with this case study, regardless of any face validity it might have, is that those CEOs who do not fully understand the total picture may latch on to a simplistic point that if they focus on their employees' satisfaction it is bound to lead to business performance improvements at some stage. Once there is unthinking obedience to such theories they degenerate very quickly into classic, HR Magic Pills. The architects of the Sears Roebuck approach could not support such slavish adherence to this most simplistic interpretation of their theory idea and the earlier B&Q story (see Chapter 6) provides further, convincing evidence that nothing in the world of human capital management can be taken for granted. So the HR-business strategist sets a much higher standard for the evidence they are prepared to accept. Better evidence not only offers a more robust and rigorous strategy, it is more likely to stand the test of time.

Before we move on though, we need to quickly review another couple of management models, this time government sponsored frameworks that have more of a societal remit than the purely commercial variety. This should help us build a more complete picture of what might have to be included in a total, human capital framework.

EFQM – EUROPEAN QUALITY AWARD/EXCELLENCE MODEL

The EU has produced a very similar but more sophisticated type of scorecard, which incorporates elements of many other management methodologies mentioned here. They are all encapsulated in their excellence model in Fig. 7.3 and can be found at http://www.efqm.org/model_awards/model/excellence_model.htm

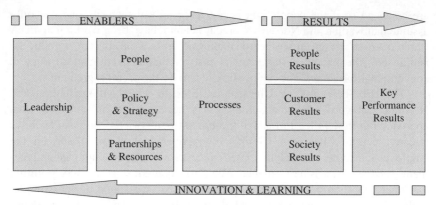

FIGURE 7.3 The European Excellence Model is more concerned with society than pure capitalism.

The most obvious difference in the EFQM model is the need to put 'enablers' in place if we are to hope to achieve the desired results. As with any scorecard each box has to have measures and there are now two specific boxes included for 'People' enablers and 'People Results'. In this model though there is also a box called 'Society Results' that is specifically designed to balance commercial results with other societal concerns. This is definitely a more socially democratic model in keeping with European, particularly northern European, traditions of welfare and fairness. These will include environmental concerns and broader indicators of corporate social responsibility (CSR). The one big question it does not help to resolve, from a CEO or boardroom perspective, is how to *reconcile* all of these goals or 'results'. For example, if you are supermarket chain Wal-Mart or Tesco, how would you reconcile the best commercial location of your stores with the wishes of local people, who may not want a store in their backyard? A hard-nosed, pure profit motive will dictate you locate them wherever local planning laws allow you to and where they can make the most profit. The EFQM model does not contain a way out of this perpetual dilemma and leaves it to be resolved by the political and legislative process.

The recommendation here is that Wal-Mart and Tesco need to articulate their value in much more societal terms if they were to satisfy the EFQM. Does Tesco's 'Finest' range of goods offer the best value for money? Does best value mean sustainable value or do they have a business model that just squeezes the life out of suppliers to reduce cost? Can they compete on value or is one of the main planks in their strategy the same as B&Q's – 'location, location, location'? Society's best interests can only be served by best value, not market manipulation.

INVESTORS IN PEOPLE (IIP)

One other framework worth mentioning, simply because it is entirely focused on people, is the UK's Investor in People scheme (see http://www.investorsinpeople.

co.uk/Standard/Introducing/Pages/Home.aspx), which has been in operation since 1991, and follows a classic, total quality, continuous improvement philosophy encapsulated in its three key principles:

- Plan – Developing strategies to improve the performance of the organization
- Do – Taking action to improve the performance of the organization
- Review – Evaluating the impact on the performance of the organization

The original version of these principles goes back at least as far as the 1920s to Walter Shewart's 'New Way' management model that had four principal steps – Plan–Do–Study–Act. Most people would now recognize this as W. Edwards Deming's model of Plan–Do–Check–Act (PDCA), which is still in daily use at Toyota. As with all management models, and as we have already seen throughout this text, what is written on paper though is only a very small part of the whole story. Any organization can achieve the Investor in People standard as long as they tick all the right boxes. Whether this means it has helped them create any value or not is another story entirely. This is not a cynical take on IiP, just an observation that the managing body – Investors in People (UK) – is still trying to convince the world that it works. It insists on commissioning interminable research that produces this sort of conclusion:

A two-year study by the Institute of Employment Studies (IES) has proved that an organisation achieving the Investors in People Standard gains, on average, an extra £176 per employee in gross profit, every year.

If any CEOs gave credence to this type of research would they see £176 per employee as a very attractive proposition? If human capital management is only worth this much we would be better off spending our time looking elsewhere for bigger opportunities, especially if more recent research into IiP is taken into account. In 2009 Professors Kim Hoque and Nicolas Bacon of Nottingham University Business School undertook research into IiP's Small Firms Initiative and concluded

The government's financial commitment to raise recognition rates and boost training levels among small firms through IiP UK's Small Firms Initiative has failed to achieve its aims

(http://www.trainingzone.co.uk/cgi-bin/item.cgi?id=194680&d=680&h=608&f=626 &dateformat=%25e-%25h-%25y)

IiP is a sound idea that has been very poorly implemented. It reinforces the view that throwing money at training initiatives has little impact if organizational immaturity renders them unable to reap the benefits on offer. Toyota does not have to commission academic research to convince itself that its management methods and use of PDCA is working or not. Its 'proof' is in the pudding and it can see, with its own eyes, measurable improvements in value every day. Cause and effect remain crystal clear because it only employs methods that start from a root cause analysis. More importantly, doing this religiously over many years translates into extraordinary market capitalization figures that convince the most hard-nosed investment analysts around.

So perhaps it is time to review your management models, your measures and how you use them. The remedy is not more measurement but more intelligent measurement. You are being encouraged here to review your existing performance measurement, not to produce any more meaningless data. In particular, as suggested by all of the proprietary models shown above, there needs to be some way of measuring the performance and value of your people; a 'people' box of measures or indicators. One way to do this is to use a very simple method for categorizing measures according to whether they tell you something about mere activity, performance or added value – there is a world of difference between them. Whatever you measure should be meaningful.

THE MEANINGFUL MEASURES TEST

- An *activity* measure tells you how active someone is (e.g. the number of calls a salesperson or social worker makes per day)
- A *performance* measure tells you that person is performing their task (i.e. they are doing what their job description demands, the salesperson sells, the social worker puts a child on the 'at-risk' register)
- An *added value* measure tells you that the organization's strategic objectives are being met (i.e. the profit margin on sales is at the right level, the incidence of child abuse is decreasing)

To try this out for yourself, simply write down about half a dozen measures that you already use to gauge 'performance' in your organization today and decide into which of these three categories they fall. You will be surprised just how many are pure activity measures and how few gauge genuine value.

To help you there is a list of common measures below, suggesting in which category they might fall, together with a brief rationale. This is not an exact science, so you have keep your brain engaged at all times; performance measures are not for automatons. You need to be clear in your own mind what you can infer or deduce from these numbers. Equally, any employees monitored against these measures need to be clear in their own minds. If they are not sure then your HR-business strategy should already have a built-in system that allows them to question and challenge the measures they are being asked to use. Employee curiosity always trumps obeisance when it comes to value creation.

COMMON MEASURES ARE WORTH REVISITING

Number of Training Days (or Hours) per Employee per Year

An activity measure – a perfect example, yet many companies set a target of between 5 and 10 days a year. Any people policy that is measured on this basis has to qualify as a stupid policy because it does not measure what it says it measures – it does not measure whether any training (i.e. learning) took place. Did the trainees listen? Did they learn anything? Did they put the lessons into practice? If it measures anything at all it could easily be the number of hours being bored stiff in the classroom or at an e-learning (sic) screen. A learning system might give this number some meaning because it would guarantee they applied what they learnt.

Output per Employee (e.g. Number of Cars Produced per Employee)

Performance – assuming that an increase is viewed as a good thing. It would need to be linked to other cost and quality metrics to reveal anything about value. Producing lots of cars at no profit is not a good idea even though GM and Ford have been doing that for years.

Average Recruitment Cost per Head

Activity – what about the quality of recruits and do you have any confident measure of that embedded in a robust performance management system? Should this measure go up or down? It depends if you are struggling to find the right people, does it not?

Profit per Employee

Added value – although even profit is not a perfect added value measure, companies that milk their cash cow to death could not be said to be creating value. We have all been in 'profitable' hotels in dire need of total refurbishment. Nevertheless, it is as near to a perfect value measure as you are going to get because it shows you managed to more than cover your costs.

HR (or Any) Department Spending per Employee

Activity – if they are doing something they have to do (hire and fire) it is a cost you cannot remove. If they are not doing anything useful then you do not need this cost at all (but see the three box system). If HR is adding value then you should invest more in it.

Calls Handled per Hour (External or Internal Customers)

Activity – could be a performance measure if you monitor the quality of the calls (e.g. 20 calls per hour to the required standard)

Sales Margin

Added value – virtually the same as profit because accountants define it by calculating sales revenue less cost of sales.

Sales Visits per Person, per Day

Activity – if the number of sales visits correlates directly with actual sales and margin then this might be useful in managing sales people (see also the Performance Curves below).

Sales Volume (e.g. 1000 Units Sold)

Performance – presuming that you want to sell more? But let us not forget about the cost of sales?

Staff Turnover

Activity – but if you want it to be a performance measure you at least have to say what you want it to be (10% or 20%?) and if you have good information on whether you are losing good people or the right people then it could be regarded as one gauge of human capital.

Customer Satisfaction (Survey or Otherwise)

Performance – definitely, keeping customers happy is always a prime concern and probably, hopefully, feeds through to profitability unless you are 'buying' customer satisfaction with prices you cannot afford.

Rework (Extra Labour Cost)

Performance – strictly speaking, although the target should always of course be 'zero defects'. While you have a rework problem any improvement could be said to be adding value, as there will be a cost saving going straight to the bottom line.

A Level Points per GCSE grade (Educational Attainment at Age 18 Relative to Attainment at 16)

Added value – a very sophisticated measure in use in the UK education system. It gauges whether a teacher manages to help students achieve what they are capable of. It also avoids unfair, league table, comparisons between state and private education as it takes into account the students' raw ability, not just their attainment level.

Hospital Patients per Bed, per Annum (e.g. 50 Patients per Bed per Year)

Activity – and very worrying that the NHS monitors this. What about corresponding mortality and re-admission rates if hospital staff feel obliged to rush patients out of their bed? What sort of behaviour does this type of measure encourage?

Even if you manage to choose the most intelligent measures available you still have to have a workforce that will use their own intelligence to work with them, rather than against them. If some of these measures do not strike you as being particularly strategic perhaps you need to ask yourself whether the average employee would understand ratios such as ROCE (return on capital employed), RONA (return on net assets) or EBIT(DA) and how they might influence their day-to-day behaviour and motivation. We should never forget that measures are at their most powerful when used as a behavioural tool rather than as a simplistic goal or target.

We would hope that all three types of measures in this taxonomy would eventually contribute value, but it is *only the added value measure that guarantees the right result has been achieved*. Only added value guarantees that human input and effort has been converted into worthwhile output. If you accept lesser measures of activity and performance as a *proxy* for value (i.e. 'as long as the social worker visited often enough and wrote enough reports then they must have been doing their job') do not be surprised if no value is added and disasters ensue (further child abuse or even death).

The only reason for concentrating on added value measures is that *added value is only achieved if everyone in the process performs well*. This is an incredibly powerful message to the whole of your workforce. High sales figures may not result in profit if the cost of after-sales support is too high, marketing have spent too much or even if the invoice clerk keeps making errors in invoicing. Attaching added value measures to each person in the chain, making them all accountable for margin, makes them all concentrate on the end result, the bottom line, not just their own task. Furthermore, how can you afford to reward any of them if no value is added at the end of the chain?

More important still, in the case of the at-risk child, in addition to social services there will be several other agencies involved including the child's school, the police and possibly the local hospital, if the child is injured. Everyone has a part to play in the chain and they should all be assessed by the single, 'bottom line' objective of ensuring the child is safe. This principle is finally dawning on the auditing profession with the UK's Audit Commission now launching a new Comprehensive Area Assessment framework that

> will provide a snapshot of how effectively local partnerships are working together to deliver local people's priorities.

http://www.audit-commission.gov.uk/caa/

even though it still has no method for measuring all of the human capital involved.

Many performance-related pay systems still fail to accept the principle that only value matters. The starkest example, of course, is the huge bonuses paid to executives of failing banks. The CEO of the Northern Rock bank in the UK, which experienced the first run on a UK bank in more than 100 years, left with a package in excess of £1 million. Such bonus schemes reward success without any corresponding consequence for the CEO taking too many risks or failing. They would do well to take a leaf out of the book of the CEO and founder of UK motor insurance company Admiral, Henry Englehardt, who receives no bonus, pension or share options and rewards his employees with shares so that everyone's interests, including shareholders, are aligned (2008 results revealed a £202 million profit on £910 million turnover).

Performance-related pay will always be contentious, especially when it is predicated on the very shaky assumption that an organization can be deconstructed into its smallest constituent parts to attribute a specific value to the contribution of individuals. This inevitably favours senior management and those at the sharpest end in sales who are deemed to be making the biggest difference. Yet, the value perspective says that value can only come from the whole system, not just parts of it. Breaking it down for performance payment purposes is incredibly divisive and creates an 'us and them' culture.

The situation would not be so bad if those who earn the most were willing to accept a corresponding level of accountability. The banking crisis showed that many CEOs did not even think they had made any mistakes, never mind shoulder any responsibility for the collapse of their business or feel it necessary to apologize. Dick Fuld was still trying to sell Lehman Brothers, with its toxic debt in place, right up until the end.

The other problem with individual performance measures is that businesses can just become 'busy fools'. This was best exemplified by a director of Rolls-Royce aero engines who declared at a conference some years ago that the good news was their order book was standing at £4 billion but the bad news was it would cost at least £4.2 billion to fulfil these orders. Performance measures (engines sold) probably gave a lot of the employees the false impression they were adding value when, in reality, nobody was. So how can you make sure your organization does not fall into the same activity and performance measurement trap? You need a much better, holistic, performance management system, one that is designed for humans.

INSTALLING A HUMAN, PERFORMANCE MANAGEMENT SYSTEM

Installing a performance management system was one of the building blocks of HR-business strategy shown in Table 3.1, but we also demonstrated how all of these systems have to be intrinsically 'human'. That means they have to be designed to work with human fallibility and patterns of motivation. Employees, more than anything else, have to want to make the system work themselves. They will only do this if they see their own interests bound up with those of the organization. They must value the performance improvements that the organization decides it needs.

This is one of those very obvious and predictable lessons about managing people that we are only just beginning to learn. In an article entitled 'Government is to rethink performance management processes in the Civil Service in a bid to encourage more innovation from public servants' as recently as 5 February 2009 http://www.personneltoday.com/articles/2009/02/05/49270/performance-rethink-to-inspire-creativity-among-civil-servants.html

A Cabinet Office Minister was quoted as saying

Success comes not from accumulating, or hoarding, or concentrating power in the hands of politicians or civil servants – it comes from giving it away to people.

This apparently is part of an attempt to find

new ways of promoting innovation, making it easier to learn from frontline workers, and delivering greater value for money to the taxpayer.

This realization only comes after many years of the Government imposing centrally dictated and driven 'performance' (sic) targets that failed to achieve performance improvements. A National Audit Office report 'Assessment of the Capability Review programme' (February 2009) also revealed that

there was little evidence that governmental capability reviews were leading to improved public services

Let us hope that whatever system replaces this is designed as a human system rather than just a new Magic Pill – probably resulting in thousands of public servants being sent on a course called something like 'Promoting Innovation' whether they want to or not. No activity driven approach will work unless the system itself is tested first.

TESTING THE SYSTEM

So how well designed is your present performance system? Here are the key criteria for human, performance management systems:

1. You need to have built a culture where performance improvement is viewed by all concerned as both a necessary and positive challenge. It will also be based on a philosophy of never-ending, continuous improvement where learning from mistakes is encouraged without seeking-to-blame anyone else.
2. The overall, strategic, value goals of the organization are communicated clearly to all employees and any changes signalled immediately (see the Value Statement in Chapter 2 and Fig. 2.1).
3. Managers have to check with their teams that they understand these goals and what contribution they might be able to make to them. If there is a lack of understanding they must be encouraged to feed this back to the executive without fear of recrimination (see item 1 above)
4. All performance indicators should have a direct connection to a value objective as we pointed out under the Meaningful Measures Test (and reread the value section in Chapter 6).

5. Where value is dependent on two separate individuals/departments/ sections they must work on the performance indicator together. If they discover that another party has to be involved (including external suppliers and other stakeholders) then they have to be allowed to involve them.

6. Any performance indicator must have a baseline measure in place before any effort is made to improve it. That baseline should be credible and accepted by those who have to improve it.

7. Any attempt at improving performance should consider how the structure, process or systems in the organization (and outside) would have to change. Clear responsibilities should be agreed in advance as to who can authorize such changes and the likely timescale involved.

8. There is nothing wrong with setting targets that have already considered the human capital implications. This includes ensuring the targets are value targets (not activity or performance only) and that the targets encourage cooperation, not division.

9. All improvements are welcomed but only serve to establish a new baseline for the next iterative, improvement.

10. All of the above is dependent on having a learning system in place (see Chapter 3) because any performance system that is not also a learning system will be a very short-term, static model.

Assuming you resolve the issues in all of these elements you also need a simple review *process* for individual employees to discuss their own personal performance issues with their boss (and anyone else who might be able to help). This does not require any formal forms, unless these might act as a guide for the manager and subordinate. These reviews should be happening on a very regular basis, even daily, as a natural way of working and not as a formal meeting once or twice a year. We should also never forget that any system has to be designed to cope with the lowest common denominator; otherwise known as the 'idiot test'. 'Idiots' will always screw up the system unless you build in controls to make sure they cannot.

You will notice that human systems do not have to over-rely on paperwork. A human system is well understood by all humans involved, just like traffic lights. It takes time to build human systems though; they can never be a Magic Pill. In fact this human performance system is so crucial to HR-business strategy that we need to delve much deeper into the subject with the aim of producing a report on how well it is working. It has to be constructed by further developing the simple performance curve we described in some detail in Fig. 6.1 (which might be worth re-reading before you move on).

ASSESSING AND REPORTING ON HUMAN CAPITAL MANAGEMENT

Although the basic building block for the next few charts is still the original performance curve in Fig. 6.1 we now need to focus on the measurement scale itself. Before, we talked about measuring shoe sizes on a 1 to 10 scale, now we are using the same scale to gauge performance and potential with 1 being the lowest and 10 being the best score. In Fig. 7.4 we plot the relative performances and management potential of the men and women in your organization. The purpose of this particular exercise is to come to a conclusion on whether the management population is comprised of the best male and female talent available. However, we are going to declare our view at the beginning, right or wrong, that there is a high probability that any given sample of 1000 men and 1000 women will produce perfectly overlapping curves. That is, women and men will perform equally well and have equal management potential. You might have a different view but as we are developing an evidence-based HR-business strategy here you had better be prepared to produce some evidence to justify your view. An assumption of equality is probably the least contentious option available for now.

Figure 7.4 is asking the question of whether you are discriminating against women in your selection of managers. Not because this is unethical or illegal (although some might argue it is both) but because you are likely to be operating suboptimally. Value is always the HR-business strategist's prime criterion.

Conceptually, it is just painting a picture of what might be happening already, a classic case of the 'glass ceiling'. Many organizations have done their best to open up opportunities for women because they think this is a problem, however ill-defined. But if we move from concept to practice then evidence needs to be gathered to support or disprove the basic hypothesis that sits behind discussions of equal opportunities. The HR-business strategist does not assume that 'more women managers' is a good thing and neither do they regard that

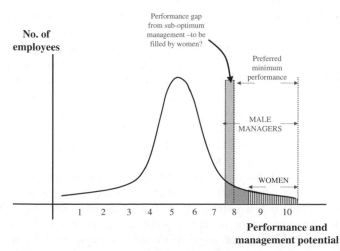

FIGURE 7.4 Do you have the same management criteria for choosing male and female managers?

proposition as inherently more 'ethical'. Promoting women into jobs that they do better than men makes perfect business sense. Promoting women who are less capable than their male colleagues, for quota purposes or even legal requirements, does not and it would be difficult to argue that diluting management capability is 'ethical' if the customer suffers as a result.

Now we move on to the question of how we support either of these contentions. Irrespective of any theory, you are where you are and already have a management group populated by a combination of men and women, inequitably or otherwise. This diagram demands that you come clean and reveal what minimum criteria you are using and how each manager is assessed against those criteria. This will not be perfect but it will at least be a start. It is this serious intent that the HR-business strategist would wholeheartedly support over any lip service to the cause of equal opportunities.

The graph shows an area of 'Preferred minimum performance' for anyone to be moved into a managerial role, but suggests that some of the male managers are not really up to this standard, as shown by the note 'Performance gap from suboptimum management – to be filled by women?' Meanwhile, the women managers are a relatively small but very capable group (shown by the lined area). So the question now would be – can you replace the lower-performing managers, below the line, with women who are rated above 7 but do not currently hold a management position?

This is no longer a hypothetical exercise. You could collect the relevant data very quickly if it does not already exist. All you need to do is ask each of your executives for a 1 to 10 score, on management capability, for all of the men and women in their team, including the existing managers. The single criterion would be 'give this person a score for how well you think they perform or would perform in management'. If you already have good people data systems and a culture of openly and regularly assessing people then you should have plenty of track record evidence to support or refute these scores. If not, then you have an immediate hurdle to overcome. So you might do this confidentially with the executive first. Let us assume you have 10 executives, with 10 direct reports and 10 potentials each, it should only take them about 20 minutes to provide the data for you to produce this curve with a sample of 200. This is not meant to be a long and drawn-out exercise. It is just a quick and dirty way of answering a serious question. If the initial data says you have all the right people in management you can move on. If it raises many questions then you need to start addressing them more seriously.

You could regard this as a very unprofessional, cavalier trick. So instead you call in some consultants to perform a thorough assessment of each candidate, including full personality and psychometric profiling. There is nothing to stop you doing so at any stage in the process, of course, but, funnily enough, you might be surprised that after all that effort the results are no more accurate or just confirm the original 1 to 10 scores. HR business strategy can be based on any data as long as it has credibility with the people concerned; intuitive data is as good as its acceptability to others. Senior managers should trust their own judgement and be able to defend their assessment of candidates. It is unlikely they will trust anyone else's judgement in preference to their own, but if they do they should not be appointing any more managers.

If you are now fully conversant with how to use this extremely simple, 300 years old, but nevertheless revealing tool you might like to move on and consider Fig 7.5. If you have not got time for this yourself then maybe it is a job for your HR director or possibly the head of talent or diversity (if you believe there is value in such positions).

Ask them to produce curve 'A' from a simple 1 to 10 score for the whole workforce. This will be problematic if you have not prepared the groundwork in advance. Here the criterion could be simply 'existing performance' or just 'how talented'? If the resulting curve is shifted to the right (i.e. nobody scores below 4) this defies the basic theory of probability, so somebody is not being entirely honest. This should then be viewed against the make up of the general population from which you can draw your talent. So if you are 'underrepresented' in either women, ethnic minorities or in any other way then the total available talent curve 'B' is bound to sit above yours. You can now ask the person producing this data to provide some clear answers as to how you attract more talent from the total pool and what needs to be done about those who are overestimating or lying about existing 'talent'. If you make any progress on this you will be moving towards curve 'C', where your workforce capability makes a beneficial shift to the right.

Simply sending people on 'diversity awareness courses', which is what every police force in the UK did 5 years ago, cannot make this shift. The

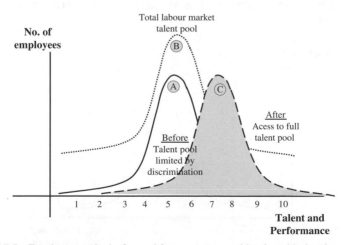

FIGURE 7.5   Equal opportunity is, first and foremost, a proposition for achieving the most value possible from the total talent pool.

Metropolitan Police in London have had a particularly poor record on diversity over the last decade. The Morris Inquiry (http://www.mpa.gov.uk/downloads/issues/morris/morris-report.pdf) looked into this in 2004 and concluded that 'there was little confidence among staff that the Met was embracing all aspects of diversity, and the majority believe diversity has yet to become part of police culture' (*Personnel Today*, 21 September 2004). The same journal reported (*Personnel Today* 8 January 2009) that two women officers were suing the Met for sexual harassment and on 25 February 2009 it had a heading "Institutional racism continues to dog Met Police as 'apartheid culture' claims come to court". More evidence that Magic Pills never work when there are deep rooted, intractable issues of human frailty involved.

A very similar proposition to Fig. 7.5 is shown in Fig. 7.6. This focuses on leadership, as opposed to management talent. Again, how you define and score leadership is up to you but any attempt at measurement is better than none. If you do not measure it you cannot manage it. Here the issues are more to do with growing the potential leadership cadre or at least making sure you identify the best.

Before we leave this fascinating subject of people performance curves, we must briefly return to a subject discussed in Chapter 6 – forced ranking. As with any management tool it can be used well or badly but the worst examples of forced ranking are those that link to pay and rewards. The performance schemes in some organizations (that shall remain nameless) predetermine that the employee population can be divided into four groupings, or sections, of the curve as in Fig. 7.7. Here the 'worst' group is D and the 'best' is A. At the end of the year each group receives a fixed percentage of the annual bonus pot; although those in D get no bonus at all. This has to be one of the most noxious 'Magic Pills' ever invented in employee performance management. It is a very unintelligent use of the theory of probability as it guarantees a divided and

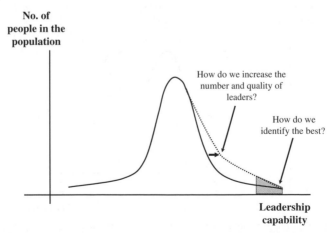

FIGURE 7.6   Are you prepared to score leadership potential to make the most of it?

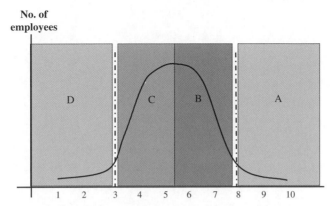

FIGURE 7.7 Predetermined performance ratios are the antithesis of performance management and very divisive.

demoralized workforce. Even some of those who receive the bonus will feel that the worst group have either been treated unfairly or just poorly managed. Rarely will anyone see this as a positive experience and it will do nothing for esprit de corps.

Chapter 8

What Factors Have the Biggest Influence on the Value of an HR-Business Strategy?

If you have been convinced enough by the arguments so far, and feel excited about the prospect of formulating a full HR-business strategy, you might want to consider what other factors you will have to take into consideration before you proceed. Here are some generic headings that require answers and you can usefully work your way through each of these first.

GREENFIELD OR BROWNFIELD?

Everything we have covered would be so much easier to implement in a greenfield situation, with a completely clean slate and a blank canvas to work on. All employees would be new, with no particular expectation. There would be no historical or attitudinal baggage and no pre-set behaviour patterns demanding re-education; the bane of an HR-business strategist's life. You, as CEO, would start with at least the minimum level of trust and respect we tend to afford people when we first meet them. From there you can declare your values and establish the principles that will form the solid basis for running the organization over many years to come. You also have the luxury of trying new ideas out because you will not have a history of failed initiatives behind you. All of this provides very fertile ground.

The primary perspective held throughout this book is really about how to introduce an HR-business strategy into a brownfield situation. This inevitably means HR-business strategy is automatically bound up with change management and organizational transformation. One of the big problems with brownfield HR strategies is that they are replete with compromises and diversions from basic principles (e.g. making allowances for unions, tolerance of underperformance, acceptance of lax attitudes) and can sway with the winds of change. Sometimes this is inevitable, but all too often it is just used as an excuse for slow progress.

This is why it is a good discipline, even if you do not have a greenfield situation, to consider what your HR-business strategy would be like if you did. It is the best way to make the most of the art of the possible, to clarify your vision without constraints, to decide on your standards and provide something to aim for. If you moved into a brand-new house you might declare a no-smoking policy, for example, and start as you mean to go on. In Jeffrey Liker's book *The Toyota Way* he tells the story of a GM light-truck factory in California that had a history of wildcat strikes. When Toyota took it over in 1984, 2 years after it was shut down by GM, Toyota decided to bring back the workers, including the 'militant' union representatives. They went over to Japan for 3 weeks and apparently came back 'converted'. No attitudes, union or otherwise, are cast in concrete.

DOES SIZE MATTER?

Perhaps the most obvious question to ask is does the size of the organization have any influence on whether HR-business strategy is appropriate or not? There has probably been an implicit assumption throughout that HR-business strategy tends to be more of an issue the bigger the organization becomes. Certainly a small organization, where the CEO knows everyone by sight if not personally, does not require a sophisticated framework. However, as we have just seen, most HR issues can be ironed out when you have the luxury of a new, start-up business and small businesses can grow into big businesses so it does no harm to try and plan accordingly.

Also, whilst the scale of value is different (a CEO in a £10 million business cannot usually have the same impact, in pure monetary terms, as the CEO managing a business worth £100 million or a £100 billion) all organizations have key people and in small organizations these can make the difference between success and failure. Furthermore, if you have no experience of using HR-business strategy then smaller organizations are probably a better place to try these ideas out first.

HOW MUCH INFLUENCE DOES LOCAL CULTURE HAVE?

At a large European HR conference in Lisbon in 2002 the feedback from about 500 delegates, the majority of whom were from Europe and the Middle East, intimated that they felt the speakers were too focused on UK and US companies and they wanted to see more speakers and case studies from other parts of the world. This may reflect a genuine need for greater cultural relevance or could simply be a matter of national pride, although it is probably a combination of both. Nevertheless, it highlights an extremely important question in HR-business strategy – is it dependent on the culture in which it has to work? This is particularly important today in an era of increasing globalization.

Certainly the UK perspective has been shaped by many factors including

- The 'Thatcherite' revolution that fundamentally changed the power of unions
- A cultural shift towards self-reliance and less dependence on the state

- A greater emphasis on the need for value that leads to stronger performance measurement and management in all walks of life (although inflated bonuses in the collapsed banking sector has brought 'performance-related pay' into disrepute)
- Increasing privatization and 'marketization' of the public sector and government agencies, where it is now the norm for utilities to be provided by commercial companies and for public services to have to go out to competitive tender
- Increasing workers' 'rights', including the minimum wage in the UK, and moves towards outlawing all forms of discrimination including 'age-ism' (whatever that is)
- Greater employment legislation both from the UK and the EU parliaments that impose tighter restrictions on an employer's freedom to hire and fire
- A growing consensus, in a developed economy, that work–life balance is an issue that needs to be addressed
- Mass migration by EU workers with a direct impact on wages

This is not meant to be an exhaustive list by any means, but it does reveal the sort of platform from which UK HR-business strategists have to work and also some of the potential opportunities that might not be available elsewhere. In the USA, the significant differences could be the readiness to pay for performance and probably a more solid belief in the purest form of capitalist values.

France and Germany's employment legislation frameworks are even tighter than the UK, which leaves less room for manoeuvre by employers, best exemplified by France's attempt to limit working hours to 35 per week. Whether these are sustainable policies in the face of global competition (France retreated from enforcing the 35-hour week in 2005) is questionable but one can discern that maybe the citizenry of developed economies are heading in this general direction?

The other dimension for consideration here has to be the influence of national identity and culture. Japan has its 'salaryman' and *karōshi* (death by overwork), America has the 'American dream', Eastern Europe has still to throw off some of its 'communist' traits, and some parts of the world still openly admit that they regard women as unequal. All of these are bound to produce differing attitudes, habits and behaviours. What is acceptable in one culture will not be in another. Yet, despite these obvious differences, it has not stopped the Toyota Way being employed all over the world and many multinational corporations run their subsidiaries on very similar lines within different cutural environments.

The only thing that is not culturally dependent is the concept of 'value'. Admittedly, on a scale of 'pure profit motive' to 'social responsibility', America is probably the most ardent version of capitalism. Philosophically, it is a million miles away from the Scandinavian, social democratic, version. Nevertheless, the concept of value is the same everywhere in the sense that organizations can only provide, ultimately, what customers and citizens *value*. HR-business strategy will always be focused on the Value Statement of the organization, whether they are for profit or not. Organizations around the world are painfully aware of environmental issues and wider notions of what constitutes a 'socially responsible organization' so the short-termist, narrow-minded, blinkered definition of profit has been under severe pressure for some years and this is only likely to increase during the present recession.

There is even a new kid on the conceptual block of the 'bottom line'. Now some commentators refer to a triple 'bottom line' of people, profit and planet that CEOs will have to contend with. None of this is likely to make a CEO's job any easier and it does not guarantee that the CEO will run the organization any better. You have to be very clear in your own mind what value really means and communicate that clearly to all employees. A clear and open discussion about what the board regards as value is the only way forward and this has to include all of the factors highlighted above. BP might try and convince the general public that it is a green organization with its green logo, but its pipeline leaks in Alaska and its oil refinery fire in Texas tell another story entirely that is bound to lead observers to contrary conclusions.

The one thing any CEO will want is some sense of certainty in their strategic plans. Effective organization abhors ambiguity and uncertainty and yet many human resource issues can be subject to endless debate. So let us consider some other contentious areas and see if we can provide a safe passage through these other minefields.

WHAT ABOUT A CLEAR PHILOSOPHY ON PAY AND REWARDS?

Probably the most contentious of all will be pay. To a simplistic economist wages are just the market price of labour, assuming a free market for labour. If that is the case then you would think that a resource that is so plentiful, 6 billion people and counting, would drive global wage rates down to very low levels. Yet, geographical mobility, political instability and education all conspire against this happening and so we are likely to see income inequality for some time. These could all be viewed as market imperfections, but the HR-business strategist will hold fast to the fundamental notion that any strategy has to be cognizant of the laws of economics. The market should always be cited as the key determinant of pay even if pay policies are notoriously inequitable and have tended to move in only one direction (up) until very recently. This is why an HR-business strategist might have a concern with minimum wage legislation, especially during a severe economic downturn.

The HR-business strategist will realize just how dynamic and contentious the whole question of pay and reward is, and it will never be an exact science, but they need to anchor their own philosophy on something that is not likely to shift. Whatever philosophy you choose it should be well conceived, consistent and deemed to be fair by everyone who is subjected to the policies that emanate from it. The number one golden rule on pay and reward is fairness. Why else would there be such an uproar about banking bonuses in failed banks?

So on what solid rocks can you anchor your own philosophy? What is your view on performance-related pay? Should somebody operating as a '4' (see Fig. 6.1) get the same pay as someone who is a '6'? Should a '9' get more than a '7'? Bearing in mind these are shifting sands and the '9' today may perform at '6' tomorrow?

Perhaps one starting point is to declare that, as a very minimum, the organization expects a 'decent day's work' from everyone if they are to earn their keep. 'Decent' on the curve could be deemed to be a 5 or a 6. Anyone not performing at this level will have to be managed up to it within a reasonable amount of time. So while a 4 might just qualify as acceptable, the message is they must keep trying harder. The 3's and less will be managed out of the organization after a reasonable amount of time allowed for them to change.

Alternatively, you could follow the idea that as long as someone is deemed as 'acceptable' then they can stay. This does not seem such a great option when you are suggesting to people that 'OK' is good enough. Where is the stretch towards greater value going to come from?

We have still not resolved the pay for performance issue. One answer is not to go down this road at all. It can be divisive and, like giving your kids pocket money for doing chores, how do you instil in them a more public-spirited mentality when they ask why they are not being paid for other menial jobs? If we only ever do things that we are directly paid for, rather than for all the other motivational reasons that are available (e.g. personal pride, self-esteem, the common good, charity), then we are not establishing a basis for getting the best value from what motivates people.

If you do choose to use performance related pay then at least make it worthwhile. A 1% performance bonus is more likely to be seen as insulting if it is expecting an extraordinary effort and can even dampen existing efforts. If extra performance is required by some, and it is valuable enough to pay for it, then make sure the 'contract' is clear to everyone and you should never reward one group (usually salespeople) if it is not solely their effort that makes the difference. The process/value chain should identify who really makes the most significant contribution.

Once you have your philosophy on pay worked out you are in a position to negotiate. However, anyone who has ever negotiated pay deals will know the pressure to 'just get a deal done' without thinking too far ahead. It is a great deal easier to concentrate on the immediate situation than to think long term; particularly when neither side knows how the wind will blow and does not want to limit their future options. Negotiators can be as short termist as anyone else and hope they are not around to have to deal with the consequences of the bargains they have struck. The best negotiators should anticipate as much as possible, otherwise the pigeons will always come home to roost at some time.

This is exactly what happened at UK-based airline bmi (British Midland International) in 2009.

The CEO had agreed a 3-year pay deal with its 5000 staff in 2006 that increased salaries by inflation plus 0.5% (we do not know what justification there was for a rise above inflation), but in 2009 he wrote to staff telling them that the final year of the pay deal would not be honoured because the airline needed to cut costs due to the worsening economic climate (see http://business. timesonline.co.uk/tol/business/industry_sectors/transport/article5650960.ece).

Presumably this CEO never anticipated a severe downturn in the industry, but why did the deal not include this possibility? Alternatively, why not produce a formula for pay deals that will cope with most eventualities, including a deflating economy, rather than one that will only apply during a period of inflation? Did no one consider a long-term formula for a long-term view of the business? Also, what does this tell us about the views of the staff working for bmi? Maybe it was simply a case, as it so often is, of a company failing to have a strategic approach to employee relations? Which leads us to the question of just how much influence should unions have on HR-business strategy?

HOW DO UNIONS FIT IN?

The UK in the 1960s and 1970s was a textbook case of how not to manage people, particularly unionized people. It was probably one of the most militant periods in UK history and we arrived at that point through very understandable, historical reasons including high inflation. Nevertheless, the general management approach to unions then was reactive, not strategic. It was also piecemeal (e.g. company by company in the car industry) when it needed to be coordinated and coordinated, in terms of industry wide collective bargaining (e.g. coal and power utilities), when it should have been fragmented. This played right into the hands of the unions by giving them more power. The unions played a much better short-term, tactical game than their CEO and political counterparts, even though their own strategy contributed to worsening the long-term employment prospects of their members.

As we all know, power corrupts and absolute power corrupts absolutely but the saddest comment of all on this sorry episode was that no one benefited from it eventually. Unions that fight for workers' rights that are not supported by economic success are doomed to failure (just go and ask Ford and GM's union leaders in the US). Even today, in the UK public sector particularly, national collective bargaining is still accepted in areas such as local government and higher education where it undermines management attempts to move forward and innovate. In doing so it not only inhibits an economy's competitive position it slows societal progress globally.

Obviously, the most damage is done when a union completely ignores the laws of economics and the market, but very rarely is a union in a position to do this today. One notable exception is the case of the RMT (rail) union, representing London Underground workers, which regularly abuses its 'monopoly' position just as much as Microsoft. It holds a 'gun to the head' of London commuters and London Transport negotiators by threatening (and taking) industrial action, including strikes. Throwing market considerations out of the window they have managed to negotiate inordinate pay rates for their members from particularly weak and ineffective management, whose political masters do not have the cojones to stand up against action that has no economic or moral justification.

This is what happens when pay negotiations are not anchored on any valid foundation. To avoid this happening you should be sending some very clear signals to yourself, never mind your workforce, that there is always a chance that somebody can do your job for less. This is not a very pleasant message but, like all home truths, it is inescapable. Anyone who thinks his or her living standard is protected from global, economic reality is already on the slippery slope to complacency. Equally, paying people too much produces prima donnas, whether they drive a tube train or kick a football.

If your goal is creating maximum value through maximizing human capital value then any unionist will have to put a case that says membership of a union creates value. One argument that might support this contention is that a union can play a dual role as a mouthpiece for the workforce and a conduit for feeding back the company's side of the negotiations. Without a coordinated response from the workforce negotiations become stymied. There is absolutely no problem with this logic except that a well-organized 'works council' can provide the same role without having to involve a union at all.

This is not intended to be an anti-union view. Just as with HR people, CEOs get the unions they deserve. The executives at Ford and GM could rightly be described as getting their just deserts for failing to manage employee relations strategically over many years and for taking the easy way out, passing costs onto customers, when competition was not as fierce as it is today. No, this is not anti-union. If it is anti-anything it is anti-poor-management, for not being able to help union members reconcile, in their own heads, that industrial disruption in a global economy will always be a lose–lose formula. Ultimately, union members will suffer more through poor leadership, both union and management, than they would do in a more cooperative, sustainable, value-driven environment. Those who call this naïve should read about the very painful lessons that Toyota management themselves had to learn, back in the 1950s, after a serious strike.

> Mutual trust is the basis of labour relations. Labour relations at Toyota were initially marked by doubts and disbelief, but with time differences were ironed out. The labour-management declaration we signed was simply a written statement of this rapprochement. …to uphold and sustain the trust that had been built up… and to prevent backsliding ….. It also was intended as a reminder to those who came after to guard the fruits won through the sacrifices made by both sides. …it took about 10 years for that relationship of mutual trust to take hold.
>
> Eiji Toyoda, 'Toyota – 50 Years in motion' Harper & Row 1987

This could easily be read as the signing of a truce after a bitter and hard-fought war. So better management–employee relations are not a pipe dream; it is more realistic than thinking the present situation can continue indefinitely. Of course, if you have inherited a situation of unionization then it is not an easy task to reverse and legislation is definitely not on your side in the left-leaning, social democratic model promoted by the EU.

However, HR-business strategy is not a static state. It is not a case of whether to have or not to have a union. All that is required is a clear understanding in your own mind that your organization will never be as successful as it could in a climate of fear and mistrust amongst your workforce. For it is a lack of trust in management that tends to foster union membership in developed countries. If employees trust their union representatives to look after their interests, more than their CEO, then that is a terrible indictment of senior management today.

What better way to start building trust than to declare your intention to remove any fear and duress from employee relations by moving towards an organizational state that is union-less. This journey will take some years, but until you make that first step you can guarantee that you will be living with distrust and unionization in your organization for the foreseeable future.

It is worth noting that the majority of HR directors living with unions today do not see it this way at all, which is rather worrying. A debate at the Public Sector People Managers Association (PPMA) annual conference in March 2006 http://www.personneltoday.com/articles/2006/04/04/34747/public-sector-strikes-fuel-heated-conference-debate.html

on whether 'Trade unions are no longer relevant in the modern workplace' (in which the author spoke for the motion) was overwhelmingly defeated. On what basis were these public sector HR directors voting? Perhaps some just accepted unions as a given and any notion of removing them as naïve? After all, they were having to deal with entrenched union and management attitudes every day. They might also know left wing councillors who may well have come from a union background. It might be a very fine line though, between a realistic vision, naïveté and sheer defeatism. What none of them offered was an alternative vision for unionism in the twenty-first century that might offer more sustainable value for the citizens they serve and the taxpayers paying their salaries. Nothing in HR-business strategy should ever be consigned to the impossible column.

Unions can still play a very important role for members in terms of education, advice and welfare. Also, in some parts of the world, they still have to fight tooth and nail for the basic human rights we now take for granted in the West (due in no small part to earlier union influence), but a combative role in developed countries tends to be an indicator of management weakness and lack of foresight. In 2008 Shell agreed a 14% pay deal with their striking UK tanker drivers, not because they deserved it (public opinion was outraged that they already earned 'high' salaries), but because they still regard industrial relations as something that can be treated like any other P&L item. If they can afford it they just pay for it. The drivers were not even directly employed by Shell because an earlier 'strategy' had been to outsource their tanker fleet, along with its attendant industrial relations problems. Obviously, that strategy failed as well and perhaps Shell should reconsider what corporate social responsibility means in the light of meeting excessive pay demands without any consideration of the knock on effect this might have for other employers who do not have such deep pockets. Neither was there any sense, amongst the tanker drivers' union leaders, that this deal was in any way inequitable for workers who would have to pay higher petrol prices as a result.

There are, of course, plenty of organizations that could be said to be getting along just fine without unions, but things can always change and even where no union exists an HR-business strategy should be prepared for that eventuality. A high-value organization is one where the employees have made a conscious and positive decision not to want a union negotiating on their behalf, simply because management have won their trust. A climate of positive employee relations is one of the most crucial elements in the psychological contract.

HR-BUSINESS STRATEGY NEEDS STRONG PSYCHOLOGICAL CONTRACTS

A great deal of effort has to go into managing the whole employment relationship if a strong and valuable psychological bond is to be formed. We all know that people come to work because they have to, but we know equally that a job can be much more than just work. Amongst a multitude of potential benefits it can provide a purpose in life, a feeling of satisfaction and self-esteem from pulling our weight, doing our bit, and it also offers us regular, social interaction. Yet, there is always a tension between these two primary drivers of needs and wants. Cold logic might tell us there is a need for profit driven businesses to provide many of the necessities of life but our human inclinations, particularly our relationships with others, make us equally aware that a 'business' relationship is totally different to a warm and natural friendship.

Some will also question whether the product or service they provide is 'right'. Do we really want to work for a company that sells powdered baby milk in Africa, makes gas-guzzling SUVs or charges high interest rates for loans? How many times have we heard the refrain 'I could only sell something that I really believed in'? Of course, not everyone is prone to such soul-searching or self-indulgent moralizing; for them it is just a case of getting on with the job of earning a living. In 2007 BAT (British American Tobacco) and Philip Morris were being sued by the Nigerian state of Kano for targeting their young people when marketing cigarettes. A report produced by Philip Morris from 1981 that included the phrase – 'Today's teenager is tomorrow's potential regular customer' – was cited in the legal action (*The Times*, 4 July 2007).

So why is this still an issue for HR-business strategists? The reason is simple, degrees of motivation. In the mind of the 'soul searcher' the strategic objectives of the organization have to be reconciled with their own, wider social concerns. However, in the mind of the steady employee, who comes to work every day and is happy to keep his or her head down, the need for greater momentum and progress has to be clearly established. So do you consciously try to motivate these people to do a better job or do you make sure that everyone is in a role where their own intrinsic motivation comes to the fore. The choice is between competing management philosophies of 'push' or 'pull'. A call centre operative can be either someone just earning a crust while answering the phone or someone who actually believes they are part of an organization providing an excellent, societal service. The HR-business strategist will aim to do everything possible to achieve a perfect match. Many employee grievances and discipline problems come from mismatched expectations between what is required and what the employee wants to give. Having the 'wrong' person in the wrong role, or a poor relationship between manager and employee, which can just as easily be a lack of chemistry as not seeing see eye to eye, is bound to diminish opportunities for value creation. Grievance and disciplinary hearings follow the 80:20 rule, 20% of cases take up 80% of an HR adviser's time (and probably the manager's as well). When the relationship has irretrievably broken down everyone loses out. Working hard at getting the psychological bond right has to be a win–win.

Game theory tells us that a 'zero sum game' is one where for every winner there has to be an equivalent loser. As with poker, every $ won by one player is a $ lost by another and the same could be said of derivatives traders. Zero-sum games are the antithesis of HR-business strategy because we want a win–win relationship. Our goal of mutual benefit, for employer and employee, is much more likely to generate greater total benefits than one in which one side wins and the other loses (which is how some management–union negotiators might still view the relationship). If our common goal is a satisfied customer then the company makes a profit and the employee gets paid. That is as much common sense as sound HR theory. In practice though, there is also the question of balance and equity; are the hard work and rewards shared out fairly?

If you run a restaurant and manage to negotiate with a prospective waiter or waitress to work in your restaurant for £1 per hour less than you could afford, then every £ per hour you gain is exactly matched by their 'loss' of a £ per hour. As a profit motivated businessperson you may feel that you have 'won' because your costs are lower than they could be but all you might be getting is a very basic service from this employee: deep down they feel they are not paid what they are worth. For a £ more in pay you might be able to find a much more capable recruit or achieve a much better performance from this same person, with more commitment and better potential value in terms of customer service and sales. They might even convince customers to enjoy another bottle of wine or add an extra course to their meal.

This might just sound like a repeat of the old dictum 'if you pay peanuts you get monkeys', but it is not intended to, we are looking at this from a different perspective altogether. What is going on in the mind of the employees when they take up your offer to work in the restaurant? They will have their own perception of the 'right rate for the job' and they will include in their instantaneous, mental calculation a very shrewd assessment of a whole range of factors. How hard will they have to work; how much will they like working with their prospective colleagues; are they a happy bunch and are you likely to be a miserable boss? This is a very complex calculation related directly to their own, unique, set of circumstances. They might join you simply because your joint has better transport links than the brasserie downtown or your opening hours fit better with their childcare arrangements.

Of course, you cannot know exactly what every prospective candidate is thinking and even the most sophisticated psychological instruments available will not necessarily unearth the most deep-seated motivators. Nevertheless, what we are highlighting is that pay is only one tiny element in the total psychological 'contract'. Being alive to that fact is what matters and ensuring your managers are equally alive to it every time they recruit someone is crucial.

They also to need to be alive to how fragile the psychological contract can be. An unkind word, a failure to empathize, not realizing someone is going through a difficult patch, are the defining moments of the underlying strength of this bond. Perhaps it should not need pointing out, but treating an employee in a shabby or inconsiderate way also damages the psychological contract with their colleagues. They will know that if you treat one employee like that you can treat anyone like that as well. They will also have their own, preconceived, performance curve of 'bosses' etched into their brains after previous experiences, many painful, and you want to make sure you get as high a score as you can if you want to have any chance of getting their best efforts.

When we considered the underlying theory of the performance curve (see Chapter 6) we readily acknowledged that it is the basis for the generalizations that we all tend to make. There is one generalization that probably ranks above all others – honesty. What sort of curve would accurately describe the honesty of people? Is it a curve that is heavily skewed to the right, with the vast majority of people being very honest? Or do you have a more jaundiced view of basic human nature? What psychological contract can be built on a foundation of distrust though? Honesty begets honesty and being dishonest with your employees is not just morally wrong, it is bad for business. Any decent employer knows that short-changing employees is just a clear sign of poor management and non-existent HR-business strategy.

There are other reasons why organizations are not more honest with their workforce and they are not all unscrupulous. Business is about risk, but most employees want security not risk and caring employers do not want to worry their people unduly. So there is a natural tendency, by both parties, to play this side of the contract down. Perhaps the best approach though is the realistic one of not trying to guarantee employment when you know there can be no such guarantees?

Some organizations, particularly in Japan, have been known for their policy of lifetime employment. The fundamental philosophy on which such employment relationships are based is that the best workforce is a stable workforce. Also, hopefully, a stable workforce is a highly motivated, productive and effective workforce; although this does not necessarily follow. If you value employee retention it should be an integral element of your HR-business strategy. You will not be able to offer complete protection to your employees from changing markets and the inevitable highs and lows of business fortune, but as long as the pretence of security continues maybe you will tend to engender greater loyalty among your staff.

Alternatively, maybe a simple, honest and straightforward message can be conveyed to employees along the following lines:

- There are no guarantees that the business will remain in business unless it continues to perform
- There is an inherent risk in any employment contract because no jobs can be guaranteed for life
- Businesses have to change in response to changing times so employees will have to change their roles, skills and even attitudes when necessary

This might not be what employees want to hear and could be in danger of encouraging more people to adopt the attitude of a mercenary rather than become an apostle. Yet, no one has to work for an employer for life to develop a strong bond. There are always good reasons why we might want to move on to further our career or simply to fit with a spouse's job move. This does not stop us having a strong attachment to our employer for the time we are there. We can have a very amicable parting when both sides know they have gained as much as they can from their time together. Even mercenaries can choose, at any particular point in time, whether they are just working for the money or they believe in the particular cause they are fighting; they are not mutually exclusive. It might not turn into a lengthy marriage, but that does not mean that the only alternative is to view it as a one-night stand. HR-business strategy is a pragmatic approach not a purist model.

Just before we leave the subject of psychological contracts, it is worth briefly mentioning something that has generally gone out of fashion – paternalism – because it tends to be seen as patronizing. Some insecure employees may well still value their CEO acting as a father figure and you might even welcome such a role but it is unlikely to form the basis of an effective HR-business strategy. Conversely, a ruthlessly hard-nosed attitude towards people is equally unlikely to work well. Neither of these terms is particularly helpful to the HR-business strategist because both plant an idea in an employee's mind that their employer is always faced with a mutually exclusive choice – look after your people or look after the business. This is a totally false dichotomy. Enlightened human capital management means caring for your employees *and* being business focused and it is this amalgam that is the only conceptual framework that makes any sense in true, strategic HR thinking. However, what options do you have if your organization is not a 'business'?

IS HR-BUSINESS STRATEGY APPROPRIATE WHEN THERE ISN'T A 'BUSINESS'?

The rewards that profit-making businesses can offer should help with motivation and even if executives are not driven solely by high rewards, per se, it certainly helps to keep them focused. Yet, even highly paid executives will tell you that it is not just the money itself but the kudos that money brings. This is why some banking executives and Wall Street traders turn their nose up at anything less than a multimillion $ payout. It is a measure of their standing amongst their peers; a phenomenon known more crudely as 'mine's bigger than yours'. But what about organizations that do not measure their success in terms of profit and do not even view their organization as a business? How much difference, in terms of strategic HR thinking, does it make when the organization works to a different economic model?

Employment in the other two sectors in the UK – the public sector and the 'third' sector (charities, trusts, voluntary organizations, not-for-profit and NGOs) is significant. The NCVO (National Council for Voluntary Organisations) Voluntary Sector Almanac, 2007, showed there were 611,000 paid workers in the UK voluntary sector, as well as an estimated 11 million volunteers. Recent figures also suggest that every year the sector contributes £7 billion to UK GDP and £25 billion to society overall. (LSC-P-NAT-080123 'Train to Gain and the Third Sector' – Learning and Skills Council 2007).

Yet volunteers have to be managed just as much as paid workers if their efforts are to be translated into actual value. So could or should these sectors have a similar approach to HR-business strategy? Or, more interestingly, could commercial organizations learn something from the way these organizations manage their people?

The employment model and psychological contract are very different in the public sector. Public sector employees know their employer cannot go bust because their customers, the taxpayers, are a captive audience. The demand for their service is regular (bins get emptied once a week, the library is open when they decide). All of this tends to create a very different relationship at work when compared to commercial employees who know they have to win customers and do whatever they can to hang on to them. There is even still talk of a 'public service ethos' that suggests many public servants do the job for some higher purpose than just making a living. The unsentimental HR-business strategist would just ask whether such an ethos provides the best value service to users and taxpayers; or at least better than the commercial sector could provide. If there were no evidence that this is the case then it would suggest that either this 'ethos' is a myth or has different aims.

Charities are a different model again with volunteers providing their labour for 'free' and therefore free to choose whether they stay if they do not like the way they are managed. The strategic questions are still the same – what is the charity trying to achieve, what are its objectives (e.g. running a hospice for the terminally ill) and how much value does it need to create (e.g. how many patients does it want to care for each year at what average cost and quality of care?). From this perspective all organizations are exactly the same to an HR-business strategist even if, at a microlevel, they may have slightly different policies (e.g. you allow volunteers to choose what hours they work). The options are exactly the same as those we have already covered, particularly the complete framework in Fig. 2.1. Even if several public sector organizations and agencies are jointly involved in, say, social services (e.g. truancy, foster care etc.) then how these organizations are structured both internally and externally, with cross-agency processes and the strength of the holistic system they create will determine how much value they can bring. Failure in any part of the complete system can be said to be a failure of everyone in the system. The system is a very unforgiving master and systemic failure is a mortal sin.

The Rogers Commission, that investigated the explosion of the Challenger Space Shuttle on January 28 1986, produced a lengthy (225 pages) report identifying all of the contributory factors that led to the disaster. It could all be neatly summed up in the two words, systemic failure, where the human elements in the system (interactions between management and engineers) were so obviously malfunctioning. So is systemic failure a rare and exceptional occurrence or is it more common than we might like to hope? What about systemic failures that are swept under the carpet, the ones we never see exposed but that cost society dearly every year in product recalls, train crashes, drug side-effects, abused children and unnecessary deaths?

Perhaps one sector that highlights just how 'joined up' the system needs to be is local government. The root cause of most disjointed organizations is an inability to reach clear agreement between all of their key stakeholders (e.g. council members, executive team, citizens, central government, employees) on a clear purpose, a clear statement of what value they are trying to create. This failing is usually followed closely by an inability to articulate their organizational objectives in a way that encourages each department to work together.

It is easy to see how and why each of the stakeholders can have a different perspective. Citizens want their streets swept, their refuse bins emptied and their children educated. They want as much value as they can get for their hard-earned taxes. Central government wants to control the purse strings, so this immediately places heavy emphasis on cost control. These two objectives are not necessarily conflicting but what is the attitude of local government employees? – To provide minimum services at minimum cost or to extract maximum value out of a limited budget? These are very different mindsets; very different attitudes. The added value mindset of the HR-business strategist says they should always be on a continuous journey to provide the *best services at the minimum cost*.

Meanwhile, council members get elected by citizens who judge them by the services they receive. This throws councillors into the melting pot who bring different priorities to bear; they compete to target resources at their own constituents. All of this has to be managed by an executive that could be forgiven for wondering who their masters are – central government, councillors, the public or their workforce? When described thus it is easy to see that a great deal of groundwork would need to be done before an effective HR-business strategy could be put in place in local government. At the moment local authorities could be accused of being configured in such a way that makes it impossible to formulate a coherent HR-business strategy.

Having run through some of the more obvious and most significant influences on your chances of developing a successful HR-business strategy we can now at last start to pull all of the ideas together in one document, a human capital report, that you could offer to any shareholder, stakeholder, auditor, analyst or other external observer to portray how well you are unleashing the value of your human capital.

Chapter 9

Due Diligence and Reporting on Human Capital

NO SIMPLE ALGORITHM BUT A COMPREHENSIVE REPORT

There is no single algorithm, no step 1–2–3 that can produce your HR-business strategy even though Google obviously think otherwise, according to the Wall Street Journal -.

> *Concerned a brain drain could hurt its long-term ability to compete, Google Inc. is tackling the problem with its typical tool: an algorithm. The Internet search giant recently began crunching data from employee reviews and promotion and pay histories in a mathematical formula Google says can identify which of its 20,000 employees are most likely to quit.*

http://online.wsj.com/article/SB124269038041932531.html.

Instead you need to create a complete picture, a human capital 'report', both for internal and external consumption, that will contain most of the necessary elements that keep you on the right track. This report is designed to be the antidote to that clichéd, 'motherhood and apple pie', sentimental gush – 'our people are our greatest asset'. That hackneyed phrase is not even factually correct; people are never an asset because you do not own them. They could leave you tomorrow at no cost to themselves but at a potentially great loss to you. They should not even be considered as a resource. No, the only accurate way to regard your people is to see them as highly valuable, yet temporary, capital that they rent out to you in return for a salary. When viewed in this way you have to accept full responsibility for maximizing the return on this capital while you have it at your disposal. Wasting human capital is as serious a crime as burning cash. So this human capital report is your opportunity to convince your toughest judges and critics that you manage your human capital better than any other CEO.

In Chapter 2 we saw that this was the thinking behind the short-lived Accounting for People Taskforce. The original ideas and intentions were right but the timing was probably wrong. In 2003 the global economy was booming and returns were already high, so there was less of an appetite for considering how to get more value out of the most difficult capital of all to manage, human capital. In the light of more recent events the time has come again to revisit HCM reporting. So this time around let us be absolutely clear what the purpose of this HCM report is and consider what different stakeholders might want from it. There are quite a few different and possibly conflicting agendas out there.

HCM AGENDAS

The Investment Analyst and Shareholder Agenda

Get-rich-quick speculators notwithstanding, serious investors (e.g. pension funds) want to maximize their returns and also want as high a level of confidence as possible that their investments are in a safe place. So they value organizations with a good track record of sound management combined with a responsiveness to market changes. Indicators such as Standard and Poor's (S&P) credit ratings should reinforce feelings of confidence about a company but deeper, complementary indicators of the quality of human capital management will provide very welcome reassurance that the business is a sound investment for the long term.

By now you should have started to develop your own mental list of what you would look for as indicators of whether an organization has an HR-business strategy or not. It is not a simple list though is it? Nevertheless, we need these other indicators of organizational effectiveness and sustainability because we now realize that most conventional, theoretical and proprietary assessment tools are not only fallible but can prove to be disastrous. Analysts were posting 'buy' notices on Enron stock just before it collapsed and some of the toxic debt purchased by major banks had an S&P 'triple A' rating, just before they realized they were worth less than 10 cents in the $. Extra perspectives are welcome if they can provide useful, due diligence, insights for investment or prior to mergers and acquisition activity.

Your Boardroom Agenda

Chairmen, CEOs and their boards of directors have to answer to their shareholders/stakeholders so we might assume they are all bound to have a similar agenda and would also like to maximize value. However, as a CEO, you have a slightly different perspective in that you are the one who will have to actually deliver it. So we should expect some conflicting views in boardrooms where HCM is discussed. Is it an opportunity or a threat to carrying on with business as usual? It is certainly not for the complacent or the faint hearted and if your colleagues are ignorant about what HCM is, or might achieve, then this will inevitably breed fear and resistance. So your HCM report had better convince them it is the best way forward.

The Corporate Governance Agenda

This agenda is much murkier. High-profile business collapses, the whole debacle over 'fat cat' remuneration and scandals surrounding misreporting have all combined to put corporate governance under a very harsh spotlight; even harsher than the strictures imposed by the Sarbanes-Oxley Act of 2002. Alongside this is the ongoing review of reporting requirements by the accounting and audit professions. These developments have conspired to place greater emphasis not only on more accurate and informative reports, but also some sense of the integrity of the company and its chief officers. Openness, for example, would be something to be welcomed whilst a culture of fear would be a contraindicator.

It is interesting to look back now at a piece in *Management Today* on 23 March 2007 about RBS forcing its staff to have their salaries paid into RBS accounts by sending out a heavy-handed memo referring to a 'breach of group policy'. As the article pointed out

> *their chosen means of enforcement hardly makes them look like a modern, caring and*
> *enlightened company. It's the charmless terms in which it has been couched as much as the*
> *message itself that is at fault here.*

The Political Economy Agenda

As with any political agenda this is likely to be a movable feast and any change in political priorities (e.g. a sudden drop in employment) could easily put a very different complexion on the purpose and possible benefits of an HCM report from a government perspective. Two espoused drivers for HCM are the obvious need to make an economy competitive, but also to promote human diversity. Governments are also employers of huge numbers of people so they need to learn whatever lessons they can from comparative HCM reports.

The HR Director's Agenda

You might think that the main supporter of this report, indeed the promoter of it, is going to be the HR director but HCM is not what conventional HR is about; regardless of what the sign on their office door says. HCM represents a big challenge for HR people, especially those that think their job is primarily about personnel administration, keeping employees happy, dealing with diversity, equal opportunities and union negotiations. To be told that their agenda now has only one item on it – value – is likely to be disconcerting to say the least. The majority of data held by the HR department currently (absence, staff turnover etc.) will have little if any relevance in the bigger scheme of things.

All of the agendas referred to above can be reduced into the single-item agenda of what factors contribute most to value? How do you explain the fact that some companies have a much higher market value than their competitors? How do you make the best use of intellectual capital? What makes some organizations more innovative than others? What is so different about the way the best organizations are structured? How come some have such a customer-responsive culture? This does not have to be rocket science though, because the first questions about human capital should always be common sense ones.

THE COMMON SENSE TEST

The first and best test is always The Common Sense Test. A clear statement that your company will always use a common sense approach should be part of the preamble to the report.

Our definition of this test is

What decision would 8 out of 10 intelligent managers take to improve the efficiency or effectiveness of their organisation, in the simplest way possible, given complete freedom to act without any constraints imposed?

This might be a very rough and ready definition but most conventional approaches to human resource management fail this test time and time again. Take the Magic Pill of 360-degree feedback. The first question posed by the test of common sense is always 'why are we doing this – how is it going to improve our efficiency or effectiveness?' Any other answer such as 'we want to improve working relationships' or 'listening to our people is a good idea' or even 'it will promote a more honest dialogue' all fail this test as they are meaningless unless and until the line of sight to value is articulated. They also fail the test of getting from A to B in the 'simplest way possible' because you can achieve all of those things without resorting to the cost and bureaucracy of a formal 360-degree procedure. You could simply say to a group of managers – 'go into a room and be as honest as you like with each other about how you need to work together to create more value'. It would not work well in an immature organization, but then again, would an artificial, 360 scheme stand any greater chance of success?

There is probably already a long list of similar activities taking place in your organization now so why not ask yourself – why are you sending people on training courses, managers on leadership development programmes, supporting MBAs, allowing the use of NLP (neurolinguistic programming) and other 'new age' and 'homeopathic' HR remedies? There are plenty of sensible people working in HR and training who would regard such methods as nothing more than the 'Emperor's new clothes'. Take this comment from TrainingZone on 18 February 2009:

Engage critical faculties

The best way to avoid fads would be for l&d (learning and development) people to apply some basic critical faculties, i.e. don't be so easily tempted by the appeal of the sales pitch or the extent to which the ideas reinforce our own subjective values; instead check the independent scientific evidence that backs up the theory, and/or the empirical studies showing successful application. If we'd applied this practice in the past, we would never have been saddled with all the new age pop psychology (nlp, learning styles, accelerated learning, etc.), which has arguably devalued the professional integrity of l&d and made us look like hopeless romantics.

EVIDENCE-BASED MANAGEMENT

The Common Sense Test will help you stop wasting time, energy and money on things that make no observable or tangible difference. However, after you have *stopped* doing things you still need to produce better returns. So the second killer test, and principle, will be that everything you do will be evidence based. Fortunately, if you reread everything so far you will find that this was always our direction of travel. There are no Magic Pills, silver bullets or off-the-shelf answers in HR-business strategy, only convincing evidence. The reality of the boardroom might be that there are no absolute truths, no 'rights' or 'wrongs', just winning arguments, but anything that helps you to win the argument has to be worthwhile if you want the organization to head in a direction of your choosing.

Your decision to subscribe to an overriding philosophy of evidence-based-management (EBM) should be an open declaration and one you would happily subject to audit. These are not just more 'apple pie' statements, so they need to be credible and supported with real examples. Perhaps we can learn some lessons from an industry that is founded on the principle of evidence-based science – the pharmaceutical industry? The drug discovery process is subjected to exhaustive clinical trials and many other challenging, regulatory, hurdles before it can market a new drug. So how do we know which drug company CEOs are managing their people best? Would current profits be good enough evidence of that or should we take a longer perspective and try to find more meaningful, organic indicators? Take a look at this story from GSK.

Some lessons in evidence-based-HCM for GSK

Over 10 years ago, drug company Smith Kline Beecham, now absorbed into GSK (GlaxoSmithKline as was) was trying to improve one of its key processes – drug discovery. This can take about 12 or more years, on average, from initial 'molecule' identification to actually getting the new drug onto the market. Total R&D can cost literally billions of dollars. One of the ways in which the HR team tried to improve the 'interface' (their words) between those involved in the process was by running a computer simulation, that could 'fast-forward' the discovery process in the classroom, thereby enabling the research teams to anticipate the long term implications of their decision making. It was a highly innovative approach but failed the common sense test of 'why exactly are we doing this?' There were no pre-measured, value objectives linked to this simulation of either increasing the number of drugs produced (O), reducing the cost (C), improving the quality (Q) or even aiming to attract a higher price (R) and nobody involved was to be held accountable for a specific improvement.

The company's drug discovery capability did not measurably improve over subsequent years. How do we know this? Because some years later their new CEO, Jean Pierre Garnier, made a presentation at his 'Inaugural Investor Meeting' in 2001, which set out his 'Strategic Platform – Top 6 Priorities' including what he called GSK's 'R&D Productivity Crisis'. Between 1980 and 2000 R&D spend increased 15-fold from $2 billion to $30 billion for an increase in new product approvals of just 50%.

Since then Garnier had tried everything to resolve this serious issue and one specific action was to reorganise the whole of R&D into separate Centres of Excellence in Drug Discovery (CEDD's) that were meant to operate like independent companies, with a more entrepreneurial and competitive spirit. Much like many of the smaller, genuinely independent, start-ups in biotechnology that GSK is increasingly having to compete with. In the Times on 2 April 2007 he remarked that "I don't think competition is bad for society. I think it makes us better, sharper,

Continued

tougher and more cost-effective. .... It's what creates drugs. We discover drugs because otherwise we die as a company." So how well did that work?

On 12 December 2007 Moncef Slaoui, who had just been appointed GSK's head of R&D (shortly before Garnier's departure in 2008) was reported in the Financial Times as 'predicting that, within a few years, half of GSK's experimental drugs would come from external partners compared with about one in 10 now'.

Against a long and very mixed history of trying to resolve this issue perhaps GSK could learn many lessons about defining the problem more clearly at the outset. If the problem is a lack of 'entrepreneurialism', as suggested by Garnier, then perhaps this is another classic HR-Catch 22; entrepreneurs, by definition, want to run their own show, they don't want to be employees. Even if GSK still wanted to follow this avenue then it should attach value measures to any attempts to improve things; even one new, blockbuster drug is worth billions of dollars so it could be worth offering these entrepreneurs very large incentives that would make everyone else's salaries look miniscule in comparison. Perhaps a better idea would be to work with the strengths of their R&D people rather than trying to turn them into something they are not. Alternatively, if GSK's strategy is based on a vision of the future that they would be better off managing a whole host of outside laboratories then it should start structuring itself accordingly. The new GSK would be totally different from the old though. This would be a revolutionary HR-business strategy.

DAMN LIES AND STATISTICAL INTEGRITY

EBM is difficult enough in operational management but in HCM it is particularly fraught simply because it is rarely linear. There is hardly ever a simple, causal connection between what employees do and how the organization produces value. If Coca Cola's success depends primarily on the strength of its brand, for example, then how can you discern whether the salespeople are selling the product well or not? Customers might buy it regardless of the sales pitch or the ability of the salesforce. Causation has always been a thorny issue in human resource management theory. The vacuum left by the academics, who failed to resolve this question satisfactorily, has been enthusiastically filled by every charlatan who has a particular Magic Pill to sell. Where academic studies suggest they have resolved the causation question we need to look very carefully at their methodology to ensure their statistics are not just more 'damn lies'.

As recently as 2008 a study entitled 'People and the bottom line' (Report 448, Tamkin, Cowling and Hunt, IES, 2008)

http://www.employment-studies.co.uk/pubs/report.php?id=448

tried to show a connection between HR practices and 'the bottom line'. The methodology was a questionnaire that was reduced down to a series of statistics that were then correlated with measures such as 'profit margin' (see section 4.3.5 of the Report). By using the statistical technique of *regression analysis* they try to convince us that good HR practices do indeed lead to better profit margins. Yet it is so easy to demonstrate how regression analysis is fatally flawed.

Regression analysis attempts to correlate many different factors that supposedly influence some of society's most intractable problems. What are the connections, for example, between sex education, poverty, welfare benefits, broken homes and teenage pregnancies? This is a murky cocktail that we try to unravel by asking the questions 'what causes what?' and of all of these 'chickens' which 'egg' hatched first? This is a bit like saying, which of the ingredients in a cocktail makes it taste like a vodka martini? Is it the vodka, the Martini, the olive, the temperature of the glass or the fact it is shaken not stirred? Of course, this is a ridiculous question that only the most theoretical academic would even try to resolve. Perhaps we just have to accept deconstruction cannot answer every question.

All the bartender needs to know is, do customers keep buying the cocktails? That's the bottom line. So an evidence-based, human capital report does not have to become embroiled in this sort of sterile debate, picking over every individual ingredient; all it has to do is produce evidence that wins the argument on human capital practices. This leads you to exactly where you need to be in terms of human capital management. Become evidence based, in the way you see the world, think and act. Evidence-based HCM offers a healthily sceptical attitude to what works and what does not. Jeffrey Pfeffer and Robert Sutton in their book 'Hard Facts' (HBS, 2006) tell us that managers

> ...are trapped by their beliefs and ideologies. Their observations are contaminated by what they expect to see.

This appears to describe conventional HR academic studies perfectly. The researchers want to see happy employees being effective employees, but life just isn't that simple and correlations, no matter how convincing they might look, cannot be transformed into causation through the sort of jiggery-pokery that regression analysis performs.

EB-HCM will not provide the perfect answer to the question of does A cause B, but what it will do is set out its stall very clearly. So if you are running an annual staff engagement survey the first thing you include in your HCM report is a statement of how it is meant to add value. If you think smiling at customers has a direct, causal impact on customer retention and referrals then the survey should not be undertaken until that hypothesis is tested. So how do you do that?

Well, first let us assume that you already have a strategic objective of needing more sales; otherwise this idea would get no further. You could then choose to employ an academic institution to carry out an IES-type study or you could do it the common sense way. First, find a group of employees who openly admit to smiling a lot at customers (this is a serious suggestion). Next, you arrange for this group, entirely with their willing agreement, to work in a business unit for a week where you already have baseline data on existing sales. If you wanted to make a nod or a wink towards academic rigour you might also monitor a similar group, a control group, where no changes were planned. Then, at the end of the week, you would compare the sales in the two units.

You might think, on first impressions, that this all sounds rather amateurish when compared to the 82-page report produced by the IES. Except that their study was ex post and yours is ex ante. It wins hands down on that basis alone, but we have not come to the most important part yet; what you do with the findings from this quick and dirty exercise. Yes, the exercise is unashamedly quick and dirty, especially the first time you try it. Pfeffer and Sutton refer to the concept of treating your organization like an 'unfinished prototype', one that is designed for and run by real people, not laboratory rats. People who are already doing what they believe is their best to sell to the customer. They will know instinctively and intuitively, by living the experience, whether something is happening but their gut reactions will mean nothing if the sales figures do not improve.

If they, themselves, conclude that they got something wrong on their first attempt they might ask permission to try it out again for another week, with a few of their own changes. One way or another, their own beliefs will eventually be confirmed or they will realize that the 'smiley' idea had no mileage in it. Either way, the lessons would be noted and shared for future use. HCM is not about statistics, correlations or regression analysis; it is about human beings being human beings, doing things that come naturally to them like trial and error (or heuristic if you prefer the jargon). The only difference, in an HCM organizational setting, is that the system should ensure all trial and error eventually results in effective practice.

The biggest, and most ironic, criticism facing academic studies into HR practices is the very fact that they have to produce any studies at all – proof itself that no one had been convinced of the value of the HR practice at the time it was enacted. Yet how many people do you know who put more faith in academic studies than they do in their own experiences? One of the sponsors of the IES study was Investors in People (see Chapter 7) because it is still trying to promote the idea that their scheme shows a causal connection to the bottom line. Would any clear-headed, CEO make a significant investment on such flimsy and questionable 'evidence'?

One very sound principle to follow is that people believe their own data. They do not trust anyone else's half as much. This is why some smokers shrug off fears of premature death by referring to their 'grandfather who smoked all his life and lived to 90' (if they did not have such a grandfather they will refer to someone else's) to justify their habit. We all see the contradictory evidence from medical researchers who seem to keep changing their minds about whether red wine or chocolate are bad for you or not. In the absence of a convincing 'truth' we might as well make up our own minds. This is another reason why performance targets imposed by central government are of little use in getting people to perform better because they are 'not invented here'. Plus, if you really want to switch people off, just give them the slightest reason to believe that they are being treated as just another, anonymous statistic.

Government departments, local authorities, the police and the NHS have come to believe that large populations can only be managed using such statistical methods. To the regression analyst we are all just so many standard deviations from the statistical norm and as such 'deviants' in need of treatment. Yet, counting numbers, such as UK teenage pregnancies, has done nothing to manage their inexorable rise. What might be a standard deviation to the statistician is a total loss of personality for the individual concerned. As a technique it makes social science numbers impersonal and encourages society to try and manage people impersonally, un-socially. This in turn results in arm's-length policy development and governments throwing money at 'problems' (e.g. Sure Start Centres to deal with child care problems) rather than actually dealing with the people themselves, as individuals and finding out the unique, root causes of their unique situation.

Perhaps all the HCM report needs under this section is a simple statement that 'we do not treat our people as a number or our customers as a statistic'. It is very easy to support this and demonstrate you are doing it in practice. Trying out the simple idea suggested above would at least be evidence that you mean what you say.

GOOD AND BAD POLITICS

One thing that could get in the way of all this common sense is office politics. Although we need to make a very clear distinction here between what could be called 'normal political discussions' and the sort of corrosive 'Yes, Minister' politics that have nothing to do with organizational performance (and are killing the civil service). One is entirely valid and to be expected in even the most mature organizations while the other is a disease that blights and frustrates those who actually want to do a good job.

Only the most naïve would assume that executive teams always get along so well that there are no politics, but there is a huge difference between 'normal' organizational politics, that stem from genuine disagreements about the best options for the future and the type of politics that is linked to the purely selfish agendas of greed, ambition and career protection. The need for Sainsbury's supermarket to want to win market share from its rival Tesco probably makes a great deal of sense. However, the commercial director at Sainsbury's will balance the company's goals with their own personal agenda ('how do I make sure I come out of this smelling of roses?') and could lead to them trying to ensure they are only measured on market share (sales volume) rather than value (margin and profitability) and therefore 'buy' the results they need with price cuts. A non-political approach would always focus on value and, ideally, long-term value at that.

So how do you pick this up in terms of HCM indicators on your report? Well the organization simply has to declare how its decisions are based on value, what that value is (e.g. increasing profitable growth in market share over the next 10 years) and that all executives are managing their own areas on this basis. To back this up, at least one example could be given of how everyone is managing value rather than resorting to their market dominance to squeeze suppliers. So to what extent are suppliers part and parcel of the value chain and do they actively engage in the process of reducing their costs without reducing the quality of their goods? Who is employed by the supermarket to work with suppliers and is there a commonly understood 'total quality' methodology in place? An even simpler check would be to monitor the quality of a particular product over time. Tesco's 'Finest' range today does not seem to be as fine as it was when it was launched. There is a strong suspicion that Tesco has a culture of squeezing suppliers that results in a downward rather than an upward trend in quality and value for money.

As with all the indicators we are exploring there will always be a natural, human tendency, from those who are not really committed, to want to 'tick the box'. The Investors in People scheme has been running for nearly 20 years and the fact that it still commissions reports on its effectiveness shows that it has not earned any kudos with CEOs who want hard evidence of its value. This must mean that plenty of organizations are achieving the standard (sic) simply by impressing the assessors who accredit the scheme, with lots of boxes ticked for their appraisal schemes, training courses and every other activity deemed to be 'good practice'.

Ticking boxes will never impress an insightful and shrewd HR-business analyst because they would very quickly get underneath the skin of such superficial schemes. Once there is evidence that the whole subject is taken seriously (at board level) there is nothing to stop us grading qualitative impressions on a 1 to 10 scale. For example, there are 'appraisal schemes' and then there are appraisal schemes. Holding these 'every six months' might get a high score from some HR traditionalists whereas the HCM report would only give a high score where there was clear evidence that

• Value objectives had been discussed
• A feedback loop was set up to check real progress
• All relevant parties were clearly involved
• All parties to the appraisal saw it as a positive and constructive experience

A score of 8 would be extremely rare and only likely to happen where everyone involved was acutely aware that an effective learning system was the bedrock of everything. To get a 10 there would be no predetermined appraisal schedule, it would still be very systematic but would happen naturally, whenever the most appropriate opportunity arose.

This would be a true indicator of HR-business strategy and an organization at Stage 6 on the HR Maturity Scale. It also reveals two more paradoxes of human capital management,

the more you focus on measurable value the less you actually have to measure,

the more mature (and sophisticated) your organisation becomes the less you have to manage it.

So, in addition to these 'impressionistic' indicators what other signs should we be looking for?

A WORKING EXAMPLE OF AN HCM REPORT

Deciding what to report internally will be a matter for your own judgement, but any reluctance to provide detailed indicators of HCM would reveal a lack of confidence. An unwillingness to share information with employees would also suggest that you have not really embraced the sort of open and honest communication philosophy that one would associate with an HCM strategy. How much you might want to report externally is a different proposition.

Any board director might be understandably reluctant to display any information that was of a highly sensitive, commercial or competitive nature. It would be naïve to suggest you reveal any more information than you have to, unless you think it would enhance your reputation and share price. Leaving those provisos to one side, Table 9.1 shows a summary HCM report containing some of the indicators that should convince any interested party whether you really have a strategic handle on your human capital. This should form part of the complete, annual company report.

NOTES, NARRATIVE AND INTERPRETATIONS OF THE HCM REPORT

The first general note is that this is not meant to be a report that adheres to any existing accounting and auditing conventions but rather enhances them by offering a totally different perspective. We could go much further and declare that HCM reporting abhors the traditional type of auditing practice that takes static snapshots of organizations and breeds fear every time it arrives for its next inspection. This report is not part of an inspection regime, more an opportunity for people in the organization to monitor their own progress. There is nothing here for any individual to fear if they are working in a highly mature organization.

It is explicitly designed to challenge those conventions with a view to shaking up complacent management thinking. An HCM analyst will already be capable of seeing through the obfuscation, smoke and mirrors of normal company reports and will want to pose many serious questions that need to be asked that check out the very heart of the enterprise.

No single piece of data should be given too much weight in isolation. This is why our recommendation is that additional notes on the more qualitative indicators need to be written (e.g. line 35: organization structure – type) and the report presented as part of a complete narrative of how the organization is developing, year on year. It is the overall picture, determined by an in-depth analysis of a range of variables and factors that will provide an accurate impression and a level of confidence as to whether the organization is managing its human capital well.

It is also worth reminding ourselves that all rating scales, whether they are credit rating agencies such as Moody's or an accredited scheme, like Investors

TABLE 9.1 XYZ plc – Human Capital Report

	Indicator	2009–2010	2010–2011	Variance +/−
1	Turnover – sales (£000's)	£100,000	£105,000	**£5,000**
2	Operating costs (£000's)	£ 90,000	£96,000	(£6,000) 6.6%
3	Operating profit (£000's)	£ 10,000	£9,000	(£1,000) − 10%
4	Share price high/low (£)	5.50/4.50	5.60/5.00	**+0.10/+0.50**
5	Market value/capitalization (£000's) – share price × total shares	£1,000,000	£1,060,000	**£60,000**
6	Book value (£000's)	£300,000	£270,000	(£30,000)
7	'Intangible' value = market value − book value (£000's)	£700,000	£790,000	**£90,000**
8	Nominal number of named 'employees' registered on 'payroll' including contractors	10,000	9800	−2%
9	Total number of hours paid (= FTEs)	18,400,000	18,032,000	−2%
10	Total number of hours actually worked	26,000,000	27,300,000	+5%
11	Employee years (46 weeks @ 35 hours)	16,149	16,956	+5%
12	Turnover per employee year (1 ÷ 11)	£6192	£6192	=
13	Operating cost per employee (2 ÷ 11)	£5573	£5661	+£88
14	Profit per employee year (3 ÷ 11)	£619	£530	(£89)
15	Intangible value per employee year (7 ÷ 11)	£43,346	£46,591	**£3245**
16	Number of key employees	300	295	−5
17	Raw staff turnover (last 12 months)/target	12% / 8%	10% / 8%	**−16.6%**
18	Staff turnover – unplanned/unwanted	4%	8%	+100%
19	Average length of service (LOS – in years)	4.00	3.75	−0.25
20	Stability 3/12/36 months (%)	95/88/60	90/85/55	−5/-3/-5

Continued

TABLE 9.1 XYZ plc – Human Capital Report—cont'd

	Indicator	2009–2010	2010–2011	Variance +/−
21	Inexperienced workers (<6 months)	1080	950	−130
22	Key employees who left this year	12	15	+3
23	New key employees added	6	8	**+2**
24	Key employee staff turnover	4%	5%	+1%
25	Key employee average LOS (years)	6.0	5.5	−0.5
26	Job offers turned down – actual / %	120/10%	150/15%	+30/+5%
27	Key employee job offers turned down – actual/%	12/60%	5/4%	**−7/−56%**
28	Average time taken to fill a vacancy (months)/target – all employees	3.0/2.5	4.0/2.5	+1.0/=
29	Average time taken to fill vacancy (months)/target – key employee	9.0/6.0	8.0/6.0	**−1.0/=**
30	HR function activity/spending – Box 1/2/3	75/5/20	70/15/15	**−5/+10/−5**
31	Training and development activity/spending – Box 1/2/3	55/5/40	70/20/10	**+15/+15/−30**
32	Performance management system – in place (years)/% jobs covered	1.0/10%	2.0/50%	**+1.0/+40%**
33	Learning system – in place (years)	1.0	2.0	**+1.0**
34	Innovation – ideas implemented per annum as % of total employees/value (£000's p.a.)	300%/£2,000	275%/£2,500	−25%/+£500
35	Organization structure – type	Classic silo	Silo to Matrix	+
36	Process changes – number/time taken	5/3 months	25/2.5 months	×5/−0.5
37	Employee engagement index (survey)	75%	80%	+5%
38	Quality assurance system	PDCA	PDCA	+
39	Unionization	80%	80%	−
40	Maturity stage – HR/Learning	2/2	3/2	+1/=

in People, are only as useful as the credibility they earn with investment analysts and market observers. The list of indicators included in this report is not exhaustive and different organizations might want to emphasize different aspects; such as a rate of innovation or a steeply declining, operating cost curve. However, if decision makers do not perceive an association between what the HCM report is saying and what the market is telling them, then it will not be worth the paper it is written on.

The variances column on an HCM Report show how problematic a '+' or a '−' can be when assessing human capital. Many of these indicators can be interpreted as both positive and negative signs depending on the specific circumstances. So each one has to be considered carefully if we are to understand what it is telling us or in which direction it is pointing. Perhaps the most obvious examples of this are the staff turnover and stability figures in lines 15 to 18. The key question you have to ask yourself is always 'did these indicators move the way we planned for them to move?' High and low staff turnover figures could be 'good' or 'bad'. Planned staff turnover, which gets rid of the right people, can be a positive sign of effective HCM. Losing people you need to keep is a negative. In order to provide a quick overview though, we have shown the items deemed to be beneficial, on this particular occasion, in bold type. Yet, even these cannot be accepted at face value and would require further investigation.

The crucial point to remember is that any HCM report will be open to a range of interpretations, which makes it no different to any other analytical report. It should convey continuity from year to year so that confidence grows over time. No business analyst likes to receive a nasty shock (e.g. a sudden loss of key people) because it shatters any confidence they had in the sound management practices of the leaders of the business. That is why some narrative on background issues such as the prevailing ethos of common sense, the quality of evidence presented and the political climate will always need to be weighed appropriately.

If we have to highlight particular features though, these would be among the top 40.

Lines 1 to 3 – Turnover, Costs, Profit

This conventional 'performance' data will already exist and is only included here in order to perform calculations in subsequent lines.

Where the 'company' is a public sector or non-profit organization, there will still have to be some simple numbers of the total, perceived value. The simplest definition of the 'value' of a commercial company is the revenue it brings in. Exactly the same argument can be applied to any state funded organisation (say a hospital) only in that case the 'value' is how much the taxpayer is willing to pay to run the hospital, even though the hospital would view this as its total 'cost'. In practice, the hospital's total value could be regarded as total state funding plus any additional charges for treatment or other revenue raised. The number of patients treated could then be divided by this number to denote 'value per patient'.

e.g.

Hospital funding (tax income)	£100 million
Additional charges and other revenue	£10 million
Private patient income	£15 million
Total	£125 million
Number of patients treated	125,000
Value per patient (£125 million ÷ 125,000)	£1000

Lines 4 to 7 – Share Price and Changes in Market Value/Capitalization

These figures are not just an acknowledgement that a distinction is often made by accountants between tangible and intangible 'assets' but to specifically attribute some of this differential value to human capital in lines 13 and 15. Referring to 'intangible value' as 'human capital value' is intended to put a very definite emphasis on the HCM slant of the whole report.

Lines 8 to 11 – Number of Employees and How Many Hours Worked

Most organizations will already measure numbers employed and full time equivalents (FTEs) based on including the hours paid for part timers and temporary workers. The HCM report also needs to include all consultants, other external suppliers and contractors that are already included in the total cost in line 8. This should help to highlight any managers that give the impression of reducing staff costs by making people redundant and bringing them back as contractors instead. The figure in line 8 would be a simplistic, nominal sum of all the different names (national insurance numbers?) on both the company's and the contractor's payroll. Line 9 then shows how many hours were paid for.

The big difference to normal reporting though comes on line 10 by showing how many *actual hours* these personnel have worked, including all overtime *and all unpaid hours*. This is a specific recommendation to record *all* worked hours properly, whether worked at home, on the road, outside the normal working day or at any other time. This should also include all travel time on company business (but not personal commuting time unless that is used for working as well).

Why do we recommend you do this? Because you need to know *literally* how hard your human capital is working to produce current value. In the 'actual hours' will be included all the re-work, mistakes and errors that arise from poor planning, design and training so you should want actual hours to decrease over time. Looking at this figure is also intended to prompt you to encourage people only to work *valuable hours* and to reduce *non-value, presenteeism*. It should also keep any tendency to a 'long hours are good' culture at bay and can be used as a pressure valve indicator of how much underlying stress is building up.

This does not mean you have to deter anyone from working as hard as they choose. It just means you have to consider how many of those hours are really productive and effective. Dedicated individuals can work very long hours and produce fantastic results but they can also make mistakes from fatigue. They also tend to expect those who work around them to be equally as committed. It is this second group that we need to manage better because they might only 'put the hours in' because they believe they have to, not because they are doing anything particularly useful.

By the way, if you think this level of detail on actual hours worked is unrecordable just go and visit a law firm to find out how they calculate and bill every 6 minutes of a lawyer's time (you will also start to realize why your legal bills are so exorbitant). They make sure they get the customer to pay for every minute they expend on a case. The HCM report is asking whether you are doing the same with your customers? If you are an engineering company, for example, are all the hours spent on design modifications generating value and being passed onto the customer? Or how about recording actual hours on any project, not for allocation of costs, but as a much better guide to how well the project is being managed? A very obvious, but nevertheless very sobering, thought that an HCM Report should drive home.

So the computation for line 11 is based on the total number of hours actually recorded divided by the number of minimum hours expected of a normal, full time employee (say 35) over say a 46-week year (52 weeks – 6 weeks for holidays and anticipated absence). This will produce a figure that shows, with much greater accuracy, how much human capital or 'employees-worth of effort' or input is being expended. The calculation would be

$$26,000,000 \text{ actual hours} \div 46 \text{ weeks} \div 35 \text{ hours per week}$$

$$= 16,149 \text{ 'employee years'}$$

You can, of course, choose whatever computation you wish and make it as sophisticated as you like as long as you follow the two principles of

- Keeping the formula the same for the baseline figure and subsequent calculations for comparison
- Ensuring everyone who sees this figure accepts that, while it may be a 'guesstimate', it is credible enough to ask some serious questions

When you fully understand these lines you can ask some simple questions as to what they reveal about the way XYZ plc has achieved a 5% increase in turnover and yet is making 10% less profits. From an employee's perspective they seem to be putting in more hours without seeing any benefit for it. This is exactly how the HCM Report should be analysed and interpreted.

Lines 12 to 15 – Profit and Value per Employee Year

These show all the key £ sign numbers related to the real employee years being expended of which only 'line 15 – Intangible value' has improved and this could be for many other reasons to do with the share price.

Lines 16 to 29 – Acquiring and Retaining Talent

This series of indicators, when taken as a group, are all concerned with the organization's ability to bring the people it needs on board and to keep them. The figures for XYZ plc reveal a picture of poor people acquisition and talent retention. The workforce is already being diluted in terms of length of experience and an apparent inability to hold key employees or replace them adequately. But before anyone rushes off and starts suggesting the Magic HR pill of offering better rewards or 'golden handcuffs' we need to stress that this is just an overview; it is not intended to lead to immediate action. Whatever conclusions we might want to jump to, the most we should expect from this report is to point us in the direction of an investigation into the problem; root-cause analysis will always be our guide and that is why HCM analysts place their absolute trust in this particular tool.

Lines 30 and 31 – HR and Training Department Activity

These are the only two lines that specifically refer to the HR and training functions and both use the simple three-box priority system (see Chapter 5) to review where they are spending their time and resources. As a rule of thumb, both departments are likely to be spending about 75% of their time on Box 1, business as usual, priorities (legislative advice, basic training etc.) The '55/5/40' figure shown on line 31 for 2009–2010 is how the training budget is currently spent between the three boxes. These figures would be a cause for serious concern because it looks much too light on necessities (Box 1) and too heavy on frivolities (Box 3). Over time, we should expect to see Box 1 efficiencies being found to save money and more time and effort devoted to Box 2; the source of most innovations and improvements. Box 3 should tend towards zero but there is always likely to be a residual amount of activity that cannot be justified in hard value terms but is still supported for other reasons. For example, you might want to try out some new HR methods (e.g. employee assessment tools) or test one or two experimental learning activities, such as more technology-based training delivery.

Lines 32 and 33 – Learning and Performance Systems

These are probably the two most important systems in any organization (see Chapters 3 and 6). The three questions that need to be asked are

- Is there a system in place?
- Is it an effective system (is it working properly)?
- How long has it been in place?

Two years would be a minimum to embed either a learning or decent performance management system. A company that maintains these systems for over 5 years would be achieving a significant advantage over their less-prescient competitors.

You might notice that we do not have a line for 'Knowledge management', a subject in which you might expect any HCM analyst to have an interest. There is a very simple reason for this, knowledge has no intrinsic value. Tacit knowledge, knowledge databases and using technology (e.g. video conferencing) to 'share knowledge' are meaningless in the absence of an applied learning system. If knowledge management is a 'system' then it is a subsystem that is always subordinated to the learning system. So a line referring to increasing use of e-learning or video conferencing would not be deemed, in itself, to be of any value. A reduction in project times, after a conscious effort to check the knowledge application of all involved, would start to suggest that knowledge is valued and used well.

Line 34 – Innovation

Of course, you will need a whole system HR-business strategy, and an innovative culture to match, if all of your employees are likely to be motivated enough to want to offer you their brainpower and show an appetite for being creative. Line 34 just looks at how you measure the results of the system. It follows a simple, well-established formula to measure ideas created and implemented.

$$\frac{\text{Ideas implemented}}{\text{Number of employees}} \times 100\%$$

$$\text{e.g.} \quad \frac{30,000 \text{ ideas}}{10,000 \text{ employees}} \times 100\% = 300\%$$

So a figure of 300% would indicate an average of three ideas per employee, fully costed and successfully implemented. That might sound a lot until you realize Toyota achieves 500% plus per year. A more detailed break down of these figures could be used, internally, to get everyone thinking about innovation. A performance curve could also easily be produced based on how many ideas each employee has generated.

Line 35 – Organizational Structure

Organizational structure is a crucial indicator of HCM. A poorly structured organization is bound to put a limit on the value of the human capital investment. It is a subject worthy of a book in its own right but despite the mass of literature available there really are only two broad options. The classic, hierarchical structure is the 'pyramid' with the board overseeing everything and the CEO controlling the operation by means of reporting lines through major functions (operations, finance, sales etc.). This passes the two common sense tests of

- Everyone knowing whom they report to and
- No one having more than one boss

This classic model is fraught with all sorts of problems though, including each function being seen as a separate empire, discouraging cross-functional cooperation and the sort of rigidity that stems from turf wars and each functional head protecting their territory.

The main alternative to this model is a matrix approach that is designed to avoid most of the weaknesses just highlighted. Except that matrix organizations have their own weaknesses built in and they break the two common sense rules just mentioned because you can end up having more than one 'boss' and multiple reporting lines.

In *Project Management* (by Gray and Larson, McGraw Hill, 2005) they try to explicate these two structural options along a continuum:

- Functional
- Weak Matrix
- Balanced Matrix
- Strong Matrix

Line 35 therefore tries to convey not only what type of organizational structure is in place but a sense of how mature the organization's attitude is towards its structure. A conventional, hierarchical organization chart does not automatically mean a 'silo' or 'stovepipe' mentality and a matrix organization does not guarantee more flexibility or cooperation. What matters is how grown up the key players are. Acknowledging this is what makes it a useful indicator, but it also has to be viewed in connection with line 40 – Maturity, to gain a more accurate impression.

You could even include more lines here to highlight how the organization is structured according to

- Geographical regions
- Product/Service lines
- Operating Divisions
- Federations
- Partnerships and/or collaborations

But each would have to provide insight into how they were working rather than just a factual statement of what they are. This would require some narrative that indicated a level of sophistication and nuance in organizational understanding. How well do the engineers work with marketing or production? This represents a particular challenge for governments wanting a range of departments and agencies to work in a 'joined up' way. How well do the police work with social services and schools, for instance? The best way to join everyone up is to treat them as one large organization and then follow the same principles of organization design, particularly the ultimate need for accountability resting with a single head.

Line 36 – Operational Process Changes

Processes are the other main organizational building block and dictate work-flow; well-designed processes should enable smooth and efficient operations. If organizational structure is the main, architectural framework then processes are the plumbing. Line 36 simply asks how many operational processes have been changed and how long, on average, they took to change. Here, XYZ plc has just started to learn this lesson and the number of processes has increased fivefold but it still takes, on average, 2.5 months to achieve a process change.

This should not be read as a simplistic activity measure. A process change will only guarantee improvement, progress and added value if it is managed well, based on premeasured, value objectives (O, C, R, Q). All process changes should save money (cost and time improvements) and/or provide better, measurable, customer service. They are only likely to do so if everyone involved in the process is aware of the purpose of the change and fully trained to operate the new process competently.

An organization's ability to change its processes, at will and with a minimum of fuss and politics, is of paramount importance in terms of responsiveness, flexibility, agility and adaptability. These words are usually regarded as intangibles but measuring the process in this way makes them all very tangible.

This line also provides an insight into organizational politics. Highly politicized organizations find it very difficult to change even the most basic processes because no one cooperates across the silos and turf wars abound.

Line 37 – Employee Engagement

We have explored the whole issue of employee engagement in some detail, but despite all the provisos and caveats it is still on the main list of HCM indicators. As we have already demonstrated (in Chapter 4), an engaged workforce will not automatically be an efficient or effective workforce. Engagement is probably a *necessary* condition for HCM, but it is certainly not sufficient. Any instrument used to complete this line should not be an off-the-shelf survey (e.g. Gallup Q12) and there should always be some questions included to make direct links between employees' views on their level of engagement and their own contribution to value.

Line 38 – Quality Assurance System

Do you have a quality assurance system in place already that builds quality into the process? Or are you still in 'quality control' mode and having to inspect everything before you try to resolve any problems arising? Is your QA system being used as a real, human *system* or is it a bureaucratic, tick-box, auditing procedure? A proprietary methodology (e.g. ISO) or accreditation might be one indicator but here we are looking for two things:

- Is it part of your learning system (if you use PDCA it should fit perfectly)
- Is it happening naturally? Would any visitor be able to see small groups working through a real PDCA exercise?

A contraindicator would be lots of quality manuals and framed certificates gathering dust.

Some organizations might be tempted to put 'lean' in this line but that, in isolation, would not be an indicator of anything. Some narrative would have to show that the organization really understands that 'lean' is not a management method in its own right but part of a complete philosophy.

Line 39 – Unionization

Unionization cannot be used as an isolated indicator either. Employees are members of unions for all sorts of reasons, some of them very valid (education and professional standards). This line is asking whether it is something you are trying to change. A drop in declared union membership will only signal a positive change in employee relations if your narrative backs this up. This requires a coherent response to unionization and one that sees the pursuit of maximum human value as being of mutual benefit to all.

Serious industrial relations problems are, of course, a strong contra-indicator, but these would usually be quite apparent to customers and even the general public without needing a specific mention (e.g. BA's strikes at Heathrow always hit the headlines and passengers know what it feels like to be stranded). Probably more important would be some acknowledgement from the executive that even when employee relations are not causing any disruption the strength of the union could still be having a negative influence on decision making and make the executive feel hidebound.

Line 40 – HR and Learning Maturity

This is a simple statement at which stage you think the organization currently stands on the two scales in Figs 3.3 and 5.2. The narrative should express what stage you need to attain and how that is linked in to your overall HR-business strategy.

CASTING A CRITICAL, HUMAN CAPITAL EYE OVER SOME REAL ORGANIZATIONS

The main intention of producing HCM reports is that one day organizations will start to attach as much importance to these indicators as they do (or used to) a Standard & Poor's triple A. This is not going to happen overnight but the collapse of companies who used to have such ratings is bound to lead observers to seek other ways of assessing underlying organizational behaviour and the long-term impact it might be having. In 2005 this approach to HCM Reporting led to the Newbury Index (www.TheNewburyIndex.com) to provide just such a readily recognized assessment of HCM and to mirror the widely accepted, 'S&P' type of rating.

To the professional HR-business strategy analyst, whose sole criterion is seeking maximum value from human capital, it is very easy to apply some of the simple lessons in this book to existing organizations. What becomes crystal clear, immediately, is just how many organizations are built on totally different foundations. You might regard some of the insights and recommendations that follow controversial. What might surprise you though is just how much evidence there is that organizations are so obviously failing to capitalize on their people.

HR-business strategy and issues of human capital management are all high-level matters (that was how the UK Government's Accounting for People Taskforce defined it) and obvious failings in this area are costing not just companies but national economies dear. So the brief analyses presented here are not meant to be revelatory, rather just a restatement of the blindingly obvious, in the hope that this might spur some effective action rather than more of the same old Magic Pills. Although they might look like a random, mixed bag, each one addresses HR-business strategy issues of epic proportions and significant lessons need to be learned sooner or later. All the issues we have highlighted suggest very simple solutions, but are in need of that extremely rare commodity, strong leadership, if they are ever to succeed.

THE UK NATIONAL HEALTH SERVICE (NHS)

The UK NHS employs approximately 1.3 million people and currently costs around £100 billion to run every year. Its biggest problem is its size. The management book on how to manage an organization this size has not been written yet. So few exist, and the Indian railways and the Chinese Red Army are not generally known for their enlightened, management expertise. The person nominally 'in charge' of the NHS is the health Secretary; currently the Right Honourable Alan Johnson, an ex-union official from the Post Office (where one of the most outdated, industrial relations environments in the UK still exists). We say 'nominally' in charge though because the de facto situation is that the medical profession rules the NHS; what the doctors say, goes. On paper, each individual NHS Trust CEO is responsible for their own Trust and you can trace a reporting line all the way up to the top, albeit through many layers of strategic health authorities and other multifarious NHS bodies. A CEO would not be allowed to directly manage doctors though because that would be unacceptable to the British

Medical Association (the doctors union). Everyone who works at a senior level in the NHS knows this to be true. Until this fundamental issue is resolved the future for the NHS is never going to be one of maximizing the value of anything, never mind its people; it cannot even have a simple objective of maximizing operating theatre utilization because of resistance from medical professionals.

Can you imagine Marriott Hotels not wanting to 'maximize room occupancy'? They have a full-time director of 'room revenue' dedicated to that singular purpose.

HONDA

Having spoken about Toyota's success story at length another well-managed automotive business is Honda. It already practises much of what is being preached here, but it also had to learn some painful lessons. Some years ago Honda was getting into financial difficulties by over-engineering its vehicles. It was a company that had a very proud and well-deserved reputation for the excellence of its engineering. The main problem was that the 'engineers' running the business were following a strategy that could not make and sell cars profitably. It only changed when it brought in more commercially minded senior executives to get the balance right between engineering excellence, fit for purpose and customer expectations.

This is a parallel lesson to the NHS, just substitute the word 'medic' for engineer'. The NHS has many, fantastically professional and dedicated consultants, doctors, nurses, directors and support staff and yet if it had to operate on commercial lines, in a fiercely competitive market, it would probably already be bankrupt.

UNIVERSITIES AND HIGHER EDUCATION

Another sector that has not fully embraced management thinking is Universities. Being populated by academics, they do not generally accept 'managerialism' as a concept and the growth in demand for a university education would suggest that their offering is faring very well. Of course, plenty of academics will produce data that correlates the number of degrees held in an economy with the size and performance of that economy. This has been driving the UK government's policy (and probably every other country) since 1997 with a declared aim of helping 50% of school leavers to enter into higher education. Hopefully, by now, we have already exposed correlations in social policy for what they are and no one has yet found a provable, causal connection between higher education and economic performance. Many top CEOs and entrepreneurs managed to become highly successful without having earned a degree (Richard Branson, Philip Green, Alan Sugar), so degrees cannot be deemed to be a necessary condition of success and many businesses have failed despite the academic qualifications of the board.

'Education, education, education' declared Tony Blair when he came to power, probably the epitome of meaningless, 'apple pie' drivel. It might have held some meaning if he had used the words 'applied learning' instead. If he had, then many university schools would be scratching their heads now wondering how to causally link their work to any meaningful economic output. This would be particularly true of postgraduate research. To many academics and politicians the question 'so what might this be worth?' is not even a valid question and yet every year billions are poured into research. Now that times have changed, the question has to be even more valid but the culture of higher education has not changed enough to start to answer it. An immediate consequence of trying to answer this question, of which all academics are only too well aware, is that there would have to be a performance curve for academic staff and researchers. This would be the equivalent, for many of them, of experiencing an earthquake under their dreamy spires of about 9 on the Richter Scale.

PRIVATE EQUITY AND HEDGE FUNDS

The depth of the recession and credit crunch might be the death knell of private equity and hedge funds. Of course, these are very different entities so why lump them together? Because they have absolutely zero interest in the way companies manage people. People are incidental to their leveraged buyouts and short selling. If companies do have a soul these 'masters of the universe' know how to surgically remove it. This is how many ordinary citizens view these people, especially if they work for a company that has become one of their victims. It is easy to adopt a similar view but the cool-headed HR-business strategist still just keeps asking the dispassionate question – what is best in value terms? Private equity partners have made billions from leveraged buyouts, loading companies with debt then selling them on at a profit, but this is not adding any value if they do not actually manage the business any better. They are working to a completely different paradigm that only sees the cold logic of short-term gain. The key issue here is why we ordinary citizens, through our governments, allow this to happen? It is certainly not in our best interests.

MONOPOLIES

Similarly, monopolies are generally not in the public interest and we have developed legislation over many years to curb their development. Microsoft shows what happens when a natural monopoly (computer operating systems) is left in the hands of one dominant player. From an HR-business strategy perspective, monopolies are also bad news because they breed complacency and contempt for the customer. So the issue here is if we have to accept monopolies, or even oligopolies, in oil, utilities and some parts of the public sector (e.g. post office) then managing their people for value becomes even more important. These organizations should be compelled to report on their human capital practices on the grounds that they are not subjected to the same pressures as competitive entities, which constantly have to seek ways of improving.

START UPS

Many HR conferences look for speakers with interesting stories to tell and the most exciting tend to come from brand new start-ups as happened with Microsoft many years ago, then Yahoo and more recently Google. When new technology businesses capture a dominant part of a new market, especially with very young and talented founders, it is bound to make their 'hip' people practices look attractive while older, more established businesses, look on with envy. Hopefully we have raised enough questions throughout this book to really challenge whether these organizations are any better at managing people than anyone else, or whether they can just afford to manage in a more liberal way. Google, for example, is a phenomenally successful business with a brilliant initial offering and most of us could not now imagine life without it. So this is not criticizing what Google does, it just asks the question – are they doing it as well as they could?

NATIONAL AND INTERNATIONAL HR-BUSINESS STRATEGY

This leads us inevitably to the biggest strategic question of all, what sort of country, economy and society do we want to live in? If we tolerate hedge funds, short-selling and bankers who have no apparent interest in the greatest happiness of the greatest number of citizens, then we get the financial systems we deserve. If we want to get the best value for the economy then it has to mean the best value for as many people as possible, otherwise we cannot expect the majority of people to want to play that particular game.

So, while HR-business strategy has been discussed, throughout this book, at the level of the individual firm it really should be viewed at both a national and international level. The reason we have a global financial meltdown, which is shaking capitalism to its very core, is because we have reaped the seeds we have sown. The Securities and Exchange Commission in the US and the Federal Reserve got it wrong just as much as the UK's authorities, not because they were inherently incapable people but because they had no global, financial system to work to. Everyone was allowed to get away with 'light touch' regulation, which was tantamount to no regulation. There is nothing wrong with enlightened capitalism, whose aim is to serve society in the best way possible. There is nothing wrong with competition, per se. There is everything wrong with a capitalist system that allows only soulless capitalists to predominate.

So will governments of all persuasions start to learn some of these lessons? Maybe we need an HR-business strategy for politicians as well. One that assesses the talents of politicians before they are allowed to enter office. A system for identifying the sort of leadership that can respond effectively and with determination to these global questions?

A system for constructing governments and civil services in the most valuable way possible. The world's leaders and financial experts are currently considering a global, financial, regulatory system and Barack Obama is supporting the removal of tax havens. These all make a great deal of sense, but it will never happen unless we can configure and organize the world to that very desirable end. Who knows? The perfect, global organization of the future might not be a hierarchy or a matrix at all but just one big cooperative?

Index